Microsoft Dynamics AX 2012 R3 Development Cookbook

Over 80 effective recipes to help you solve real-world Microsoft Dynamics AX development problems

Mindaugas Pocius

BIRMINGHAM - MUMBAI

Microsoft Dynamics AX 2012 R3 Development Cookbook

Copyright © 2015 Packt Publishing

All rights reserved. No part of this book may be reproduced, stored in a retrieval system, or transmitted in any form or by any means, without the prior written permission of the publisher, except in the case of brief quotations embedded in critical articles or reviews.

Every effort has been made in the preparation of this book to ensure the accuracy of the information presented. However, the information contained in this book is sold without warranty, either express or implied. Neither the author, nor Packt Publishing, and its dealers and distributors will be held liable for any damages caused or alleged to be caused directly or indirectly by this book.

Packt Publishing has endeavored to provide trademark information about all of the companies and products mentioned in this book by the appropriate use of capitals. However, Packt Publishing cannot guarantee the accuracy of this information.

First published: December 2009

Second edition: May 2012

Third edition: April 2015

Production reference: 1230415

Published by Packt Publishing Ltd.
Livery Place
35 Livery Street
Birmingham B3 2PB, UK.

ISBN 978-1-78528-169-3

www.packtpub.com

Credits

Author
Mindaugas Pocius

Reviewers
Palle Agermark
Pankaj Chaturvedi
Fatih Demirci
Stefan Ebert
Rodrigo Fraga
Kishor Jadhav
Umesh Pandit

Commissioning Editor
Amarabha Banerjee

Acquisition Editor
Vinay Argekar

Content Development Editor
Amey Varangaonkar

Technical Editor
Ankita Thakur

Copy Editors
Charlotte Carneiro
Dipti Kapadia

Project Coordinator
Suzanne Coutinho

Proofreaders
Simran Bhogal
Bridget Braund
Maria Gould
Paul Hindle

Indexer
Tejal Soni

Production Coordinator
Manu Joseph

Cover Work
Manu Joseph

About the Author

Mindaugas Pocius is currently a freelance Dynamics AX technical and functional consultant and trainer at DynamicsLab Limited (www.dynamicslab.com). The company specializes in providing development, consulting, and training services for Microsoft Dynamics AX resellers and customers.

Mindaugas started his IT consulting career back in 2001 while he was still pursuing his master's degree in information technology at Kaunas University of Technology in Lithuania. Since then, he has become a recognized Microsoft Certified Professional for Dynamics AX in all major areas, such as development, configuration and installation, financials, projects, and trade and logistics. He is also a Certified Microsoft Trainer for Dynamics AX and has delivered numerous Dynamics AX trainings.

Mindaugas has participated in over 20 Dynamics AX implementations. He has held a wide range of development, consulting, and lead roles while always maintaining the significant role of a business application developer.

In December 2009, he released his first book, *Microsoft Dynamics AX 2009 Development Cookbook*, and then in May 2012, its second edition, *Microsoft Dynamics AX 2012 Development Cookbook*, both of which are published by Packt Publishing.

> First of all, I would like to thank my wife, Rasa, and my two boys, Dominykas and Augustas, for their support and understanding during the long hours that I spent on this book. I also want to apologize for the time I've stolen from them to make this book a reality.
>
> Secondly, I wish to thank all the reviewers, who provided very valuable comments to improve the code in this book and who helped to make the code's explanations clearer.
>
> Lastly, a special thanks goes to the Packt Publishing team who made this book possible.

About the Reviewers

Palle Agermark has worked as a developer and technical consultant with Concorde XAL and Microsoft Dynamics AX for more than 20 years. He has worked for a number of years at the Microsoft Development Center, Copenhagen, primarily developing the financial, accounts payable, and accounts receivable modules; he has also worked on other things, such as the Unit Test framework.

Currently, Palle works for one of Scandinavia's largest Microsoft Dynamics AX partners, EG, in Copenhagen.

In 2006, Palle wrote a chapter titled *Extending Microsoft Dynamics AX* for *Inside Microsoft Dynamics AX 4.0*, *Microsoft Press*. He has been a reviewer of several books from Packt Publishing, including *Microsoft Dynamics AX 2012 R2 Services*.

> I'd like to thank the author and publisher for putting their time and money into this excellent book, which will be very helpful to the entire Dynamics AX developer community.

Pankaj Chaturvedi is an experienced Dynamics AX technical consultant. He is currently working with Sonata Software Ltd. in Bangalore, India.

Pankaj began working with AX in 2006 and has a wide range of expertise, both technical and functional. Apart from Dynamics AX, he also works with other Microsoft technologies, including Microsoft NAV, SharePoint, Reporting Services, Analysis Services, and Visual Studio.

Pankaj has worked on many Dynamics AX implementations, which specialize in business solutions design, X++ programming, reporting, and business intelligence. He is a Microsoft Certified Professional for AX (development, installation, and configuration) as well as for key modules (finance and trade and logistics). He is also a Microsoft Certified Trainer for AX.

Fatih Demirci (MCT) is a technical consultant and trainer. He has been working professionally on Dynamics AX since 2006. He has worked with many Microsoft partners and customers. He has over 9 years of consulting experience, where he has played a variety of roles, including senior software engineer, team leader, trainer, and technical consultant in Dynamics AX. He is one of the cofounders of DMR Consultancy, which is the most promising ERP consultancy company in Turkey, and he works with some of the most experienced and creative Dynamics AX professionals.

Fatih runs a professional and technical blog at `www.fatihdemirci.net`, and shares his thoughts and readings on Twitter and LinkedIn.

> I would like to thank my family and friends for motivating me and for always pushing me to do my best.

Stefan Ebert started his Dynamics AX career in 2007 after studying computer science at Hochschule Darmstadt. As a consequence of working on IT projects for a large manufacturing company for more than 10 years, he has a deep and wide knowledge of the company's business and economic activities.

He is experienced in the overall software development cycle, from designing, implementing, and integrating to testing, building, and deploying applications and tools. He is a thorough professional and loves topics such as quality, performance, testing, reviewing, and version control systems.

Stefan can be contacted via LinkedIn at `http://de.linkedin.com/in/dynamicsaxbusiness`.

> I would like to thank Mindaugas and Packt Publishing for letting me be a part of the making of this book. It was a great experience.

Rodrigo Fraga has been working with Dynamics AX since 2006 and has participated in different projects, implementing AX, across South and North America.

Currently, Rodrigo works for Hewlett-Packard, allocated at Suncor, one of the largest AX implementations in the world.

Kishor Jadhav is currently working as a Microsoft Dynamics AX senior technical consultant with 42 Hertz INC. He has completed his master's degree in computer application from the University of Mumbai, and his bachelor's degree in information technology from Vidyalankar School of Information Technology, Mumbai.

Kishor has around 6 years of IT experience. He has worked with Godrej Infotech Ltd., Mumbai, as a Dynamics AX technical consultant. He has a deep understanding of Microsoft Dynamics AX ERP systems. He has worked with different versions of AX, such as AX 5.0 (AX 2009) and AX 6.0 (AX 2012, AX 2012 R2, and AX 2012 R3). He has a good knowledge of Microsoft technologies such as SQL, VB 6.0, C#, SSRS, and SSAS.

He can be contacted via Skype (`kishorworld`) or e-mail (`kishoworld1@gmail.com`), and he blogs at `http://kdynamics.blogspot.in`.

> I would like to thank Mindaugas Pocius, Suzanne Coutinho, and Packt Publishing team for giving me the opportunity to review this book.

Umesh Pandit is a Microsoft Dynamics AX deployment senior specialist who currently works with Hitachi Solutions, India. He has completed his master's degree in computer applications, with first division, having specialized in ERP from Ideal Institute of Technology, Ghaziabad.

Umesh is also a Microsoft Certified Professional for Microsoft Dynamics AX 2009 Installation and Configuration, Microsoft Dynamics AX 2012 Installation and Configuration, Server Virtualization with Windows Server Hyper-V and System Center, Microsoft Dynamics AX 2012 Development Introduction I, Microsoft Dynamics POS 2009, Administering Microsoft SQL Server 2012 Databases, and Implementing Microsoft Azure Infrastructure Solutions.

In the past, he has successfully reviewed *Microsoft Dynamics AX 2012 Reporting Cookbook* by Kamalakannan Elangovan, *Developing SSRS Reports for Dynamics AX* by Mukesh Hirwani, *Microsoft Dynamics AX 2012 Programming: Getting Started* by Mohammed Rasheed and Erlend Dalen, and *Reporting in TFS* by Dipti Chhatrapati, all by Packt Publishing.

He has worked with top IT giants, such as KPIT Technologies, Capgemini India, and Google India, as well as with a cable manufacturing company called Cords Cable Industries Limited.

Umesh has a deep understanding of ERP systems, such as Microsoft Dynamics AX and SAP. He has worked with different versions of Microsoft Dynamic AX, starting with Axapta versions, such as AX 3.0, AX 4.0, AX 2009, AX 2012, AX 2012 R2, AX 2012 R3, and AX 2012 R3 CU8. He has vast knowledge of Microsoft Technologies, such as SQL 2014, CRM, TFS, Office 2013, Windows Server 2003, Window Server 2008, Windows Server 2012, Office 365, Microsoft Dynamics NAV, SSRS, Cubes, Management Reporter, SSAS, and Visual Studio.

He can be reached at `pandit.umesh@hotmail.com`, and he blogs at `http://msdynamicsaxtips.blogspot.in/`.

> I would like to give special thanks to my close friend Pramila who supported me a lot, and best buddies at work—Sunil Wadhwa, Rohan Sodani, Fareeda Begum, Aman Bhatia, Gyan Chand Kabra, Debashish Ray, Arjita Choudhury, and Meenakshi Pandey—who have guided me and encouraged my passion.

www.PacktPub.com

Support files, eBooks, discount offers, and more

For support files and downloads related to your book, please visit www.PacktPub.com.

Did you know that Packt offers eBook versions of every book published, with PDF and ePub files available? You can upgrade to the eBook version at www.PacktPub.com and as a print book customer, you are entitled to a discount on the eBook copy. Get in touch with us at service@packtpub.com for more details.

At www.PacktPub.com, you can also read a collection of free technical articles, sign up for a range of free newsletters and receive exclusive discounts and offers on Packt books and eBooks.

https://www2.packtpub.com/books/subscription/packtlib

Do you need instant solutions to your IT questions? PacktLib is Packt's online digital book library. Here, you can search, access, and read Packt's entire library of books.

Why subscribe?

- Fully searchable across every book published by Packt
- Copy and paste, print, and bookmark content
- On demand and accessible via a web browser

Free access for Packt account holders

If you have an account with Packt at www.PacktPub.com, you can use this to access PacktLib today and view 9 entirely free books. Simply use your login credentials for immediate access.

Instant updates on new Packt books

Get notified! Find out when new books are published by following @PacktEnterprise on Twitter or the *Packt Enterprise* Facebook page.

Table of Contents

Preface	**v**
Chapter 1: Processing Data	**1**
Introduction	2
Creating a new number sequence	2
Renaming the primary key	8
Merging two records	11
Adding a document handling note	14
Using a normal table as a temporary table	17
Copying a record	19
Building a query object	23
Using a macro in a SQL statement	27
Executing a direct SQL statement	29
Enhancing the data consistency check	36
Exporting data to an XML file	40
Importing data from an XML file	43
Creating a comma-separated value file	45
Reading a comma-separated value file	48
Using the date effectiveness feature	52
Chapter 2: Working with Forms	**57**
Introduction	57
Creating dialogs using the RunBase framework	58
Handling a dialog event	63
Building a dynamic form	68
Adding a form splitter	73
Creating a modal form	78
Modifying multiple forms dynamically	80
Storing user selections	82

Table of Contents

Using a Tree control	86
Building a checklist	97
Adding the View details link	106

Chapter 3: Working with Data in Forms — 109

Introduction	109
Using a number sequence handler	110
Creating a custom filter control	113
Creating a custom instant search filter	118
Building a selected/available list	121
Preloading images	130
Creating a wizard	137
Processing multiple records	150
Coloring records	151
Adding an image to records	153

Chapter 4: Building Lookups — 163

Introduction	163
Creating an automatic lookup	164
Creating a lookup dynamically	167
Using a form to build a lookup	169
Building a tree lookup	175
Displaying a list of custom options	179
Displaying custom options in another way	181
Building a lookup based on the record description	185
Building the browse for folder lookup	192
Building a lookup to select a file	196
Creating a color picker lookup	200

Chapter 5: Processing Business Tasks — 207

Introduction	207
Using a segmented entry control	208
Creating a general journal	214
Posting a general journal	222
Processing a project journal	224
Creating and posting a ledger voucher	228
Changing an automatic transaction text	233
Creating a purchase order	236
Posting a purchase order	239
Creating a sales order	244
Posting a sales order	247
Creating an electronic payment format	252

Chapter 6: Integration with Microsoft Office — 261
- Introduction — 261
- Creating an Excel file — 262
- Reading an Excel file — 265
- Creating a Word document from a template — 268
- Creating a Word document with repeating elements — 272
- Creating a Microsoft Project file — 276
- Sending an e-mail using Outlook — 281

Chapter 7: Using Services — 285
- Introduction — 285
- Consuming the system query service — 286
- Consuming the system metadata service — 291
- Consuming an existing document service — 293
- Creating a document service — 297
- Consuming a document service — 302
- Using an enhanced document service — 305
- Creating a custom service — 310
- Consuming a custom service — 313
- Consuming an external service — 315

Chapter 8: Improving Development Efficiency — 319
- Introduction — 319
- Creating a code editor template — 320
- Modifying the Tools menu — 325
- Modifying the right-click context menu — 327
- Searching for an object in a development project — 333
- Modifying the Personalization form — 336
- Modifying the About Microsoft Dynamics AX dialog — 340

Chapter 9: Improving Dynamics AX Performance — 343
- Introduction — 343
- Calculating code execution time — 343
- Writing efficient SQL statements — 346
- Caching a display method — 348
- Using Dynamics AX Trace Parser — 351
- Using SQL Server Database Engine Tuning Advisor — 357

Index — 361

Preface

As a Dynamics AX developer, your responsibility is to deliver all kinds of application customizations, whether it is a small adjustment or a bespoke module. Dynamics AX is a highly customizable system and requires a significant amount of knowledge and experience to deliver quality solutions. One goal can be achieved in multiple ways, and there is always the question of which way is the best.

This book takes you through numerous recipes to help you with daily development tasks. Each recipe contains detailed step-by-step instructions along with the application screenshots and in-depth explanations. The recipes cover multiple Dynamics AX modules, so at the same time, the book provides an overview of the functional aspects of the system for developers.

What this book covers

The book's content is presented in nine chapters that cover various aspects of Dynamics AX.

Chapter 1, Processing Data, focuses on data manipulation. It explains how to build data queries, how to check and modify existing data, how to read and write external files, and how to use date effectiveness.

Chapter 2, Working with Forms, covers various aspects of building forms in Dynamics AX. In this chapter, dialogs and their events are explained. Also, various useful features such as splitters, tree controls, and checklists are explained here.

Chapter 3, Working with Data in Forms, basically supplements *Chapter 2, Working with Forms*, and explains about data organization in forms. Examples in this chapter include instructions about how to build filter controls on forms, process multiple records, and work with images and colors.

Chapter 4, Building Lookups, covers all kinds of lookups in the system. The chapter starts with a simple, automatically generated lookup, continues with more advanced ones, and finishes with standard Windows lookups, such as the file selection dialog or color picker.

Preface

Chapter 5, Processing Business Tasks, explains the usage of the Dynamics AX business logic API. In this chapter, topics such as how to process journals, as well as purchase and sales orders are discussed. Other features such as posting ledger vouchers, modifying transaction texts and creating electronic payment formats are included as well.

Chapter 6, Integration with Microsoft Office, shows how Word, Excel, Outlook, and Project applications can be integrated with Dynamics AX.

Chapter 7, Using Services, explains how to use services in Dynamics AX. The chapter covers standard query, metadata, and document system services. It also demonstrates how to create custom services and how to consume external services.

Chapter 8, Improving Development Efficiency, presents a few ideas on how to make daily development tasks easier. The chapter demonstrates how to build code templates, modify the tools and the right-click context menus, use search in development projects, and customize the Personalization form.

Chapter 9, Improving Dynamics AX Performance, discusses how system performance can be improved by following several simple rules. The chapter explains how to calculate code execution time, how to write efficient SQL statements, how to properly cache display methods, and how to use Dynamics AX Trace Parser and SQL Server Database Engine Tuning Advisor.

Exceptions and considerations

The code in this book follows the best practice guidelines provided by Microsoft, but there are some exceptions:

- No text labels were used to make the code clear
- No three-letter code was used in front of each new AOT object
- No configuration or security keys were used
- Object properties that are not relevant to the topic being discussed are not set

Also, here are some considerations that you need to keep in mind when reading the book:

- Each recipe only demonstrates the principle and is not a complete solution
- The data in your environment might not match the data used in the recipes, so the code might have to be adjusted appropriately
- For each recipe, the assumption is that no other modifications are present in the system, unless it is explicitly specified
- The code might not have all the possible validations that are not relevant to the principle being explained

- The code might have more variables than required in order to ensure that it is clear for all audiences
- Sometimes, unnecessary code wrapping is used to make sure the code fits into the page width of this book and is easy readable

What you need for this book

All the coding examples were performed in a virtual Microsoft Dynamics AX 2012 R3 image downloaded from the Microsoft CustomerSource or PartnerSource websites. The following list of software from the virtual image was used in this book:

- Microsoft Dynamics AX 2012 R3 (kernel: 6.3.164.0, application: 6.3.164.0)
- Microsoft Dynamics AX Trace Parser (version: 6.3.164.0)
- Microsoft Windows Server 2012 R2 Datacenter
- Microsoft SQL Server 2014
- Microsoft Office Excel 2013
- Microsoft Office Word 2013
- Microsoft Office Outlook 2013
- Microsoft Office Project 2013
- Microsoft Internet Explorer 11
- Windows Notepad

Although all the recipes have been tested on the previously-mentioned software, they might work on older or newer software versions without any implications or with minor code adjustments.

Who this book is for

This book is for Dynamics AX developers primarily focused on delivering time-proven application modifications. Although new X++ developers can use this book along with their beginner guides, this book is more focused on people who are willing to raise their programming skills above beginner level and, at the same time, learn the functional aspects of Dynamics AX. So, some Dynamics AX coding experience is expected.

Sections

In this book, you will find several headings that appear frequently (Getting ready, How to do it, How it works, There's more, and See also).

Preface

To give clear instructions on how to complete a recipe, we use these sections as follows:

Getting ready

This section tells you what to expect in the recipe, and describes how to set up any software or any preliminary settings required for the recipe.

How to do it...

This section contains the steps required to follow the recipe.

How it works...

This section usually consists of a detailed explanation of what happened in the previous section.

There's more...

This section consists of additional information about the recipe in order to make the reader more knowledgeable about the recipe.

See also

This section provides helpful links to other useful information for the recipe.

Conventions

In this book, you will find a number of text styles that distinguish between different kinds of information. Here are some examples of these styles and an explanation of their meaning.

Code words in text, all Application Object Tree (AOT) object names like tables, forms, extended data types, classes and others, folder names, filenames, file extensions, pathnames, dummy URLs, and user input are shown as follows: "We start the recipe by adding a number sequence initialization code into the `NumberSeqModuleCustomer` class."

A block of code is set as follows:

```
datatype.parmDatatypeId(extendedTypeNum(CustGroupId));
datatype.parmReferenceHelp("Customer group ID");
datatype.parmWizardIsContinuous(false);
datatype.parmWizardIsManual(NoYes::No);
datatype.parmWizardIsChangeDownAllowed(NoYes::Yes);
datatype.parmWizardIsChangeUpAllowed(NoYes::Yes);
```

```
datatype.parmWizardHighest(999);
datatype.parmSortField(20);
datatype.addParameterType(
    NumberSeqParameterType::DataArea, true, false);
this.create(datatype);
```

New terms and **important words** are shown in bold. Words that you see on the screen, for example, in menus or dialog boxes, appear in the text like this: "Click on **Details** to view more information."

Reader feedback

Feedback from our readers is always welcome. Let us know what you think about this book—what you liked or disliked. Reader feedback is important for us as it helps us develop titles that you will really get the most out of.

To send us general feedback, simply e-mail `feedback@packtpub.com`, and mention the book's title in the subject of your message.

If there is a topic that you have expertise in and you are interested in either writing or contributing to a book, see our author guide at `www.packtpub.com/authors`.

Customer support

Now that you are the proud owner of a Packt book, we have a number of things to help you to get the most from your purchase.

Downloading the example code

You can download the example code files from your account at `http://www.packtpub.com` for all the Packt Publishing books you have purchased. If you purchased this book elsewhere, you can visit `http://www.packtpub.com/support` and register to have the files e-mailed directly to you.

Downloading the color images of this book

We also provide you with a PDF file that has color images of the screenshots/diagrams used in this book. The color images will help you better understand the changes in the output. You can download this file from: `http://www.packtpub.com/sites/default/files/downloads/1693EN_ColorImages.pdf`.

Errata

Although we have taken every care to ensure the accuracy of our content, mistakes do happen. If you find a mistake in one of our books—maybe a mistake in the text or the code—we would be grateful if you could report this to us. By doing so, you can save other readers from frustration and help us improve subsequent versions of this book. If you find any errata, please report them by visiting http://www.packtpub.com/submit-errata, selecting your book, clicking on the **Errata Submission Form** link, and entering the details of your errata. Once your errata are verified, your submission will be accepted and the errata will be uploaded to our website or added to any list of existing errata under the Errata section of that title.

To view the previously submitted errata, go to https://www.packtpub.com/books/content/support and enter the name of the book in the search field. The required information will appear under the **Errata** section.

Piracy

Piracy of copyrighted material on the Internet is an ongoing problem across all media. At Packt, we take the protection of our copyright and licenses very seriously. If you come across any illegal copies of our works in any form on the Internet, please provide us with the location address or website name immediately so that we can pursue a remedy.

Please contact us at copyright@packtpub.com with a link to the suspected pirated material.

We appreciate your help in protecting our authors and our ability to bring you valuable content.

Questions

If you have a problem with any aspect of this book, you can contact us at questions@packtpub.com, and we will do our best to address the problem.

1
Processing Data

In this chapter, we will cover the following recipes:

- Creating a new number sequence
- Renaming the primary key
- Merging two records
- Adding a document handling note
- Using a normal table as a temporary table
- Copying a record
- Building a query object
- Using a macro in a SQL statement
- Executing a direct SQL statement
- Enhancing the data consistency check
- Exporting data to an XML file
- Importing data from an XML file
- Creating a comma-separated value file
- Reading a comma-separated value file
- Using the date effectiveness feature

Processing Data

Introduction

This chapter focuses on data manipulation exercises. These exercises are very useful when doing data migration, system integration, custom reporting, and so on. Here, we will discuss how to work with query objects from the X++ code. We will also discuss how to reuse macros in X++ SQL statements and how to execute SQL statements directly in the database. This chapter will explain how to rename primary keys, how to merge and copy records, how to add document handling notes to selected records, and how to create and read XML and **comma-separated value** (**CSV**) files. The chapter ends with a recipe about the date effectiveness feature.

Creating a new number sequence

Number sequences in Dynamics AX are used to generate specifically formatted numbers used for various identification. These number sequences can be anything from voucher numbers or transaction identification numbers to customer or vendor account codes.

When developing custom functionality, often one of the tasks is to add a new number sequence to the system in order to support newly created tables and forms. Adding a number sequence to the system is a two-step process. First, we create the number sequence itself; second, we start using it in some particular form or from the code. Number sequences can be created either manually or automatically by the wizard.

Dynamics AX contains a list of `NumberSeqApplicationModule` derivative classes, which hold the number sequence's setup data for the specific module. These classes are read by the number sequence wizard, which detects already created number sequences and proposes to create the missing ones. The wizard is normally run as part of the application initialization. It can also be rerun any time later when expanding the Dynamics AX functionality used. The wizard also has to be rerun if new custom number sequences are added to the system.

In this recipe, we will do the first step, that is, add a new number sequence to the system. In a standard application, the customer group number is not driven by a number sequence, so we will enhance this by creating a new number sequence for customer groups. The second step is explained later in the *Using a number sequence handler* recipe in *Chapter 3, Working with Data in Forms*.

How to do it...

Carry out the following steps in order to complete this recipe:

1. Open the `NumberSeqModuleCustomer` class in the **Application Object Tree** (**AOT**) and add the following code snippet at the bottom of the `loadModule()` method:

    ```
    datatype.parmDatatypeId(extendedTypeNum(CustGroupId));
    datatype.parmReferenceHelp("Customer group ID");
    datatype.parmWizardIsContinuous(false);
    ```

```
datatype.parmWizardIsManual(NoYes::No);
datatype.parmWizardIsChangeDownAllowed(NoYes::Yes);
datatype.parmWizardIsChangeUpAllowed(NoYes::Yes);
datatype.parmWizardHighest(999);
datatype.parmSortField(20);
datatype.addParameterType(
    NumberSeqParameterType::DataArea, true, false);
this.create(datatype);
```

> **Downloading the example code**
> You can download the example code files for all Packt books you have purchased from your account at http://www.packtpub.com. If you purchased this book elsewhere, you can visit http://www.packtpub.com/support and register to have the files e-mailed directly to you.

2. Create a new job with the following lines of code and run it:

```
static void NumberSeqLoadAll(Args _args)
{
    NumberSeqApplicationModule::loadAll();
}
```

3. Navigate to **Organization administration** | **Common** | **Number sequences** and open the **Number sequences** list page. Run the number sequence wizard by clicking on the **Generate** button. On the first wizard's page, click on the **Next** button, as shown in the following screenshot:

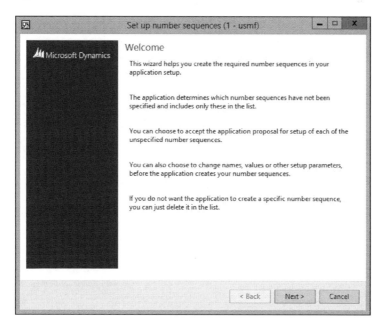

Processing Data

4. On the next page, click on **Details** to view more information. Delete everything apart from the rows where **Area** is **Accounts receivable** and **Reference** is **Customer group**. Note the number sequence codes and click on the **Next** button, as shown here:

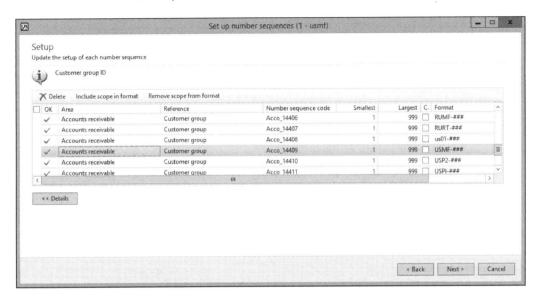

5. On the last page, click on the **Finish** button to complete the setup, as shown in the following screenshot:

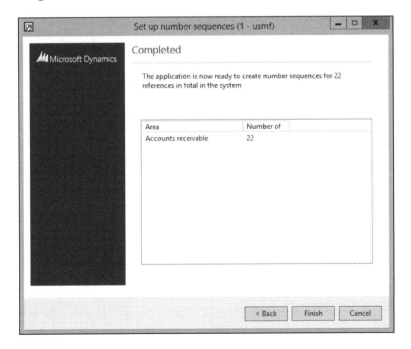

6. The newly created number sequences can now be found in the **Number sequences** list page, as shown in the following screenshot:

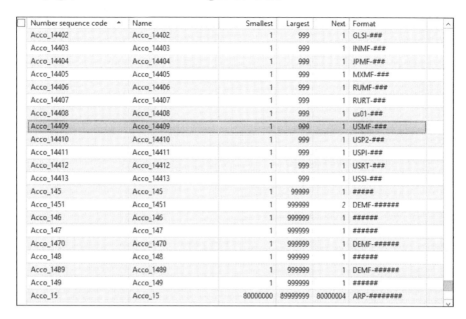

7. Navigate to **Organization administration | Number sequences | Segment configuration** and notice the new **Customer group** reference under the **Accounts receivable** area:

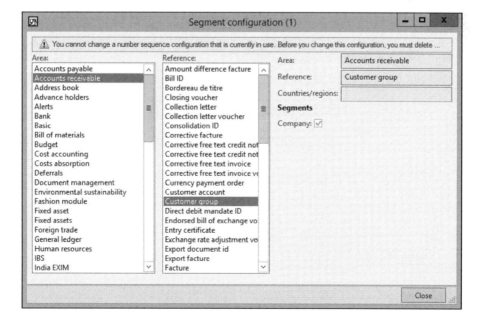

Processing Data

8. Navigate to **Accounts receivable | Setup | Accounts receivable parameters** and select the **Number sequences** tab page. Here, you should see the new number sequence code:

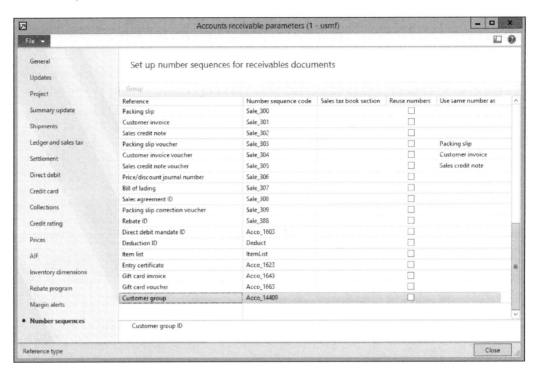

9. The last thing to be done is to create a helper method for this number sequence. Locate the `CustParameters` table in the AOT by navigating to **Data Dictionary | Tables** and create the following method:

```
client server static NumberSequenceReference numRefCustGroupId()
{
    return NumberSeqReference::findReference(
        extendedTypeNum(CustGroupId));
}
```

How it works...

We start the recipe by adding a number sequence initialization code into the `NumberSeqModuleCustomer` class. This class holds all the definitions of the number sequence parameters that belong to the **Accounts receivable** module. There are many other similar classes, such as `NumberSeqModuleVendor` or `NumberSeqModuleLedger`, that holds the number sequence definitions for other modules.

The code in the `loadModule()` method defines the default number sequence settings to be used in the wizard, such as the data type, description, and highest possible number. Additional options such as the starting sequence number, number format, and others can also be defined here. All the mentioned options can be changed while running the wizard. The `addParameterType()` method is used to define the number sequence scope. In the example, we created a separate sequence for each Dynamics AX company.

Before we start the wizard, we initialize number sequence references. The references are those records that are normally located under the **Number sequences** tab pages in the parameters forms in most of the Dynamics AX modules. This is normally done as a part of the Dynamics AX initialization checklist, but in this example, we execute it manually by calling the `loadAll()` method of the `NumberSeqApplicationModule` class.

Next, we execute the wizard that will create the number sequence codes for us. We skip the welcome page, and in the second step of the wizard, the **Details** button can be used to display more options. The options can also be changed later in the **Number sequences** form before or even after the number sequence codes actually used. The last page shows an overview of what will be created. Once completed, the wizard creates new records in the **Number sequences** form for each company.

The newly created number sequence reference appears in the **Segment configuration** form. Here, we can see that the **Data area** checkbox is checked, which means that we will have separate number lists for each company.

See also

- The *Using a number sequence handler* recipe in *Chapter 3, Working with Data in Forms*

Processing Data

Renaming the primary key

Most of you who are familiar with the Dynamics AX application have probably used the standard **Rename** function. This function allows you to rename the primary key of almost any record. With this function, you can fix records that were saved or created by mistake. The **Rename** function ensures data consistency, that is, all the related records are renamed as well. The function can be accessed from the **Record information** form (shown in the following screenshot), which can be opened by selecting **Record info** in the record's right-click context menu:

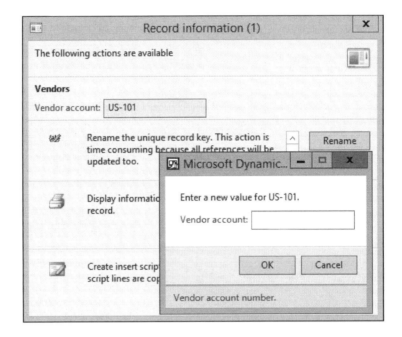

When it comes to mass renaming, this function might be very time-consuming as you need to run it on every record. An alternative way of doing this is to create a job that automatically runs through all the required records and calls this function automatically.

This recipe will explain how a record's primary key can be renamed through the code. As an example, we will create a job that renames a vendor account.

Chapter 1

How to do it...

Carry out the following steps in order to complete this recipe:

1. Navigate to **Accounts payable | Common | Vendors | All vendors** and find the account that you want to rename, as shown here:

Vendor account	Name	Vendor hold	Phone	Extension
JP-001	Contoso Chemicals Japan	No		
US-111	Contoso office supply	No		
US-105	Datum Receivers	No	123-555-0100	
✓ US-101	Fabrikam Electronics	No		
US-104	Fabrikam Supplier	No	612-5550121	
US_TX_023	Federal Tax Authority	No	111-555-1040	
US_TX_002	Florida State Tax Authority	No	111-555-9988	
US_TX_004	Georgia State Tax Authority	No	111-555-2929	
US-106	Humongous Insurance	No	111-555-1060	
US-107	Idaho Department of Family Services	No	111-555-9375	
US_TX_005	Idaho State Tax Authority	No	111-555-9090	
US_TX_006	Illinois State Tax Authority	No	111-555-9876	
US_TX_007	Iowa State Tax Authority	No	111-555-6543	
1002	Lande Packaging Supplies	No		
US_TX_008	Maryland State Tax Authority	No	111-555-4321	
US_TX_009	Massachusetts State Tax Authority	No	111-555-0987	

2. Click on **Transactions** in the action pane to check the existing transactions, as shown in the following screenshot:

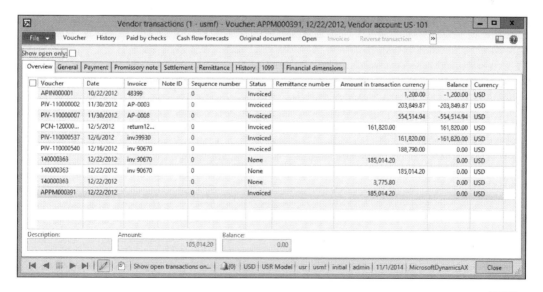

9

Processing Data

3. Open the AOT, create a new job named `VendAccountRename`, and enter the following code snippet. Use the previously selected account:

```
static void VendAccountRename(Args _args)
{
    VendTable vendTable;

    ttsBegin;

    select firstOnly vendTable
        where vendTable.AccountNum == 'US-101';

    if (vendTable)
    {
        vendTable.AccountNum = 'US-101_';
        vendTable.renamePrimaryKey();
    }

    ttsCommit;
}
```

4. Run the job and check whether the renaming was successful by navigating to **Accounts payable | Common | Vendors | All vendors** again and finding the new account. The new account should have retained all its transactions and other related records, as shown in the following screenshot:

Vendor account	Name	Vendor hold	Phone	Extension
JP-001	Contoso Chemicals Japan	No		
US-111	Contoso office supply	No		
US-105	Datum Receivers	No	123-555-0100	
✓ US-101_	Fabrikam Electronics	No		
US-104	Fabrikam Supplier	No	612-5550121	
US_TX_023	Federal Tax Authority	No	111-555-1040	
US_TX_002	Florida State Tax Authority	No	111-555-9988	
US_TX_004	Georgia State Tax Authority	No	111-555-2929	
US-106	Humongous Insurance	No	111-555-1060	
US-107	Idaho Department of Family Services	No	111-555-9375	
US_TX_005	Idaho State Tax Authority	No	111-555-9090	
US_TX_006	Illinois State Tax Authority	No	111-555-9876	
US_TX_007	Iowa State Tax Authority	No	111-555-6543	
1002	Lande Packaging Supplies	No		
US_TX_008	Maryland State Tax Authority	No	111-555-4321	
US_TX_009	Massachusetts State Tax Authority	No	111-555-0987	

5. Click on **Transactions** in the action pane in order to see whether the existing transactions are still in place, as shown here:

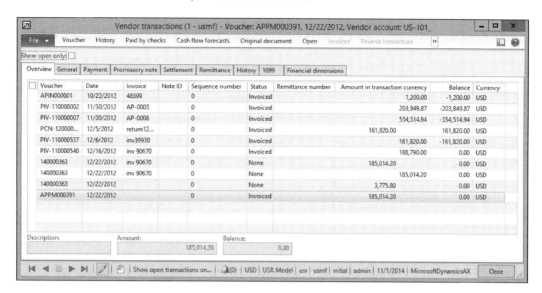

How it works...

In this recipe, we first select the desired vendor record and set its account number to the new value. Note that only the fields belonging to the table's primary key can be renamed in this way.

Then, we call the table's `renamePrimaryKey()` method, which does the actual renaming. The method finds all the related records for the selected vendor account and updates them with the new value. The operation might take a while, depending on the volume of data, as the system has to update multiple records located in multiple tables.

Merging two records

For various reasons, the data in a system—such as customers, ledger accounts, configuration settings, and similar data—may become obsolete. This can be because of changes in the business or it can simply be a user input error. For example, two sales people can create two records for the same customer, start entering sales orders, and post invoices. One of the ways to solve this problem is to merge both the records into a single record.

In this recipe, we will explore how to merge one record into another, including all the related transactions. For this demonstration, we will merge two ledger reason codes into a single one.

Processing Data

How to do it...

Carry out the following steps in order to complete this recipe:

1. Navigate to **General ledger | Setup | Ledger reasons** in order to find the reasons that you want to merge. Pick any two ledger reasons. In this example, we will use **ADJ** and **OTHER**, as shown in the following screenshot:

2. Open the AOT and create a new job named `LedgerReasonMerge` with the following code snippet (replace the reason codes with your own values):

```
static void LedgerReasonMerge(Args _args)
{
    ReasonTable reasonTableDelete;
    ReasonTable reasonTable;

    ttsBegin;

    select firstOnly forUpdate reasonTableDelete
        where reasonTableDelete.Reason == 'ADJ';

    select firstOnly forUpdate reasonTable
        where reasonTable.Reason == 'OTHER';

    reasonTableDelete.merge(reasonTable);
    reasonTable.doUpdate();
```

```
        reasonTableDelete.doDelete();

        ttsCommit;
    }
```

3. Run the job to merge the records.
4. Open the **Ledger reasons** form again; you will notice that both the reasons were merged into one and all the related transactions have also been updated to reflect the change:

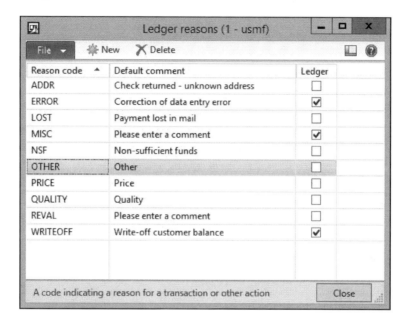

How it works...

First, we retrieve both the records from the database and prepare them for updating.

The key method in this recipe is merge(). This method will ensure that all the data from one record will be copied into the second one and all the related transactions will be updated to reflect the change.

Finally, we save the changes of the destination record and delete the first record.

All the code has to be within the ttsBegin/ttsCommit pair as we perform several database update operations in one go.

Such a technique can be used to merge two or more records of any type.

Adding a document handling note

Document handling in Dynamics AX is a feature that allows you to add notes, links, documents, images, files, and other related information to almost any record in the system. For example, we can track all the correspondence sent out to our customers by attaching the documents to their records in the system. Document handling on most of the forms can be accessed either from the action pane by clicking on the **Attachments** button, selecting **Document handling** from the **Command** menu under **File**, or selecting the **Document handling** icon from the status bar.

Document handling has a number of configuration parameters that you can find by navigating to **Organization administration** | **Setup** | **Document management**. Please refer to Dynamics AX documentation to find out more.

Dynamics AX also allows you to add document handling notes from the code. This can be useful when you need to automate the document handling process. In this recipe, we will demonstrate this by adding a note to a vendor account.

Getting ready

Before you start, ensure that document handling is enabled on the user interface. Open **Document management parameters** by navigating to **Organization administration** | **Setup** | **Document management** and make sure that **Use Active document tables** is not marked, as shown in the following screenshot:

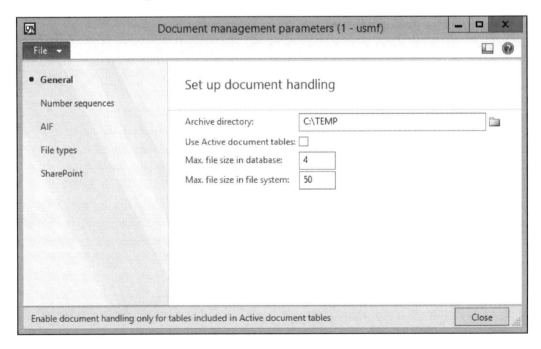

Chapter 1

Then, open the **Document types** form from the same location and locate or create a new document type with its **Group** set to **Note**, as shown in the following screenshot. In our demonstration, we will use a document type called **Note**:

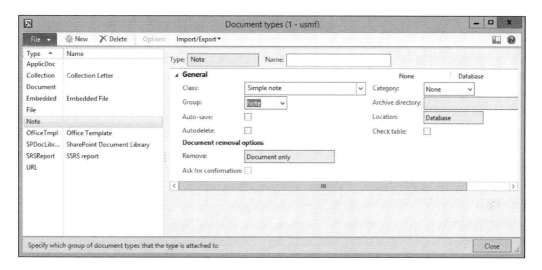

How to do it...

Carry out the following steps in order to complete this recipe:

1. Navigate to **Accounts payable** | **Common** | **Vendors** | **All vendors** and locate any vendor account to be updated, as shown here:

Processing Data

2. Open the AOT, create a new job named `VendAccountDocu`, and enter the following code snippet. Use the previously selected vendor account and document type:

```
static void VendAccountDocu(Args _args)
{
    VendTable   vendTable;
    DocuType    docuType;
    DocuRef     docuRef;

    vendTable = VendTable::find('US-108');
    docuType  = DocuType::find('Note');

    if (!docuType ||
        docuType.TypeGroup != DocuTypeGroup::Note)
    {
        throw error("Invalid document type");
    }


    docuRef.RefCompanyId = vendTable.dataAreaId;
    docuRef.RefTableId   = vendTable.TableId;
    docuRef.RefRecId     = vendTable.RecId;
    docuRef.TypeId       = docuType.TypeId;
    docuRef.Name         = 'Automatic note';
    docuRef.Notes        = 'Added from X++';
    docuRef.insert();

    info("Document note has been added successfully");
}
```

3. Run the job to create the note.
4. Go back to the vendor list and click on the **Attachments** button in the form's action pane or expand the **File** menu and navigate to **Command | Document handling** to view the note added by our code, as shown in the following screenshot:

Chapter 1

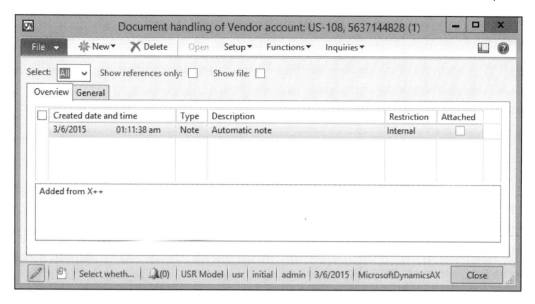

How it works...

All the document handling notes are stored in the `DocuRef` table, where three fields, `RefCompanyId`, `RefTableId`, and `RefRecId`, are used to identify the parent record. In this recipe, we set these fields to the vendor company ID, vendor table ID, and vendor account record ID, respectively. Then, we set the type, name, and description and insert the document handling record. Notice that we have validated the document type before using it. In this way, we added a note to the record.

Using a normal table as a temporary table

Temporary tables in Dynamics AX are used in numerous places. In forms and reports, they are used as data sources when it is too complicated to query normal tables. In code, they can be used for storing intermediate results while running complex operations.

Temporary tables can be either created from scratch or existing regular tables could be reused as temporary. The goal of this recipe is to demonstrate the latter approach. As an example, we will use the vendor table to insert and display a couple of temporary records without affecting the actual data.

Processing Data

How to do it...

Carry out the following steps in order to complete this recipe:

1. In the AOT, create a new class named `VendTableTmp` with the following code snippet:

    ```
    class VendTableTmp
    {
    }

    server static void main(Args _args)
    {
        VendTable    vendTable;

        vendTable.setTmp();

        vendTable.AccountNum = '1000';
        vendTable.Blocked    = CustVendorBlocked::No;
        vendTable.Party      = 1;
        vendTable.doInsert();

        vendTable.clear();
        vendTable.AccountNum = '1002';
        vendTable.Blocked    = CustVendorBlocked::All;
        vendTable.Party      = 2;
        vendTable.doInsert();

        while select vendTable
        {
            info(strFmt(
                "%1 - %2",
                vendTable.AccountNum,
                vendTable.Blocked));
        }
    }
    ```

2. Run the class and check the results, which may be similar to this:

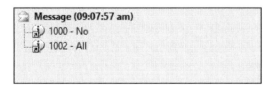

18

How it works...

The key method in this recipe is `setTmp()`. This method is available on all the tables, and it makes the current table instance behave as a temporary table in the current scope. Basically, it creates an `InMemory` temporary table that has the same schema as the original table.

In this recipe, we create a new class and place all the code in its `main()` method. The reason why we create a class and not a job is that the `main()` method can be set to run on the server tier by specifying the `server` modifier. This will improve the code's performance.

In the code, we first call the `setTmp()` method on the `vendTable` table to make it temporary in the scope of this method. This means that any data manipulations will be lost once the execution of this method is over and the actual table content will not be affected.

Next, we insert a couple of test records. Here, we use the `doInsert()` method to bypass any additional logic, which normally resides in the table's `insert()` method. We have to keep in mind that even the table becomes temporary; all the code in its `insert()`, `update()`, `delete()`, `initValue()`, and other methods is still present and we have to make sure that we don't call it unintentionally.

The last thing to do is to check for newly created records by showing them on the screen. We can see that although the table contains many actual records, only the records that we inserted were displayed in the **Infolog** window. Additionally, the two records we inserted do not appear in the actual table.

Copying a record

Copying existing data is one of the data manipulation tasks in Dynamics AX. There are numerous places in the standard Dynamics AX application where users can create new data entries just by copying existing data and then modifying it. A few examples are the **Copy** button on the **Costing versions** form located in **Inventory management | Setup | Costing** and the **Copy project** button on the **All projects** list page located in **Project management and accounting | Common | Projects**. Also, although the mentioned copying functionality might not be that straightforward, the idea is clear: the existing data is reused while creating new entries.

In this recipe, we will learn two ways to copy records in X++. We will discuss the usage of the table's `data()` method, the global `buf2buf()` function, and their differences. As an example, we will copy one of the existing main account records into a new record.

Processing Data

How to do it...

Carry out the following steps in order to complete this recipe:

1. Navigate to **General ledger | Common | Main accounts** and find the account to be copied. In this example, we will use **130100**, as shown here:

Main account	Name	Main account type	Main account category
120500	BOE Remitted for Discount	Asset	CASHEQUIV
120600	Protested BOE	Asset	CASHEQUIV
129999	TOTAL SECURITIES	Total	
130100	Accounts Receivable - Domestic	Asset	AR
130110	Accounts Receivable - Foreign	Asset	AR
130300	Accounts Receivable - Not Invoiced	Asset	AR
130400	Credit Card Receivable	Asset	AR
130500	Interest Receivable	Asset	AR
130600	Notes Receivable	Asset	NOTESREC
130700	Other Receivables	Asset	AR
130701	Accrued Vendor Rebates Receivable	Asset	AR
130725	Bridging	Asset	AR
130730	Received PDC	Asset	AR
130750	Use Tax Receivable	Asset	AR
130800	VAT Tax Receivable	Asset	AR
130999	TOTAL ACCOUNTS RECEIVABLE	Total	
132100	Prepaid Insurance	Asset	PREPAIDEXP

2. Open the AOT, create a new job named `MainAccountCopy` with the following code snippet, and run it:

   ```
   static void MainAccountCopy(Args _args)
   {
       MainAccount mainAccount1;
       MainAccount mainAccount2;

       mainAccount1 = MainAccount::findByMainAccountId(
           '130100');

       ttsBegin;

       mainAccount2.data(mainAccount1);

       mainAccount2.MainAccountId = '130101';
       mainAccount2.Name += ' - copy';

       if (!mainAccount2.validateWrite())
   ```

```
        {
                throw Exception::Error;
        }

        mainAccount2.insert();

        ttsCommit;
}
```

3. Navigate to **General ledger | Common | Main accounts** again and notice that there are two identical records now, as shown in the following screenshot:

Main account	Name	Main account type	Main account category
120500	BOE Remitted for Discount	Asset	CASHEQUIV
120600	Protested BOE	Asset	CASHEQUIV
129999	TOTAL SECURITIES	Total	
☑ 130100	Accounts Receivable - Domestic	Asset	AR
☑ 130101	Accounts Receivable - Domestic - copy	Asset	AR
130110	Accounts Receivable - Foreign	Asset	AR
130300	Accounts Receivable - Not Invoiced	Asset	AR
130400	Credit Card Receivable	Asset	AR
130500	Interest Receivable	Asset	AR
130600	Notes Receivable	Asset	NOTESREC
130700	Other Receivables	Asset	AR
130701	Accrued Vendor Rebates Receivable	Asset	AR
130725	Bridging	Asset	AR
130730	Received PDC	Asset	AR
130750	Use Tax Receivable	Asset	AR
130800	VAT Tax Receivable	Asset	AR
130999	TOTAL ACCOUNTS RECEIVABLE	Total	
132100	Prepaid Insurance	Asset	PREPAIDEXP

How it works...

In this recipe, we have two variables: `mainAccount1` for the original record and `mainAccount2` for the new record. First, we find the original record by calling `findMainAccountId()` in the `MainAccount` table.

Next, we copy the original record into the new one. Here, we use the table's `data()` method, which copies all the data fields from one variable into another.

After that, we set a new main account number, which is a part of the table's unique index.

Finally, we call `insert()` on the table if `validateWrite()` is successful. In this way, we create a new main account record that is exactly the same as the existing one apart from the account number.

Processing Data

There's more...

As we saw before, the `data()` method copies all the table fields, including the system fields such as the record ID or company account. Most of the time it is OK because when the new record is saved, the system fields are overwritten with the new values. However, this function may not work for copying records across companies. In this case, we can use another function called `buf2Buf()`. This function is a global function and is located in the `Global` class, which you can find by navigating to **AOT | Classes**. The `buf2Buf()` function is very similar to the table's `data()` method with one major difference. The `buf2Buf()` function copies all the data fields excluding the system fields. The code in the function is as follows:

```
static void buf2Buf(
    Common     _from,
    Common     _to,
    TableScope _scope = TableScope::CurrentTableOnly)
{
    DictTable  dictTable = new DictTable(_from.TableId);
    FieldId    fieldId   = dictTable.fieldNext(0, _scope);

    while (fieldId && ! isSysId(fieldId))
    {
        _to.(fieldId)   = _from.(fieldId);
        fieldId         = dictTable.fieldNext(fieldId, _scope);
    }
}
```

We can clearly see that during the copying process, all the table fields are traversed, but the system fields, such as `RecId` or `dataAreaId`, are excluded. The `isSysId()` helper function is used for this purpose.

In order to use the `buf2Buf()` function, the code of the `MainAccountCopy` job can be amended as follows:

```
static void MainAccountCopy(Args _args)
{
    MainAccount mainAccount1;
    MainAccount mainAccount2;

    mainAccount1 = MainAccount::findByMainAccountId('130100');

    ttsBegin;

    buf2Buf(mainAccount1, mainAccount2);

    mainAccount2.MainAccountId = '130101';
```

```
        mainAccount2.Name += ' - copy';

        if (!mainAccount2.validateWrite())
        {
            throw Exception::Error;
        }

        mainAccount2.insert();

        ttsCommit;
    }
```

Building a query object

Query objects in Dynamics AX are used to build SQL statements for reports, views, forms, and other AOT objects. They are normally created in the AOT using the drag and drop functionality and by defining various properties. Query objects can also be created from the code at runtime. This is normally done when AOT tools cannot handle complex and/or dynamic queries.

In this recipe, we will create a query from the code to retrieve project records from the **Project management** module. We will select the records where project ID starts with 00005, project type is time & material and project has at least one transaction of type hour registered.

How to do it...

Carry out the following steps in order to complete this recipe:

1. Open the AOT, create a new job named ProjTableQuery, and enter the following code snippet:

```
static void ProjTableQuery(Args _args)
{
    Query                   query;
    QueryBuildDataSource    qbds1;
    QueryBuildDataSource    qbds2;
    QueryBuildRange         qbr1;
    QueryBuildRange         qbr2;
    QueryRun                queryRun;
    ProjTable               projTable;

    query = new Query();

    qbds1 = query.addDataSource(tableNum(ProjTable));
```

```
            qbds1.addSortField(
                fieldNum(ProjTable, Name),
                SortOrder::Ascending);

            qbr1 = qbds1.addRange(fieldNum(ProjTable,Type));
            qbr1.value(queryValue(ProjType::TimeMaterial));

            qbr2 = qbds1.addRange(fieldNum(ProjTable,ProjId));
            qbr2.value(
                SysQuery::valueLikeAfter(queryValue('00005')));

            qbds2 = qbds1.addDataSource(tableNum(ProjEmplTrans));
            qbds2.relations(true);
            qbds2.joinMode(JoinMode::ExistsJoin);

            queryRun = new QueryRun(query);

            while (queryRun.next())
            {
                projTable = queryRun.get(tableNum(ProjTable));
                info(strFmt(
                    "%1, %2, %3",
                    projTable.ProjId,
                    projTable.Name,
                    projTable.Type));
            }
        }
```

2. Run the job and you will get a screen similar to the following screenshot:

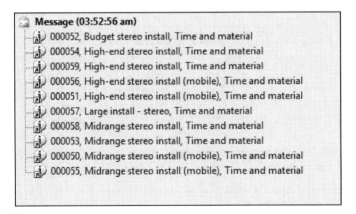

How it works...

First, we create a new `query` object. Next, we add a new `ProjTable` data source to the `query` object by calling its `addDataSource()` method. The method returns a reference to the `QueryBuildDataSource` object—`qbds1`. Here, we call the `addSortField()` method to enable sorting by the project name.

Next we create two ranges. The first range filters only the projects of the `ProjType::TimeMaterial` type and the second one lists only the records where the project number starts with `00005`. These two ranges are automatically added together using SQL's `AND` operator. The `QueryBuildRange` objects are created by calling the `addRange()` method of the `QueryBuildDataSource` object with the field ID number as the argument. The range value is set by calling `value()` on the `QueryBuildRange` object itself. We use the `queryValue()` function from the `Global` class and the `valueLikeAfter()` function from the `SysQuery` class to prepare the values before applying them as a range. More functions, such as `queryNotValue()` and `queryRange()`, can be found in the `Global` application class, which is located in **AOT | Classes**. Note that these functions are actually shortcuts to the `SysQuery` application class, which in turn has even more interesting helper methods that might be handy for every developer.

Adding another data source to an existing one connects both the data sources using SQL's `JOIN` operator. In this example, we are displaying projects that have at least one posted hour line. We start by adding the `ProjEmplTrans` table as another data source.

Next, we need to add relationships between the tables. If relationships are not defined on tables, we will have to use the `addLink()` method. In this example, relations in the tables are already defined, so you only need to enable them by calling the `relations()` method with `true` as an argument.

Calling `joinMode()` with `JoinMode::ExistsJoin` as a parameter ensures that only the projects that have at least one transaction of type hour will be selected. In situations like this, where we do not need any data from the second data source, performance-wise it is better to use an `exists` join instead of the `inner` join. This is because the `inner` join fetches the data from the second data source and therefore takes longer to execute.

The last thing that needs to be done is to create and run the `queryRun` object and show the selected data on the screen.

There's more...

It is worth mentioning a couple of specific cases when working with query objects from the code. One of them is how to use the `OR` operator and the other one is how to address array fields.

Processing Data

Using the OR operator

As you have already noted, regardless of how many ranges are added, all of them will be added together using SQL's AND operator. In most cases, this is fine, but sometimes complex user requirements demand ranges to be added using SQL's OR operator. There might be a number of workarounds, such as using temporary tables or similar tools, but we can use the Dynamics AX feature that allows you to pass a part of a raw SQL string as a range.

In this case, the range has to be formatted in a manner similar to a fully-qualified SQL WHERE clause, including field names, operators, and values. The expressions have to be formatted properly before you use them in a query. Here are some of the rules:

- The expression must be enclosed within single quotes and then inside the quotes—within parenthesis
- Each subexpression must also be enclosed within parentheses
- String values have to be enclosed within double quotes
- For enumerations, use their numeric values

For value formatting, use various Dynamics AX functions, such as `queryValue()` and `date2StrXpp()`, or methods from the `SysQuery` class.

Let's replace the code snippet from the previous example with the following lines of code:

```
qbr2.value(SysQuery::valueLikeAfter(queryValue('00005')));
with the new code:
qbr2.value(strFmt(
    '((%1 like "%2") || (%3 = %4))',
    fieldStr(ProjTable,ProjId),
    queryvalue('00005')+'*',
    fieldStr(ProjTable,Status),
    ProjStatus::InProcess+0));
```

Notice that by adding zero to the enumeration in the previous code, we can force the `strFmt()` function to use the numeric value of the enumeration. The `strFmt()` output should be similar to the following line:

```
((ProjId like "00005*") || (Status = 3))
```

Now if you run the code, besides all the projects starting with 00005, the result will also include all the active projects, as shown in the following screenshot:

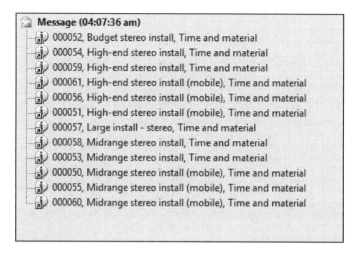

See also

- The *Creating a custom filter control* recipe in *Chapter 3, Working with Data in Forms*
- The *Using a form to build a lookup* recipe in *Chapter 4, Building Lookups*

Using a macro in a SQL statement

In a standard Dynamics AX application, there are macros, such as InventDimJoin and InventDimSelect, that are reused numerous times across the application. These macros are actually full or partial X++ SQL queries that can be called with various arguments. Such approaches save development time by allowing you to reuse pieces of X++ SQL queries.

In this recipe, we will create a small macro that holds a single WHERE clause to display only the active vendor records. Then, we will create a job that uses the created macros to display a vendor list.

Processing Data

How to do it...

Carry out the following steps in order to complete this recipe:

1. Open the AOT and create a new macro named `VendTableNotBlocked` with the following code snippet:

   ```
   (%1.Blocked == CustVendorBlocked::No)
   ```

2. In the AOT, create a new job called `VendTableMacro` with the following code snippet:

   ```
   static void VendTableMacro(Args _args)
   {
       VendTable    vendTable;

       while select vendTable
           where #VendTableNotBlocked(vendTable)
       {
           info(strFmt(
               "%1 - %2",
               vendTable.AccountNum,
               vendTable.name()));
       }
   }
   ```

3. Run the job and check the results, as shown in the following screenshot:

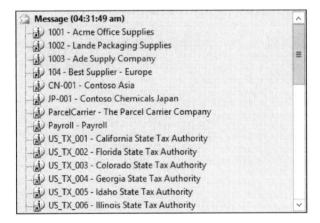

How it works...

In this recipe, first we define a macro that holds the WHERE clause. Normally, the purpose of defining SQL in a macro is to reuse it a number of times in various places. We use `%1` as an argument. More arguments formatted as `%2`, `%3`, and so on can be used.

Next, we create a job with the `SELECT` statement. Here, we use the previously created macro in the `WHERE` clause and pass `vendTable` as an argument.

The query works like any other query, but the advantage is that the code in the macro can be reused elsewhere.

Remember that before we start using macros in SQL queries, we should be aware of the following caveats:

- Too much code in a macro might reduce the SQL statement's readability for other developers
- Cross-references do not take into account the code inside the macro
- Changes in the macro will not be reflected in the objects where the macro is used until the objects are recompiled

Executing a direct SQL statement

Dynamics AX allows developers to build X++ SQL statements that are flexible enough to fit into any custom business process. However, in some cases, the usage of X++ SQL is either not effective or not possible at all. One such case is when we run data upgrade tasks during an application version upgrade. A standard application contains a set of data upgrade tasks to be completed during the version upgrade. If the application is highly customized, then most likely, standard tasks have to be modified in order to reflect data dictionary customizations, or a new set of tasks have to be created to make sure data is handled correctly during the upgrade.

Normally, at this stage, SQL statements are so complex that they can only be created using database-specific SQL and executed directly in the database. Additionally, running direct SQL statements dramatically increases data upgrade performance because most of the code is executed on the database server where all the data resides. This is very important when working with large volumes of data.

Another case when we will need to use direct SQL statements is when we want to connect to an external database using the ODBC connection. In this case, X++ SQL is not supported at all.

This recipe will demonstrate how to execute SQL statements directly. We will connect to the current Dynamics AX database directly using an additional connection and retrieve a list of vendor accounts.

Processing Data

How to do it...

Carry out the following steps in order to complete this recipe:

1. In the AOT, create a new class named `VendTableSql` using the following code snippet:

    ```
    class VendTableSql
    {
    }

    server static void main(Args _args)
    {
        UserConnection                      userConnection;
        Statement                           statement;
        str                                 sqlStatement;
        SqlSystem                           sqlSystem;
        SqlStatementExecutePermission       sqlPermission;
        ResultSet                           resultSet;
        DictTable                           tblVendTable;
        DictTable                           tblDirPartyTable;
        DictField                           fldParty;
        DictField                           fldAccountNum;
        DictField                           fldDataAreaId;
        DictField                           fldBlocked;
        DictField                           fldRecId;
        DictField                           fldName;

        tblVendTable     = new DictTable(tableNum(VendTable));
        tblDirPartyTable = new DictTable(tableNum(DirPartyTable));

        fldParty = new DictField(
            tableNum(VendTable),
            fieldNum(VendTable,Party));

        fldAccountNum = new DictField(
            tableNum(VendTable),
            fieldNum(VendTable,AccountNum));

        fldDataAreaId = new DictField(
            tableNum(VendTable),
            fieldNum(VendTable,DataAreaId));

        fldBlocked = new DictField(
            tableNum(VendTable),
    ```

```
        fieldNum(VendTable,Blocked));

    fldRecId = new DictField(
        tableNum(DirPartyTable),
        fieldNum(DirPartyTable,RecId));

    fldName = new DictField(
        tableNum(DirPartyTable),
        fieldNum(DirPartyTable,Name));

    sqlSystem = new SqlSystem();

    sqlStatement = 'SELECT %1, %2 FROM %3 ' +
        'JOIN %4 ON %3.%5 = %4.%6 ' +
        'WHERE %7 = %9 AND %8 = %10';

    sqlStatement = strFmt(
        sqlStatement,
        fldAccountNum.name(DbBackend::Sql),
        fldName.name(DbBackend::Sql),
        tblVendTable.name(DbBackend::Sql),
        tblDirPartyTable.name(DbBackend::Sql),
        fldParty.name(DbBackend::Sql),
        fldRecId.name(DbBackend::Sql),
        fldDataAreaId.name(DbBackend::Sql),
        fldBlocked.name(DbBackend::Sql),
        sqlSystem.sqlLiteral(curext(), true),
        sqlSystem.sqlLiteral(CustVendorBlocked::No, true));

    userConnection = new UserConnection();
    statement      = userConnection.createStatement();

    sqlPermission = new SqlStatementExecutePermission(
        sqlStatement);

    sqlPermission.assert();

    resultSet      = statement.executeQuery(sqlStatement);

    CodeAccessPermission::revertAssert();

    while (resultSet.next())
    {
        info(strFmt(
```

Processing Data

```
            "%1 - %2",
            resultSet.getString(1),
            resultSet.getString(2)));
    }
}
```

2. Run the class to retrieve a list of vendors directly from the database, as shown in the following screenshot:

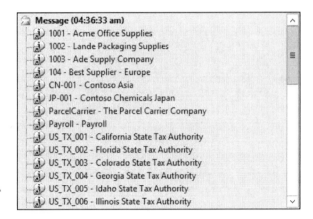

How it works...

We start the code by creating the `DictTable` and `DictField` objects to handle the vendor table and its fields, which are used later in the query. The `DirPartyTable` is used to get an additional vendor information.

A new `SqlSystem` object is also created. It is used to convert Dynamics AX types to SQL types.

Next, we set up a SQL statement with a number of placeholders for the table or field names and field values to be inserted later.

The main query creation takes place next, when the query placeholders are replaced with the right values. Here, we use the previously created `DictTable` and `DictField` objects . We call their name() methods with the `DbBackend::Sql` enumeration as an argument. This ensures that we use the table and field names exactly as they are defined in the database. This is because due to some technical restrictions, the names in SQL database sometimes might slightly differ from their names in the Dynamics AX application.

We also use the `sqlLiteral()` method of the previously created `sqlSystem` object to properly format SQL values in order to ensure that they do not have any unsafe characters.

The value of the `sqlStatement` variable that holds the prepared SQL query depending on your environment is as follows:

```
SELECT ACCOUNTNUM, NAME FROM VENDTABLE
    JOIN DIRPARTYTABLE ON VENDTABLE.PARTY = DIRPARTYTABLE.RECID
    WHERE DATAAREAID = 'usmf' AND BLOCKED = 0
```

Once the SQL statement is ready, we initialize a direct connection to the database and run the statement. The results are returned in the `resultSet` object, and we get them by using the `while` statement and calling the `next()` method until no records left.

Note that we created an `sqlPermission` object of the type `SqlStatementExecutePermission` here and called its `assert()` method before executing the statement. This is required in order to comply with Dynamics AX's trustworthy computing requirements.

Another thing that needs to be mentioned is that when building direct SQL queries, special attention has to be paid to license, configuration, and security keys. Some tables or fields might be disabled in the application and may contain no data in the database.

The code in this recipe also can be used to connect to external ODBC databases. We only need to replace the `UserConnection` class with the `OdbcConnection` class and use text names instead of the `DictTable` and `DictField` objects.

There's more...

The standard Dynamics AX application provides an alternate way of building direct SQL statements by using a set of `SQLBuilder` classes. By using these classes, we can create SQL statements as objects, as opposed to text. Next, we will demonstrate how to use the `SQLBuilder` classes. We will create the same SQL statement as we did before.

First, in AOT, create another class named `VendTableSqlBuilder` using the following code snippet:

```
class VendTableSqlBuilder
{
}

server static void main(Args _args)
{
    UserConnection                    userConnection;
    Statement                         statement;
    str                               sqlStatement;
    SqlStatementExecutePermission     sqlPermission;
    ResultSet                         resultSet;
```

```
SQLBuilderSelectExpression     selectExpr;
SQLBuilderTableEntry           vendTable;
SQLBuilderTableEntry           dirPartyTable;
SQLBuilderFieldEntry           accountNum;
SQLBuilderFieldEntry           dataAreaId;
SQLBuilderFieldEntry           blocked;
SQLBuilderFieldEntry           name;

selectExpr = SQLBuilderSelectExpression::construct();
selectExpr.parmUseJoin(true);

vendTable = selectExpr.addTableId(
    tablenum(VendTable));

dirPartyTable = vendTable.addJoinTableId(
    tablenum(DirPartyTable));

accountNum = vendTable.addFieldId(
    fieldnum(VendTable,AccountNum));

name = dirPartyTable.addFieldId(
    fieldnum(DirPartyTable,Name));

dataAreaId = vendTable.addFieldId(
    fieldnum(VendTable,DataAreaId));

blocked = vendTable.addFieldId(
    fieldnum(VendTable,Blocked));

vendTable.addRange(dataAreaId, curext());
vendTable.addRange(blocked, CustVendorBlocked::No);

selectExpr.addSelectFieldEntry(
    SQLBuilderSelectFieldEntry::newExpression(
        accountNum,
        'AccountNum'));

selectExpr.addSelectFieldEntry(
    SQLBuilderSelectFieldEntry::newExpression(
        name,
        'Name'));
```

```
        sqlStatement     = selectExpr.getExpression(null);

        userConnection = new UserConnection();
        statement        = userConnection.createStatement();

        sqlPermission = new SqlStatementExecutePermission(
            sqlStatement);

        sqlPermission.assert();

        resultSet = statement.executeQuery(sqlStatement);

        CodeAccessPermission::revertAssert();

        while (resultSet.next())
        {
            info(strfmt(
                "%1 - %2",
                resultSet.getString(1),
                resultSet.getString(2)));
        }
    }
```

In the preceding method, we first create a new `selectExpr` object, which is based on the `SQLBuilderSelectExpression` class. It represents the object of the SQL statement.

Next, we add the `VendTable` table to it by calling its member method `addTableId()`. This method returns a reference to the `vendTable` object of the type `SQLBuilderTableEntry`, which corresponds to a table node in a SQL query. We also add `DirPartyTable` as a joined table.

Then, we create a number of field objects of the `SQLBuilderFieldEntry` type to be used later and two ranges to show only this company account and only the active vendor accounts.

We use `addSelectFieldEntry()` to add two fields to be selected. Here, we use the previously created field objects.

The SQL statement is generated once the `getExpression()` method is called, and the rest of the code is the same as in the previous example.

Running the class will give us the results that are similar to the ones we got earlier.

Processing Data

Enhancing the data consistency check

It is highly recommended for system administrators to run the standard Dynamics AX data consistency checks from time to time, which can be found by navigating to **System administration | Periodic | Database | Consistency check**, to evaluate the system's data integrity. This function finds orphan data, validates parameters, and checks many other things.

In this recipe, we will see how we can enhance the standard Dynamics AX consistency check to include more tables in their data integrity validation.

Getting ready

Before we start, we need to create an invalid setup in order to make sure that we can simulate data inconsistency. Navigate to **Fixed assets | Setup | Value models** and create a new model, for instance, TEST, as shown in the following screenshot:

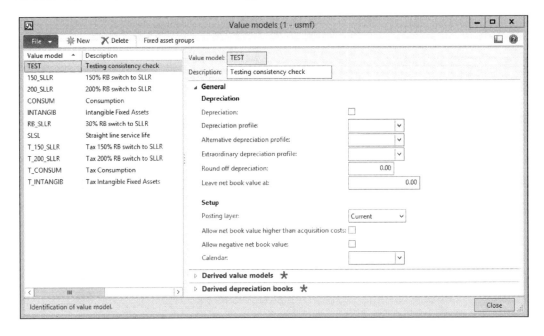

Navigate to **Fixed assets | Setup | Fixed asset posting profiles** and under the **Ledger accounts** tab page, create a new record with the newly created value model for any of the posting types, as shown here:

Chapter 1

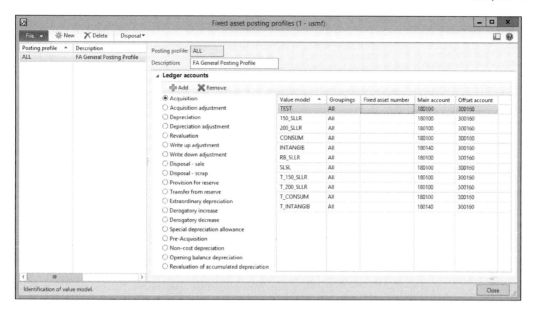

Go back to the **Value models** form and delete the previously created value model. Now, we have a nonexistent value model in the fixed asset posting settings.

How to do it...

Carry out the following steps in order to complete this recipe:

1. In the AOT, create a new class named `AssetConsistencyCheck` with the following code snippet:

   ```
   class AssetConsistencyCheck extends SysConsistencyCheck
   {
   }

   client server static ClassDescription description()
   {
       return "Fixed assets";
   }

   client server static HelpTxt helpText()
   {
       return "Consistency check of the fixed asset module";
   }

   Integer executionOrder()
   ```

Processing Data

```
    {
        return 1;
    }

    void run()
    {
        this.kernelCheckTable(tableNum(AssetLedgerAccounts));
    }
```

2. Navigate to **System administration** | **Periodic** | **Database** | **Consistency check**, select the newly created **Fixed assets** option from the **Module** drop-down list, and click on **OK** to run the check, as shown here:

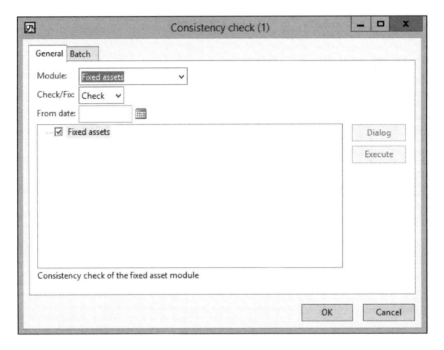

3. Now, the message displayed in the **Infolog** window should complain about the missing value model in the fixed assets posting settings, as shown in the following screenshot:

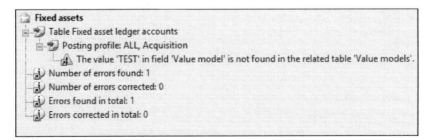

How it works...

The consistency check in Dynamics AX validate only the predefined list of tables for each module. The system contains a number of classes derived from `SysConsistencyCheck`. For example, the `CustConsistencyCheck` class is responsible for validating the **Accounts receivable** module, `LedgerConsistencyCheck` for validating **General ledger**, and so on.

In this recipe, we created a new class named `AssetConsistencyCheck`, extending the `SysConsistencyCheck` class for the fixed asset module. The following methods were created:

- `description()`: This provides a name to the consistency check form.
- `helpText()`: This displays some explanation about the check.
- `executionOrder()`: This determines where the check is located in the list.
- `run()`: This holds the code to perform the actual checking. Here, we use the `kernelCheckTable()` method, which validates the given table.

There's more...

The classes that we just mentioned can only be executed from the main **Consistency check** form. Individual checks can also be invoked as standalone functions. We just need to create an additional method to allow the running of the class:

```
static void main(Args _args)
{
    SysConsistencyCheckJob consistencyCheckJob;
    AssetConsistencyCheck  assetConsistencyCheck;

    consistencyCheckJob = new SysConsistencyCheckJob(
        classIdGet(assetConsistencyCheck));

    if (!consistencyCheckJob.prompt())
    {
        return;
    }

    consistencyCheckJob.run();
}
```

Processing Data

Exporting data to an XML file

Briefly, XML defines a set of rules for encoding documents electronically. It allows the creation of all kinds of structured documents that can be exchanged between systems. In Dynamics AX, XML files are widely used across the application.

Probably the main thing that is associated with XML in Dynamics AX is the **Application Integration Framework** (**AIF**). It is an infrastructure that allows you to expose business logic or exchange data with other external systems. The communication is done by using XML-formatted documents. By using the existing XML framework's application classes prefixed with Axd, you can export or import data into the system. It is also possible to create new Axd classes using **AIF Document Service Wizard** from the **Tools** menu to support the export and import of newly created tables.

Dynamics AX also contains a set of application classes prefixed with Xml, such as XmlDocument and XmlNode. Basically, these classes are wrappers around the System.XML namespace in the .NET Framework.

In this recipe, we will create a new simple XML document by using the Xml classes in order to show the basics of XML. We will create a file with the data from the main account table and save it as an XML file.

How to do it...

Carry out the following steps in order to complete this recipe:

1. Open the AOT and create a new class named CreateXmlFile with the following code snippet:

```
class CreateXmlFile
{
}

static void main(Args _args)
{
    XmlDocument doc;
    XmlElement  nodeXml;
    XmlElement  nodeTable;
    XmlElement  nodeAccount;
    XmlElement  nodeName;
```

```
MainAccount mainAccount;
#define.filename(@'C:\Temp\accounts.xml')

doc      = XmlDocument::newBlank();

nodeXml = doc.createElement('xml');

doc.appendChild(nodeXml);

while select RecId, MainAccountId, Name from mainAccount
    order by mainAccountId
    where mainAccount.LedgerChartOfAccounts ==
        LedgerChartOfAccounts::current()
{
    nodeTable = doc.createElement(tableStr(MainAccount));

    nodeTable.setAttribute(
        fieldStr(MainAccount, RecId),
        int642str(mainAccount.RecId));

    nodeXml.appendChild(nodeTable);

    nodeAccount = doc.createElement(
        fieldStr(MainAccount, MainAccountId));

    nodeAccount.appendChild(
        doc.createTextNode(mainAccount.MainAccountId));

    nodeTable.appendChild(nodeAccount);

    nodeName = doc.createElement(
        fieldStr(MainAccount, Name));

    nodeName.appendChild(
        doc.createTextNode(mainAccount.Name));

    nodeTable.appendChild(nodeName);
}

doc.save(#filename);

info(strFmt("File %1 created.", #filename));
}
```

Processing Data

2. Run the class. The XML file named `accounts.xml` will be created in the specified folder. Open the XML file using any XML editor or viewer, such as Microsoft Internet Explorer, and review the created XML structure, as shown in the following screenshot:

```xml
<?xml version="1.0" encoding="UTF-8"?>
<xml>
    <MainAccount RecId="22565421316">
        <MainAccountId>110110</MainAccountId>
        <Name>Bank Account - USD</Name>
    </MainAccount>
    <MainAccount RecId="22565421317">
        <MainAccountId>110115</MainAccountId>
        <Name>Bank Account - CAD</Name>
    </MainAccount>
    <MainAccount RecId="22565421318">
        <MainAccountId>110120</MainAccountId>
        <Name>Bank Account - CNY</Name>
    </MainAccount>
    <MainAccount RecId="22565421319">
        <MainAccountId>110130</MainAccountId>
        <Name>Bank Account - EUR</Name>
    </MainAccount>
    <MainAccount RecId="22565421320">
        <MainAccountId>110140</MainAccountId>
        <Name>Bank Account - DKK</Name>
    </MainAccount>
    <MainAccount RecId="22565421321">
        <MainAccountId>110150</MainAccountId>
        <Name>Bank Account - GBP</Name>
    </MainAccount>
    <MainAccount RecId="22565421322">
        <MainAccountId>110160</MainAccountId>
        <Name>Bank Account - Payroll</Name>
    </MainAccount>
```

How it works...

We start the recipe by creating a new `XmlDocument` using the `newBlank()` method, which represents an XML structure. Then, we create its root node named `xml` using the `createElement()` method and add the node to the document by calling the document's `appendChild()` method.

Next, we go through all the main accounts in the current chart of accounts and perform the following tasks for each record:

- Create a new `XmlElement` node, which is named exactly the same as the table name, and add this node to the root node.
- Create a node that represents the account number field and a child node representing its value. The account number node is created using `createElement()` and its value is created using `createTextNode()`. The `createTextNode()` method basically adds a value as text with no XML tags.
- Add the account number node to the table node.

- Create a node representing the account name field and a child node representing its value.
- Add the account name node to the table node.

Finally, we save the created XML document as a file.

In this way, we create an XML document that contains the current chart of accounts.

Importing data from an XML file

In Dynamics AX, an XML file is imported in a similar way as it is exported. In this recipe, we will continue using the XML application classes. We will create a new class that reads XML files and displays their content on the screen. As the source file, we will use the previously created `accounts.xml` file.

How to do it...

Carry out the following steps in order to complete this recipe:

1. Open the AOT and create a new class named `ReadXmlFile` with the following code snippet. Use the document created in the previous recipe:

    ```
    class ReadXmlFile
    {
    }
    static void main(Args _args)
    {
        XmlDocument  doc;
        XmlNodeList  data;
        XmlElement   nodeTable;
        XmlElement   nodeAccount;
        XmlElement   nodeName;
        #define.filename(@'C:\Temp\accounts.xml')

        doc = XmlDocument::newFile(#filename);

        data = doc.selectNodes('//'+tableStr(MainAccount));

        nodeTable = data.nextNode();

        while (nodeTable)
        {
            nodeAccount = nodeTable.selectSingleNode(
                fieldStr(MainAccount, MainAccountId));
    ```

Processing Data

```
            nodeName = nodeTable.selectSingleNode(
                fieldStr(MainAccount, Name));

            info(strFmt(
                "%1 - %2",
                nodeAccount.text(),
                nodeName.text()));

            nodeTable = data.nextNode();
        }
    }
```

2. Run the class. The **Infolog** window will display the contents of the `accounts.xml` file on the screen, as shown here:

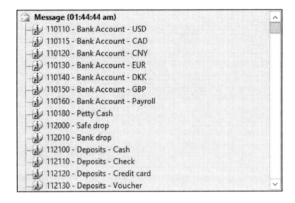

How it works...

In this recipe, we first create a new `XmlDocument` object. We create it from the file and hence we use the `newFile()` method for this. Then, we get all the document nodes of the `MainAccount` table as `XmlNodeList`. We also obtain its first element by calling the `nextNode()` function.

Next, we loop through all the list elements and perform the following tasks:

- Get an account number node as an `XmlElement`.
- Obtain an account name node as an `XmlElement`.
- Display the text of both the nodes in the **Infolog** window. Normally, this should be replaced with more sensible code to process the data.
- Get the next list element.

In this way, we retrieve data from the XML file. A similar approach can be used to read any other XML file.

Creating a comma-separated value file

CSV files are widely used across various systems. Although nowadays modern systems use XML formats for data exchange, CSV files are still popular because of the simplicity of their format.

Normally, the data in a file is organized, so one line corresponds to one record and each line contains a number of values, normally separated by commas. Record and value separators can be any other symbol, depending on the system requirements.

In this recipe, we will learn how to create a custom CSV file from the code. We will also export a list of main accounts—account number and name from the current chart of accounts.

How to do it...

Carry out the following steps in order to complete this recipe:

1. Open the AOT and create a new class named `CreateCommaFile` with the following code snippet:

```
class CreateCommaFile
{
}
static client void main(Args _args)
{
    CommaTextIo         file;
    container           line;
    MainAccount         mainAccount;
    #define.filename(@'C:\Temp\accounts.csv')
    #File

    file = new CommaTextIo(#filename, #io_write);

    if (!file || file.status() != IO_Status::Ok)
    {
        throw error("File cannot be opened.");
    }

    file.outRecordDelimiter('\r\n');
    file.outFieldDelimiter(',');

    while select MainAccountId, Name from mainAccount
        order by MainAccountId
        where mainAccount.LedgerChartOfAccounts ==
```

Processing Data

```
                LedgerChartOfAccounts::current()
    {
        line = [
            mainAccount.MainAccountId,
            mainAccount.Name];
        file.writeExp(line);
    }

    info(strFmt("File %1 created.", #filename));
}
```

2. Run the class. A new file named accounts.csv should be created in the specified folder. Open this file with Notepad or any other text editor to view the results, as shown in the following screenshot:

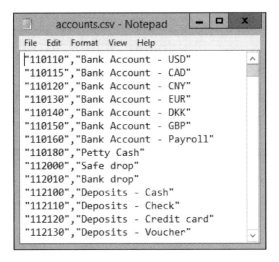

How it works...

In the variable declaration section of the main() method of the newly created CreateCommaFile class, we define a name for the output file along with other variables. Here, we also declare the standard #File macro, which contains a number of file-handling definitions like modes, such as #io_read, #io_write, #io_append, file types, and delimiters.

Then, we create a new CSV file by calling the `new()` method on a standard `CommaTextIo` class. It accepts two parameters: filename and mode. For mode, we use `#io_write` from the `#File` macro to make sure that a new file is created and opened for further writing. If a file with the given name already exists, then it will be overwritten. In order to make sure that a file is created successfully, we check whether the file object exists and its status is valid, otherwise we show an error message.

In multilingual environments, it is better to use the `CommaTextIo` class. It behaves the same way as the `CommaIo` class does, plus it supports Unicode, which allows you to process data with various language-specific symbols.

Next, we specify the delimiters for the output file. As the name suggests, by default, a CSV file contains a number of rows separated by line breaks and a number of values in each line separated by commas. The two methods `outRecordDelimiter()` and `outFieldDelimiter()` allow you to specify those delimiters for output files. In this example, we called these two methods just for demonstration purposes as the values we specify are the default values anyway.

Finally, we loop through all the main accounts in the current chart of accounts, store all the account numbers and their names into a container, and write them to the file using the `writeExp()` method.

In this way, we create a new CSV file with a list of main accounts inside.

There's more...

You probably might have already noticed that the `main()` method has the `client` modifier, which forces its code to run on the client. When dealing with large amounts of data, it is more effective to run the code on the server. In order to do this, we need to change the modifier to `server`. The following class generates exactly the same file as before, except that this file is created in the folder on the server's file system:

```
class CreateCommaFileServer
{
}

static server void main(Args _args)
{
    CommaTextIo          file;
    container            line;
    MainAccount          mainAccount;
    FileIoPermission     perm;
    #define.filename(@'C:\Temp\accounts.csv')
    #File
```

```
    perm = new FileIoPermission(#filename, #io_write);
    perm.assert();

    file = new CommaTextIo(#filename, #io_write);

    if (!file || file.status() != IO_Status::Ok)
    {
        throw error("File cannot be opened.");
    }

    file.outRecordDelimiter('\r\n');
    file.outFieldDelimiter(',');

    while select MainAccountId, Name from mainAccount
        order by MainAccountId
        where mainAccount.LedgerChartOfAccounts ==
            LedgerChartOfAccounts::current()
    {
        line = [
            mainAccount.MainAccountId,
            mainAccount.Name];
        file.writeExp(line);
    }

    CodeAccessPermission::revertAssert();

    info(strFmt("File %1 created.", #filename));
}
```

File manipulation on the server is protected by Dynamics AX code access security, and we must use the `FileIoPermission` class to make sure that we match the requirements.

At the end, we call `CodeAccessPermission::revertAssert()` to revert the previous assertion.

Reading a comma-separated value file

Besides data import/export, CSV files can be used for integration between systems. It is probably the most simple integration approach, when one system generates CSV files in some network folder and another system reads those files at specified intervals. Although this is not a very sophisticated real-time integration, in most cases, it does the job and does not require any additional components, such as Dynamics AX AIF or similar.

In this recipe, you will learn how to read CSV files from the code. As an example, we will process the file created in the previous recipe.

How to do it...

Carry out the following steps in order to complete this recipe:

1. In the AOT, create a new class named `ReadCommaFile` with the following code snippet:

   ```
   class ReadCommaFile
   {
   }

   static client void main(Args _args)
   {
       CommaTextIo       file;
       container         line;
       #define.filename(@'C:\Temp\accounts.csv')
       #File

       file = new CommaTextIo(#filename, #io_read);

       if (!file || file.status() != IO_Status::Ok)
       {
           throw error("File cannot be opened.");
       }

       file.inRecordDelimiter('\r\n');
       file.inFieldDelimiter(',');

       line = file.read();

       while (file.status() == IO_Status::Ok)
       {
           info(con2Str(line, ' - '));
           line = file.read();
       }
   }
   ```

Processing Data

2. Run the `ReadCommaFile` class to view the file's content, as shown in the following screenshot:

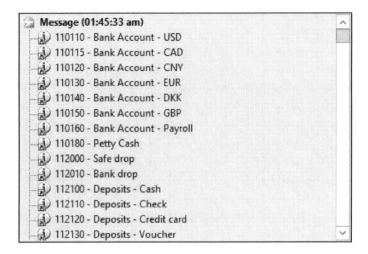

How it works...

As in the previous recipe, we first create a new file object using the `CommaTextIo` class. This time, we use `#io_read` as the mode to ensure that the existing file is opened for reading only. We also perform the same validations to make sure that the file object is correctly created; otherwise, an error message is displayed.

Finally, we read the file line by line until we reach the end of the file. Here, we use the `while` loop until the file status changes from `IO_Status::OK` to any other status, which means we reached the end of the file or something unexpected had happened. Inside the loop, we call the `read()` method on the file object, which returns the current line as a container and moves the internal file cursor to the next line. The data in the file is then simply shown on the screen using the standard global `info()` function in conjunction with the `con2Str()` function, which converts a container to a string.

There's more...

File reading can also be executed in a way similar to file writing on the server tier in order to improve performance. The `client` modifier has to be changed to `server`, and the code with the `FileIoPermission` class has to be added to fulfill the code access security requirements.

Chapter 1

The modified class will look similar to the following code snippet:

```
class ReadCommaFileServer
{
}

static server void main(Args _args)
{
    CommaTextIo         file;
    container           line;
    FileIoPermission    perm;
    #define.filename(@'C:\Temp\accounts.csv')
    #File

    perm = new FileIoPermission(#filename, #io_read);
    perm.assert();

    file = new CommaTextIo(#filename, #io_read);

    if (!file || file.status() != IO_Status::Ok)
    {
        throw error("File cannot be opened.");
    }

    file.inRecordDelimiter('\r\n');
    file.inFieldDelimiter(',');

    line = file.read();

    while (file.status() == IO_Status::Ok)
    {
        info(con2Str(line, ' - '));
        line = file.read();
    }

    CodeAccessPermission::revertAssert();
}
```

Processing Data

Using the date effectiveness feature

Date effectiveness is a feature in Dynamics AX 2012 that allows developers to easily create date range fields. Date ranges are used to define record validity between the specified dates, for example, defining employee contract dates.

This feature significantly reduces the amount of time that developers spend on writing code and also provides a consistent approach to implementing data range fields.

This recipe will demonstrate the basics of the date effectiveness feature. We will implement the date effectiveness functionality for e-mail templates on the **E-mail templates** forms.

How to do it...

Carry out the following steps in order to complete this recipe:

1. In the AOT, find the `SysEmailTable` table and change its property, as shown in the following table:

Property	Value
`ValidTimeStateFieldType`	Date

2. Note the two new fields that are automatically added to the table, as shown in the following screenshot:

Chapter 1

3. Add the newly created `ValidFrom` and `ValidTo` fields to the existing `emailIdIdx` index and change its properties, as shown in the following table:

Property	Value
AlternateKey	Yes
ValidTimeStateKey	Yes
ValidTimeStateMode	NoGap

4. Save the table. The system should prompt you to synchronize the table. Click on **Continue**, as shown here:

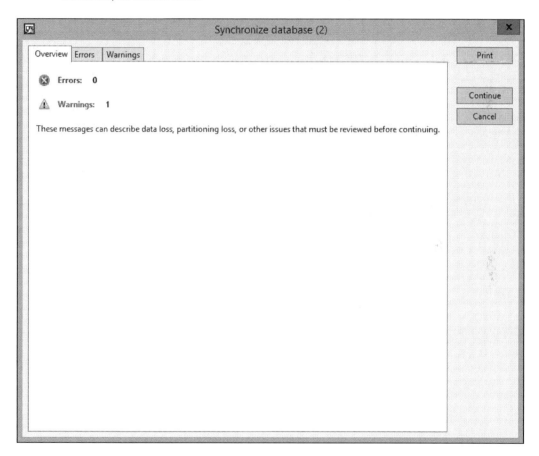

Processing Data

5. After the changes, the index should look similar to the following screenshot:

6. Next, add the `ValidFrom` and `ValidTo` fields to the table's `Identification` group, as shown in the following screenshot:

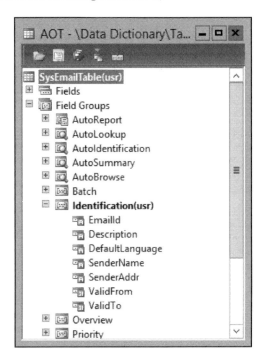

Chapter 1

7. In the AOT, find the `SysEmailTable` form, refresh it using the **Restore** command from the right-click context menu, then locate its data source named `SysEmailTable` and change its properties, as follows:

Property	Value
`ValidTimeStateAutoQuery`	`DateRange`
`ValidTimeStateUpdate`	`Correction`

8. In order to test the results, navigate to **Organization administration | Setup | E-mail templates** and notice the newly created fields: **Effective** and **Expiration**. Try creating records with the same **E-mail ID** and overlapping date ranges—you will notice how the system is proposing to maintain valid date ranges, as shown in the following screenshot:

How it works...

We start the recipe by setting the `ValidTimeStateFieldType` property of `SysEmailTable` to `Date`. This automatically creates two new fields, `ValidFrom` and `ValidTo`, that are used to define a date range.

Next, we add the created fields to the primary index where the `EmailId` field is used and adjust the index's properties.

We set the `AlternateKey` property to `Yes` in order to ensure that this index is part of an alternate key.

We set the `ValidTimeStateKey` property to `Yes` in order to specify that the index is used to determine valid date ranges.

Processing Data

We also set the `ValidTimeStateMode` property to `NoGap` in order to ensure that e-mail templates with the same identification number can be created within continuous periods only. This property can also be set to `Gap`, allowing noncontinuous date ranges.

Finally, we adjust the `SysEmailTable` form to reflect the changes. We add the newly created `ValidFrom` and `ValidTo` fields to the `SysEmailTable` table's `Identification` group so that they automatically appear in the form's `Overview` grid. We also change a few properties of the `SysEmailTable` data source, as follows:

1. Set the `ValidTimeStateAutoQuery` property to `DateRange` in order to ensure that all the records are visible. The default `AsOfDate` value can be used if you want to display only the records for the current period.
2. Set the `ValidTimeStateUpdate` property to `Correction`, allowing the system to automatically adjust the dates of the associated records.

There's more...

Forms with date-effective records can be enhanced with an automatically generated toolbar for filtering the records. This can be done with the help of the `DateEffectivenessPaneController` application class.

In order to demonstrate this, let's modify the previously used `SysEmailTable` form and add the following code snippet at the bottom of the form's `init()` method:

```
DateEffectivenessPaneController::constructWithForm(
    this,
    SysEmailTable_ds);
```

Now, when you open the form, it contains an automatically generated date effectiveness filter at the top, as shown in the following screenshot:

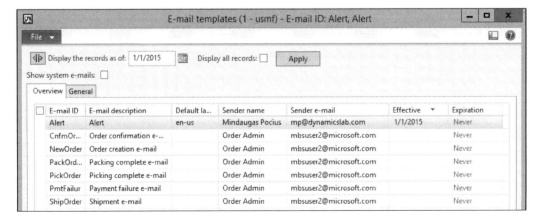

2
Working with Forms

In this chapter, we will cover the following recipes:

- Creating dialogs using the RunBase framework
- Handling a dialog event
- Building a dynamic form
- Adding a form splitter
- Creating a modal form
- Modifying multiple forms dynamically
- Storing user selections
- Using a Tree control
- Building a checklist
- Adding the View details link

Introduction

Forms in Dynamics AX represent the user interface and are mainly used to enter or modify data. They are also used to run reports, execute user commands, validate data, and so on.

Normally, forms are created using the AOT by creating a form object and adding various controls into it, such as tabs, tab pages, grids, groups, data fields, and others. The form's behavior is controlled by its properties or the code in its methods. The behavior and layouts of form controls are also controlled by their properties and the code in their methods. Although it is very rare, forms can also be created dynamically from the code.

Working with Forms

In this chapter, we will cover various aspects of using Dynamics AX forms. We start by building Dynamics AX dialogs, and discuss how to handle their events. The chapter will also show you how to build dynamic forms, how to add dynamic controls to existing forms, and how to make modal forms.

This chapter also discusses the usage of splitters and tree controls as well as how to create checklists, save user selections, and other things.

Creating dialogs using the RunBase framework

Dialogs are a way to present users with a simple input form. They are commonly used for small user tasks, such as filling in report values, running batch jobs, and presenting only the most important fields to the user when creating new records. Dialogs are normally created from X++ code without storing the actual layout in the AOT.

The application class called `Dialog` is used to build dialogs. Other application classes, such as `DialogField`, `DialogGroup`, `DialogTabPage` and others, are used to create dialog controls. The easiest way to create dialogs is to use the `RunBase` framework. This is because the framework provides a set of predefined methods, which make the creation and handling of the dialog well-structured as opposed to having all the code in a single place. Although in Dynamics AX 2012 the `RunBase` framework was replaced by the `SysOperation` framework, the `RunBase` framework is still widely used across the application.

In this example, we will demonstrate how to build a dialog from the code using the `RunBase` framework class. The dialog will contain customer table fields shown in different groups and tabs for creating a new record. There will be two tab pages, **General** and **Details**. The first page will have the **Customer account** and **Name** input controls. The second page will be divided into two groups, **Setup** and **Payment**, with the relevant fields inside each group. The actual record will not be created, as it is out of the scope of this example. However, for demonstration purposes, the information specified by the user will be displayed in the **Infolog** window.

How to do it...

Carry out the following steps in order to complete this recipe:

1. Open the AOT and create a new class `CustCreate` with the following code snippet:

    ```
    class CustCreate extends RunBase
    {
        DialogField     fieldAccount;
        DialogField     fieldName;
        DialogField     fieldGroup;
        DialogField     fieldCurrency;
    ```

```
        DialogField    fieldPaymTermId;
        DialogField    fieldPaymMode;
        CustAccount    custAccount;
        CustName       custName;
        CustGroupId    custGroupId;
        CurrencyCode   currencyCode;
        CustPaymTermId paymTermId;
        CustPaymMode   paymMode;
    }

    container pack()
    {
        return conNull();
    }

    boolean unpack(container _packedClass)
    {
        return true;
    }

    protected Object dialog()
    {
        Dialog         dialog;
        DialogGroup    groupCustomer;
        DialogGroup    groupPayment;

        dialog = super();

        dialog.caption("Customer information");

        fieldAccount    = dialog.addField(
            extendedTypeStr(CustVendAC),
            "Customer account");

        fieldName       =
           dialog.addField(extendedTypeStr(CustName));

        dialog.addTabPage("Details");

        groupCustomer   = dialog.addGroup("Setup");
        fieldGroup      = dialog.addField(
            extendedTypeStr(CustGroupId));
        fieldCurrency   = dialog.addField(
            extendedTypeStr(CurrencyCode));
```

```
        groupPayment    = dialog.addGroup("Payment");
        fieldPaymTermId = dialog.addField(
            extendedTypeStr(CustPaymTermId));
        fieldPaymMode   = dialog.addField(
            extendedTypeStr(CustPaymMode));

        return dialog;
    }

    boolean getFromDialog()
    {
        custAccount   = fieldAccount.value();
        custName      = fieldName.value();
        custGroupId   = fieldGroup.value();
        currencyCode  = fieldCurrency.value();
        paymTermId    = fieldPaymTermId.value();
        paymMode      = fieldPaymMode.value();
        return super();

    }

    void run()
    {
        info("You have entered customer information:");
        info(strFmt("Account: %1", custAccount));
        info(strFmt("Name: %1", custName));
        info(strFmt("Group: %1", custGroupId));
        info(strFmt("Currency: %1", currencyCode));
        info(strFmt("Terms of payment: %1", paymTermId));
        info(strFmt("Method of payment: %1", paymMode));
    }

    static void main(Args _args)
    {
        CustCreate custCreate = new CustCreate();

        if (custCreate.prompt())
        {
            custCreate.run();
        }
    }
```

Chapter 2

2. In order to test the dialog, run the `CustCreate` class. The following form will appear, with the **General** tab page open initially:

3. Click on the **Details** tab page; you will see a screen similar to the following screenshot:

Working with Forms

4. Enter information in all the fields and click on **OK**. The results will be displayed in the **Infolog** window, as shown here:

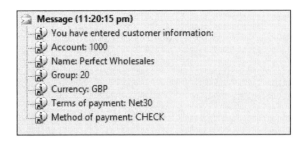

How it works...

First, we create a new class named `CustCreate`. By extending it from `RunBase`, we utilize a standard approach to develop data manipulation functions in Dynamics AX. The `RunBase` framework will define a common structure and automatically add additional controls, such as the **OK** and **Cancel** buttons, to the dialog.

Then, we declare class variables, which will be used later. The `DialogField` type variables are actual user input controls. The rest of the variables are used to store the values returned from the user input.

The `pack()` and `unpack()` methods are normally used to convert an object into a container and convert the container back into an object, respectively. A container is a common format used to store objects in the user cache (`SysLastValue`) or to transfer the object between the server and client tiers. The `RunBase` framework needs these two methods to be implemented in all its subclasses. In this example, we are not using any of the `pack()` or `unpack()` features, but because these methods are mandatory, we still create them and return an empty container from `pack()` and we return `true` from `unpack()`.

The layout of the actual dialog is constructed in the `dialog()` method. Here, we define local variables for the dialog itself and the control groups inside the dialog. The `super()` method creates the initial dialog object for us and automatically adds the relevant controls, including the **OK** and **Cancel** buttons.

Additional dialog controls are added to the dialog by using the `addField()`, `addGroup()`, and `addTabPage()` methods. There are more methods, such as `addText()`, `addImage()`, and `addMenuItemButton()`, to add different types of controls. All the controls have to be added to the dialog object directly. Adding an input control to groups or tabs is done by calling `addField()` right after `addGroup()` or `addTabPage()`. In the previous example, we added tab pages, groups, and fields in a top down logical sequence. Note that it is enough only to add a second tab page, and the first tab page labeled **General** is added automatically by the `RunBase` framework.

Values from the dialog controls are assigned to the variables by calling the `value()` method of `DialogField`. If a dialog is used within the `RunBase` framework, as it is used in this example, the best place to assign dialog control values to variables is the `getFormDialog()` method. The `RunBase` framework calls this method right after the user clicks on **OK**.

The main processing is done in the `run()` method. For demonstration purposes, this class only shows the user input in the **Infolog** window.

In order to make this class runnable, the `main()` static method has to be created. Here, we create a new `CustCreate` object and invoke the user dialog by calling the `prompt()` method. Once the user has finished entering customer details by clicking on **OK**, we call the `run()` method to process the data.

See also

- The *Handling a dialog event* recipe

Handling a dialog event

Sometimes, in the user interface, it is necessary to change the status of one field, depending on the status of another field. For example, if the user marks the **Show filter** checkbox, then another field, **Filter**, appears or becomes enabled. In AOT forms, this can be done using the `modified()` input control event. However, if this feature is required on runtime dialogs, handling events are not that straightforward.

Often, existing dialogs have to be modified in order to support events. The easiest way to do this is, of course, to convert the dialog into an AOT form. However, when the existing dialog is complex enough, probably a more cost-effective solution would be to implement dialog event handling instead of converting to an AOT form. Event handling in dialogs is not flexible, as in the case of AOT forms, but in most cases, it does the job.

In this recipe, we will create a dialog similar to the previous dialog, but instead of entering the customer number, we will be able to select the number from the list. Once the customer is selected, the rest of the fields will be filled in automatically by the system from the customer record.

Working with Forms

How to do it...

Carry out the following steps in order to complete this recipe:

1. In the AOT, create a new class named `CustSelect` with the following code snippet:

    ```
    class CustSelect extends RunBase
    {
        DialogField fieldAccount;
        DialogField fieldName;
        DialogField fieldGroup;
        DialogField fieldCurrency;
        DialogField fieldPaymTermId;
        DialogField fieldPaymMode;
    }

    container pack()
    {
        return conNull();
    }

    boolean unpack(container _packedClass)
    {
        return true;
    }

    protected Object dialog()
    {
        Dialog          dialog;
        DialogGroup     groupCustomer;
        DialogGroup     groupPayment;

        dialog = super();

        dialog.caption("Customer information");
        dialog.allowUpdateOnSelectCtrl(true);

        fieldAccount    = dialog.addField(
            extendedTypeStr(CustAccount),
            "Customer account");

        fieldName       = dialog.addField(extendedTypeStr(CustName));
        fieldName.enabled(false);
    ```

```
        dialog.addTabPage("Details");

        groupCustomer    = dialog.addGroup("Setup");
        fieldGroup       = dialog.addField(
            extendedTypeStr(CustGroupId));
        fieldCurrency    = dialog.addField(
            extendedTypeStr(CurrencyCode));
        fieldGroup.enabled(false);
        fieldCurrency.enabled(false);

        groupPayment     = dialog.addGroup("Payment");
        fieldPaymTermId  = dialog.addField(
            extendedTypeStr(CustPaymTermId));
        fieldPaymMode    = dialog.addField(
            extendedTypeStr(CustPaymMode));
        fieldPaymTermId.enabled(false);
        fieldPaymMode.enabled(false);

        return dialog;
    }

    void dialogSelectCtrl()
    {
        CustTable custTable;

        custTable = CustTable::find(fieldAccount.value());
        fieldName.value(custTable.name());
        fieldGroup.value(custTable.CustGroup);
        fieldCurrency.value(custTable.Currency);
        fieldPaymTermId.value(custTable.PaymTermId);
        fieldPaymMode.value(custTable.PaymMode);
    }

    static void main(Args _args)
    {
        CustSelect custSelect = new CustSelect();

        if (CustSelect.prompt())
        {
            CustSelect.run();
        }
    }
```

Working with Forms

2. Run the `CustSelect` class, select any customer from the list, and move the cursor to the next control. Notice how the rest of the fields were populated automatically with the customer's information, as shown in the following screenshot:

3. When you click on the **Details** tab page, you will see more information about the customer, as shown in the following screenshot:

How it works...

The new class named `CustSelect` is actually a copy of the `CustCreate` class from the previous recipe, with a few changes. In its class declaration, we leave all the `DialogField` declarations and remove the rest of the variables.

The `pack()` and `unpack()` methods remain the same as we are not using any of their features.

In the `dialog()` member method, we call the `allowUpdateOnSelectCtrl()` method with the `true` parameter to enable input control event handling. We also disable all the controls apart from **Customer account** by calling `enable()` with the `false` parameter for each control.

The `dialogSelectCtrl()` member method of the `RunBase` class is called every time the user modifies any input control in the dialog. It is the place where we have to add all the required code to ensure that in our case, all the controls are populated with the correct data from the customer record—once **Customer account** is selected.

The `main()` method ensures that the class is runnable.

There's more...

Sometimes, the usage of the `dialogSelectCtrl()` method might appear a bit limited, as this method is only invoked when the dialog control loses its focus. Also, no other events can be controlled, and it can become messy if the events on multiple controls need to be processed.

The `Dialog` class does not provide direct access to the underlying form's event handling functions, but we can still control this in a slightly different way. Let's modify the previous example to include more events. We will add an event to the second tab page, which is triggered once the page is activated.

First, we have to override the `dialogPostRun()` method in the `CustSelect` class, as shown here:

```
void dialogPostRun(DialogRunbase dialog)
{
    dialog.formRun().controlMethodOverload(true);
    dialog.formRun().controlMethodOverloadObject(this);
    super(dialog);
}
```

Working with Forms

Here, we enable event overloading in the runtime form after it is fully initialized and is ready to be displayed on the screen. We also pass the `CustSelect` object as an argument to the `controlMethodOverloadObject()` method in order to ensure that the form *knows* where the overloaded events are located.

Next, we have to create a method that will be executed once the tab page is opened:

```
void TabPg_1_pageActivated()
{
    info('Tab page activated');
}
```

The method name consists of the control name and the event name joined by an underscore. Now, run the class again and select the **Details** tab page. The message should be displayed in the **Infolog** window.

Before creating such methods, we first have to obtain the name of the runtime control. This is because the dialog form is created dynamically and the system defines control names automatically without allowing the user to define them. In this example, we have to temporarily add the following code snippet to the bottom of the `dialog()` method, which displays the name of the **Details** tab page control. Just replace `dialog.addTabPage("Details");` with `info(dialog.addTabPage("Details").name());`.

Running the class will display the name of the control in the **Infolog** window.

Note that this approach may not work properly if the dialog contains an automatically generated query. In such cases, control names will change if the user adds or removes query ranges.

See also

> - The *Creating dialogs using the RunBase framework* recipe

Building a dynamic form

A normal approach for creating forms in Dynamics AX is to build and store form objects in the AOT. It is possible to achieve a high level of complexity using this approach. However, in a number of cases, it is necessary to have forms created dynamically. In a standard Dynamics AX application, we can see that application objects, such as the **Table browser** form, various lookups, or dialogs, are built dynamically.

In this recipe, we will create a dynamic form. In order to show how flexible the form can be, we will replicate the layout of the existing **Customer groups** form located in the **Accounts receivable** module under **Setup | Customers**.

Chapter 2

How to do it...

Carry out the following steps in order to complete this recipe:

1. In the AOT, create a new class called `CustGroupDynamic` with the following code snippet:

```
class CustGroupDynamic
{
}

static void main(Args _args)
{
    DictTable                        dictTable;
    Form                             form;
    FormBuildDesign                  design;
    FormBuildDataSource              ds;
    FormBuildActionPaneControl       actionPane;
    FormBuildActionPaneTabControl    actionPaneTab;
    FormBuildButtonGroupControl      btngrp1;
    FormBuildButtonGroupControl      btngrp2;
    FormBuildCommandButtonControl    cmdNew;
    FormBuildCommandButtonControl    cmdDel;
    FormBuildMenuButtonControl       mbPosting;
    FormBuildFunctionButtonControl   mibPosting;
    FormBuildFunctionButtonControl   mibForecast;
    FormBuildGridControl             grid;
    FormBuildGroupControl            grpBody;
    Args                             args;
    FormRun                          formRun;
    #Task

    dictTable = new DictTable(tableNum(CustGroup));

    form = new Form();
    form.name("CustGroupDynamic");

    ds = form.addDataSource(dictTable.name());
    ds.table(dictTable.id());

    design = form.addDesign('Design');
    design.caption("Customer groups");
    design.style(FormStyle::SimpleList);
    design.titleDatasource(ds.id());
```

Working with Forms

```
actionPane = design.addControl(
    FormControlType::ActionPane, 'ActionPane');
actionPane.style(ActionPaneStyle::Strip);
actionPaneTab = actionPane.addControl(
    FormControlType::ActionPaneTab, 'ActionPaneTab');
btngrp1 = actionPaneTab.addControl(
    FormControlType::ButtonGroup, 'NewDeleteGroup');
btngrp2 = actionPaneTab.addControl(
    FormControlType::ButtonGroup, 'ButtonGroup');

cmdNew = btngrp1.addControl(
    FormControlType::CommandButton, 'NewButton');
cmdNew.buttonDisplay(FormButtonDisplay::TextAndImageLeft);
cmdNew.normalImage('11045');
cmdNew.imageLocation(SysImageLocation::EmbeddedResource);
cmdNew.primary(NoYes::Yes);
cmdNew.command(#taskNew);

cmdDel = btngrp1.addControl(
    FormControlType::CommandButton, 'NewButton');
cmdDel.text("Delete");
cmdDel.buttonDisplay(FormButtonDisplay::TextAndImageLeft);
cmdDel.normalImage('10121');
cmdDel.imageLocation(SysImageLocation::EmbeddedResource);
cmdDel.saveRecord(NoYes::Yes);
cmdDel.primary(NoYes::Yes);
cmdDel.command(#taskDeleteRecord);

mbPosting = btngrp2.addControl(
    FormControlType::MenuButton, 'MenuButtonPosting');
mbPosting.helpText("Set up related data for the group.");
mbPosting.text("Setup");

mibPosting = mbPosting.addControl(
    FormControlType::MenuFunctionButton, 'Posting');
mibPosting.text('Item posting');
mibPosting.saveRecord(NoYes::No);
mibPosting.dataSource(ds.id());
mibPosting.menuItemName(menuitemDisplayStr(InventPosting));

mibForecast = btngrp2.addControl(
    FormControlType::MenuFunctionButton, 'SalesForecast');
mibForecast.text('Forecast');
mibForecast.saveRecord(NoYes::No);
```

```
    mibForecast.menuItemName(
        menuitemDisplayStr(ForecastSalesGroup));

    grpBody = design.addControl(FormControlType::Group, 'Body');
    grpBody.heightMode(FormHeight::ColumnHeight);
    grpBody.columnspace(0);
    grpBody.style(GroupStyle::BorderlessGridContainer);

    grid = grpBody.addControl(FormControlType::Grid, "Grid");
    grid.dataSource(ds.name());
    grid.showRowLabels(false);
    grid.widthMode(FormWidth::ColumnWidth);
    grid.heightMode(FormHeight::ColumnHeight);

    grid.addDataField(
        ds.id(), fieldNum(CustGroup,CustGroup));

    grid.addDataField(
        ds.id(), fieldNum(CustGroup,Name));

    grid.addDataField(
        ds.id(), fieldNum(CustGroup,PaymTermId));

    grid.addDataField(
        ds.id(), fieldnum(CustGroup,ClearingPeriod));

    grid.addDataField(
        ds.id(), fieldNum(CustGroup,BankCustPaymIdTable));

    grid.addDataField(
        ds.id(), fieldNum(CustGroup,TaxGroupId));

    args = new Args();
    args.object(form);

    formRun = classFactory.formRunClass(args);
    formRun.init();
    formRun.run();

    formRun.detach();
}
```

2. In order to test the form, run the `CustGroupDynamic` class. Notice that the dynamic form is similar to the static **Customer groups** form, which can be obtained by navigating to **Accounts receivable | Setup | Customers**, as shown in the following screenshot:

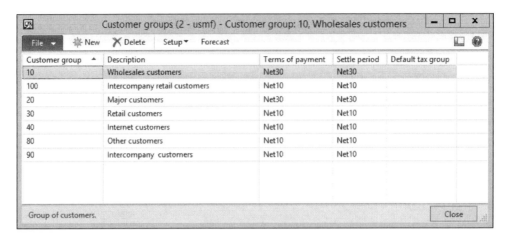

How it works...

We start the code by declaring our variables. Note that most of the variable types begin with `FormBuild`, which are a part of a set of application classes used to build dynamic forms. Each of these types corresponds to the control types that are manually used when building forms in the AOT.

Right after the variable declaration, we create a `dictTable` object based on the `CustGroup` table. We will use this object several times later in the code. Then, we create a `form` object and set a name by calling the following lines of code:

```
form = new Form();
form.name("CustGroupDynamic");
```

The name of the form is not important as this is a dynamic form. The form should have a data source, so we add one by calling the `addDataSource()` method to the `form` object and by providing a previously created `dictTable` object, as shown here:

```
ds = form.addDataSource(dictTable.name());
ds.table(dictTable.id());
```

Every form has a design, so we add a new design, define its style as a simple list, and set its title data source, as shown in the following code snippet:

```
design = form.addDesign('Design');
design.caption("Customer groups");
design.style(FormStyle::SimpleList);
design.titleDatasource(ds.id());
```

Once the design is ready, we can start adding controls from the code as if we were doing this from the AOT. The first thing you need to do is to add an action pane of `Strip` type with its buttons:

```
actionPane = design.addControl(
    FormControlType::ActionPane, 'ActionPane');
actionPane.style(ActionPaneStyle::Strip);
actionPaneTab = actionPane.addControl(
    FormControlType::ActionPaneTab, 'ActionPaneTab');
btngrp1 = actionPaneTab.addControl(
```

Right after the action pane, we add an automatically expanding grid that points to the previously mentioned data source. Just to follow the best practices, we place the grid inside a `Group` control:

```
grpBody = design.addControl(FormControlType::Group, 'Body');
grpBody.heightMode(FormHeight::ColumnHeight);
grpBody.columnspace(0);
grpBody.style(GroupStyle::BorderlessGridContainer);

grid = grpBody.addControl(FormControlType::Grid, "Grid");
grid.dataSource(ds.name());
grid.showRowLabels(false);
grid.widthMode(FormWidth::ColumnWidth);
grid.heightMode(FormHeight::ColumnHeight);
```

Next, we add a number of grid controls that point to the relevant data source fields by calling `addDataField()` on the `grid` object. The last thing is to initialize and run the form. Here, we use a recommended approach to create and run forms using the globally available `classFactory` object.

Adding a form splitter

In Dynamics AX, complex forms consist of one or more sections. Each section may contain grids, groups, or any other element. In order to maintain section sizes while resizing the form, the sections are normally separated by the so-called **splitter**. Splitters are not special Dynamics AX controls; they are `Group` controls with their properties modified so that they look like splitters. Most of the multisection forms in Dynamics AX already contain splitters.

Working with Forms

In this recipe, in order to demonstrate the usage of the splitters, we will modify one of the existing forms that does not have a splitter. We will modify the **Account reconciliation** form. To open this form, navigate to **Cash and bank management** | **Common** | **Bank accounts**, select any bank account, and click on the **Account reconciliation** button under the **Reconcile** group in the action pane. Then, select any of the existing records, and click on the **Transactions** button. From the following screenshot, you can see that it is not possible to control the size of each grid individually and that they are resized automatically using a fixed ratio when resizing the form:

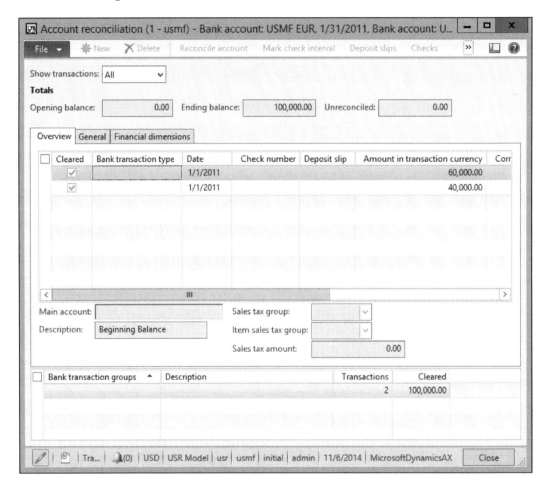

In this recipe, we will demonstrate how to add a splitter to the **Account reconciliation** form. We will add a form splitter between the two grids. This will allow users to set the sizes of both the grids in order to ensure that the data is displayed optimally.

How to do it...

Carry out the following steps in order to complete this recipe:

1. Open the `BankReconciliation` form in the AOT, and in the form's design, add a new `Group` control right after the `ActionPane` control with the following properties:

Property	Value
Name	Top
AutoDeclaration	Yes
Width	Column width
FrameType	None

2. Move the `AllReconciled`, `Balances`, and `Tab` controls into the newly created group.

3. Change the following properties of the existing `BankTransTypeGroup` group:

Property	Value
Top	Auto
Height	Column height

4. Change the following property of the exiting `TypeSums` grid located inside the `BankTransTypeGroup` group:

Property	Value
Height	Column height

5. Add a new `Group` control immediately below the `Top` group with the following properties:

Property	Value
Name	Splitter
Style	SplitterHorizontalContainer
AutoDeclaration	Yes

6. Add the following line of code at the bottom of the form's class declaration:

   `SysFormSplitter_Y formSplitter;`

Working with Forms

7. Add the following line of code at the bottom of the form's `init()` method:
   ```
   formSplitter = new SysFormSplitter_Y(Splitter, Top, element);
   ```

8. In the AOT, the modified `BankReconciliation` form should look similar to the following screenshot:

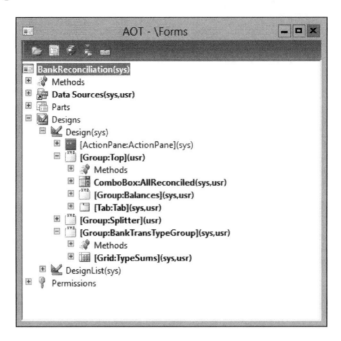

9. Now, in order to test the results, navigate to **Cash and bank management | Common | Bank accounts**, select any bank account, click on **Account reconciliation**, select an existing or create a new bank statement, and click on the **Transactions** button. Note that now the form has a splitter in the middle, which makes the form look better and allows you to resize both the grids, as shown in the following screenshot:

Chapter 2

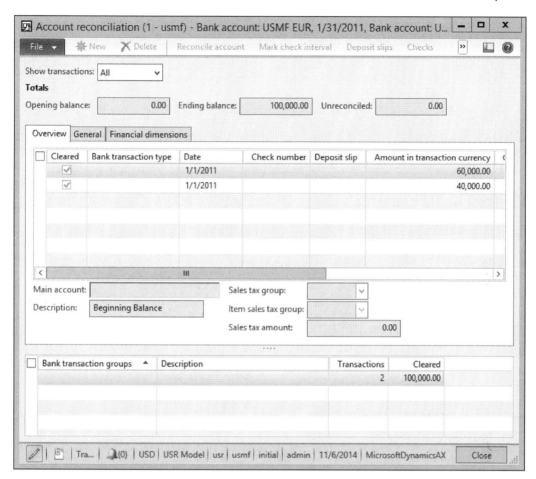

How it works...

Normally, a splitter has to be placed between two form groups. In this recipe, to follow this rule, we need to adjust the `BankReconciliation` form's design. The `AllReconciled`, `Balances`, and `Tab` controls are moved to a new group called `Top`. We set the group's `FrameType` property to `None` to make sure its border is not visible to the user. We also change its `AutoDeclaration` property to `Yes` allowing you to access this object from the code. Finally, we make this group automatically expand in the horizontal direction by setting its `Width` property to `Column width`. At this stage, the visual form layout does not change.

Next, we change the `BankTransTypeGroup` group. We set its `Top` behavior to `Auto` and make it fully expandable in the vertical direction by setting its `Height` property to `Column height` in order to fill all the vertical space.

Working with Forms

Now, we add a new `Group` control in between the `Top` and `BankTransTypeGroup` groups. We set its `Style` property to `SplitterHorizontalContainer`, which makes this group look like a proper form splitter.

Finally, we have to declare and initialize the `SysFormSplitter_Y` application class, which does the rest of the tasks.

In this way, horizontal splitters can be added to any form. Vertical splitters can also be added to forms using a similar approach. For this, we need to use another application class called `SysFormSplitter_X`.

Creating a modal form

Often, people who are not familiar with computers and software tend to get lost among open application windows. The same can be applied to Dynamics AX. Often, a user opens a form, clicks on a button to open another form, and then goes back to the first form without closing the second form. Sometimes this happens intentionally, sometimes not, but the result is that the second form gets hidden behind the first one and the user starts wondering why it is not possible to close or edit the first form.

Although it is not the best practice, sometimes such issues can be easily solved by making the second form a modal window. In other words, the second form always stays on top of the first one until it is closed. In this recipe, we will make the **Create sales order** form to behave as a modal window.

How to do it...

Carry out the following steps in order to complete this recipe:

1. Open the `SalesCreateOrder` form in the AOT and change its design's property, as follows:

Property	Value
WindowType	Popup

2. In order to test the modal form, navigate to **Sales and marketing | Common | Sales orders | All sales orders** and start creating a new order. Notice that now the **Create sales order** form always stays on top:

Chapter 2

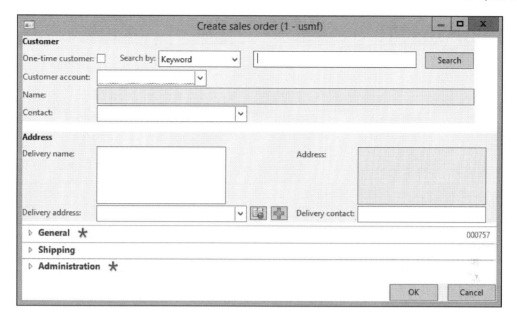

How it works...

The form's design has the `WindowType` property, which is set to `Standard` by default. In order to make a form behave as a modal window, we have to change it to `Popup`. Such forms will always stay on top of the parent form.

There's more...

We already know that some of the Dynamics AX forms are created dynamically using the `Dialog` class. If we take a look deeper into the code, we can find that the `Dialog` class actually creates a runtime form. This means that we can apply the same principle—change the `WindowType` property to `Popup` on the form's `Design` node. The following lines of code can be added to the dialog creation code:

```
dialog.dialogForm().buildDesign().windowType(
    FormWindowType::Popup);
```

Here, we get a reference to the form's design by first using the `dialogForm()` method of the `Dialog` object to get a reference to the `DialogForm` object, and then we call `buildDesign()` on the latter object. Lastly, we set the design's window type by calling its `windowType()` method with the `FormWindowType::Popup` as an argument.

See also

- The *Creating dialogs using the RunBase framework* recipe

79

Working with Forms

Modifying multiple forms dynamically

In the standard Dynamics AX application, there is a class called `SysSetupFormRun`. The class is called during the run of every form; therefore, it can be used to override some of the common behaviors for all Dynamics AX forms at once. For example, different form background colors can be set for different company accounts, some controls can be hidden or added depending on specific circumstances, and so on.

In this recipe, we will modify the `SysSetupFormRun` class to automatically add the **About Microsoft Dynamics AX** button to every form in Dynamics AX.

How to do it...

Carry out the following steps in order to complete this recipe:

1. In the AOT, open the `SysSetupFormRun` class and create a new method with the following code snippet:

```
private void addAboutButton()
{
    FormActionPaneControl     actionPane;
    FormActionPaneTabControl  actionPaneTab;
    FormCommandButtonControl  cmdAbout;
    FormButtonGroupControl    btngrp;
    #define.taskAbout(259)

    actionPane = this.design().controlNum(1);
    if (!actionPane ||
        !(actionPane is FormActionPaneControl) ||
        actionPane.style() == ActionPaneStyle::Strip)
    {
        return;
    }

    actionPaneTab = actionPane.controlNum(1);
    if (!actionPaneTab ||
        !(actionPaneTab is FormActionPaneTabControl))
    {
        return;
    }

    btngrp = actionPaneTab.addControl(
        FormControlType::ButtonGroup, 'ButtonGroup');
    btngrp.caption("About");
```

Chapter 2

```
    cmdAbout = btngrp.addControl(
        FormControlType::CommandButton, 'About');
    cmdAbout.command(#taskAbout);
    cmdAbout.imageLocation(SysImageLocation::EmbeddedResource);
    cmdAbout.normalImage('412');
    cmdAbout.big(NoYes::Yes);
    cmdAbout.saveRecord(NoYes::No);
}
```

2. In the same class, override its `run()` method with the following code snippet:

```
void run()
{
    this.addAboutButton();
    super();
}
```

3. In order to test the results, open any list page; for example, go to **General ledger | Common | Main accounts** and notice a new button named **About Microsoft Dynamics AX** in the action pane, as shown in the following screenshot:

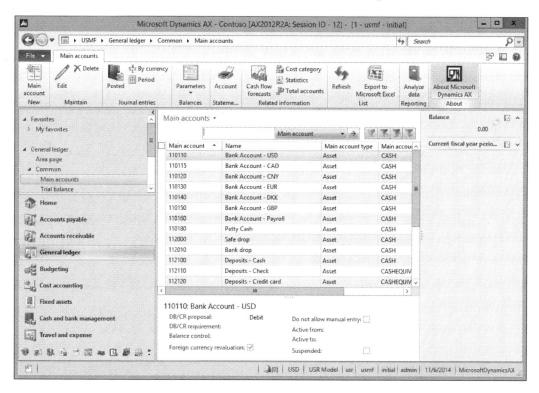

Working with Forms

How it works...

The `SysSetupFormRun` is the application class that is called by the system every time a user runs a form. The best place to add our custom control is in its `run()` method.

We use the `this.design()` method to get a reference to the form's design and then we check whether the first control in the design is an action pane. We continue by adding a new separate button group and the **About Microsoft Dynamics AX** command button. Now, every form in Dynamics AX with an action pane will have one more button.

In this way, any other control or controls can be added or changed in all Dynamics AX form at once.

Storing user selections

Dynamics AX has a very useful feature that allows you to save the latest user choices for forms, reports, and other objects. This feature is already implemented across a number of standard forms, reports, periodic jobs, and other objects, which require user input. When developing a new functionality for Dynamics AX, it is recommended that you keep it that way.

In this recipe, we will demonstrate how to save the latest user selections. In order to make it as simple as possible, we will use the existing filter on the **Bank statement** form, which can be opened by navigating to **Cash and bank management** | **Common** | **Bank accounts**, selecting any bank account, and then clicking on the **Account reconciliation** button in the action pane. This form contains one filter called **View**, which allows you to display bank statements based on their status. We will enhance this form so the system will remember the latest user's choice when the form is opened next time.

How to do it...

Carry out the following steps in order to complete this recipe:

1. In the AOT, find the `BankAccountStatement` form and add the following code snippet at the bottom of its class declaration:

    ```
    AllNotReconciled showAllReconciled;
    #define.CurrentVersion(1)
    #localmacro.CurrentList
        showAllReconciled
    #endmacro
    ```

2. Create the following additional form methods:

    ```
    void initParmDefault()
    {
        showAllReconciled = AllNotReconciled::NotReconciled;
    }
    ```

```
container pack()
{
    return [#CurrentVersion, #CurrentList];
}

boolean unpack(container _packedClass)
{
    int version = RunBase::getVersion(_packedClass);

    switch (version)
    {
        case #CurrentVersion:
            [version, #CurrentList] = _packedClass;
            return true;
        default:
            return false;
    }
    return false;
}

IdentifierName lastValueDesignName()
{
    return element.args().menuItemName();
}

IdentifierName lastValueElementName()
{
    return this.name();
}

UtilElementType lastValueType()
{
    return UtilElementType::Form;
}

UserId lastValueUserId()
{
    return curUserId();
}

DataAreaId lastValueDataAreaId()
{
    return curext();
}
```

Working with Forms

3. Override the form's `run()` method and add the following lines of code right before its `super()` method:

   ```
   xSysLastValue::getLast(this);
   AllReconciled.selection(showAllReconciled);
   ```

4. Override the form's `close()` method and add the following lines of code at the bottom of this method:

   ```
   showAllReconciled = AllReconciled.selection();
   xSysLastValue::saveLast(this);
   ```

5. Finally, delete the following line of code from the `init()` method of the `BankAccountStatement` data source:

   ```
   allReconciled.selection(1);
   ```

6. Now to test the form, navigate to **Cash and bank management | Common | Bank accounts**, select any bank account, click on **Account reconciliation**, change the filter's value, close the form, and then open it again. The previous choice should stay, as shown in the following screenshot:

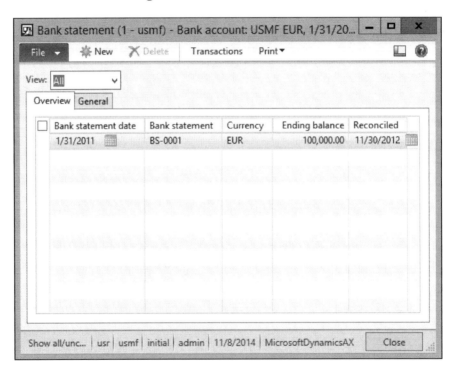

How it works...

First, we define a variable that will store the value of the filter control and the `#CurrentList` macro, which defines a list of variables that we are going to save in the usage data storage (the `SysLastValue` table). Currently, we have our single variable inside it.

The `#CurrentVersion` macro defines a version of the saved values. In other words, it says that the variables defined by the `#CurrentList` macro, which will be stored in the system usage data storage, can be addressed using the number 1.

Normally, when implementing this feature for the first time for a particular object, `#CurrentVersion` is set to 1. Later on, if you decide to add new values or change the existing ones, you have to change the value of `#CurrentVersion`, normally increasing it by 1. This ensures that the system addresses the correct list of variables in the usage data storage.

The `initParmDefault()` method specifies the default values if nothing is found in the usage data storage. Normally, this happens if we run a form for the first time, we change `#CurrentVersion`, or clear the usage data. This method is called automatically by the `xSysLastValue` class.

The `pack()` and `unpack()` methods are responsible for formatting a storage container from the variables and extracting variables from a storage container, respectively. In our case, `pack()` returns a container consisting of two values: version number and the **View** filter's value. These values will be saved in the system usage data storage after the form is closed. When the form is opened, the `xSysLastValue` class calls `unpack()` to extract the values from the stored container. In this method, first of all the container version of the stored data is checked against the version number defined by `#CurrentVersion`, and only if both numbers match, the values in the container are considered correct and are assigned to the form's variables.

The return values of `lastValueDesignName()`, `lastValueElementName()`, `lastValueType()`, `lastValueUserId()`, and `lastValueDataAreaId()` represent a unique combination that is used to identify the stored usage data. This ensures that different users can store their selections for different objects in different companies without overriding each other's values.

The `lastValueDesignName()` method is meant to return the name of the object's current design in the cases where the object can have several designs. In this recipe, there is only one design, so instead of leaving it empty, we used it for a slightly different purpose. The method returns the name of the menu item used to open this form. In this case, separate usage datasets will be stored for each menu item that opens the same form.

The last two pieces of code need to be added to the form's `run()` and `close()` methods. In the `run()` method, `xSysLastValue::getLast(this)` retrieves the saved user values from the usage data and assigns them to the form's variables.

Finally, the code in the `close()` method is responsible for assigning user selections to the variables and saving them to the usage data by calling `xSysLastValue::saveLast(this)`.

Working with Forms

Using a Tree control

Frequent users will notice that some of the Dynamics AX forms use `Tree` controls instead of the commonly used grids. In some cases, it is extremely useful, especially when there are parent-child relationships among records. It is a much clearer way to show the whole hierarchy as compared to a flat list. For example, product categories are organized as a hierarchy and give a much better overview when displayed in a tree layout.

This recipe will discuss the principles of how to build tree-based forms. As an example, we will use the **Budget model** form, which can be found by navigating to **Budgeting | Setup | Basic Budgeting | Budget models**. This form contains a list of budget models and their submodels, and although the data is organized using a parent-child structure, it is still displayed as a grid. In this recipe, in order to demonstrate the usage of the `Tree` control, we will convert the grid into the tree.

How to do it...

Carry out the following steps in order to complete this recipe:

1. In the AOT, create a new class called `BudgetModelTree` with the following code snippet:

    ```
    class BudgetModelTree
    {
        FormTreeControl  tree;
        BudgetModelId    modelId;
    }

    void new(
        FormTreeControl _formTreeControl,
        BudgetModelId   _budgetModelId)
    {
        tree    = _formTreeControl;
        modelId = _budgetModelId;
    }

    static BudgetModelTree construct(
        FormTreeControl _formTreeControl,
        BudgetModelId   _budgetModelId = '')
    {
        return new BudgetModelTree(
            _formTreeControl,
            _budgetModelId);
    }
    ```

```
TreeItemIdx createNode(
    TreeItemIdx   _parentIdx,
    BudgetModelId _modelId,
    RecId         _recId)
{
    TreeItemIdx itemIdx;
    BudgetModel model;
    BudgetModel submodel;

    model = BudgetModel::find(HeadingSub::Heading, _modelId);

    itemIdx = SysFormTreeControl::addTreeItem(
        tree,
        _modelId + ' : ' + model.Txt,
        _parentIdx,
        _recId,
        0,
        true);
    if (modelId == _modelId)
    {
        tree.select(itemIdx);
    }
    while select submodel
        where submodel.ModelId == _modelId &&
              submodel.Type    == HeadingSub::SubModel
    {
        this.createNode(
            itemIdx,
            submodel.SubModelId,
            submodel.RecId);
    }
    return itemIdx;
}

void buildTree()
{
    BudgetModel model;
    BudgetModel submodel;
    TreeItemIdx itemIdx;

    tree.deleteAll();
    tree.lock();
    while select RecId, ModelId from model
        where model.Type == HeadingSub::Heading
```

Working with Forms

```
            notExists join submodel
                where submodel.SubModelId == model.ModelId &&
                      submodel.Type       == HeadingSub::SubModel
        {
            itemIdx = this.createNode(
                FormTreeAdd::Root,
                model.ModelId,
                model.RecId);
            SysFormTreeControl::expandTree(tree, itemIdx);
        }
        tree.unLock(true);
    }
}
```

2. In the AOT, open the `BudgetModel` form's design, expand the `Body` group, then expand the `GridContainer` group, and change the following property of the `BudgetModel` grid control:

Property	Value
Visible	No

3. Create a new `Tree` control right below the `BudgetModel` grid with the following properties, along with their values:

Property	Value
Name	Tree
Width	Column width
Height	Column height
Border	Single line
RowSelect	Yes

4. Add the following line of code to the bottom of the form's class declaration:

   `BudgetModelTree modelTree;`

5. Add the following lines of code at the bottom of the form's `init()` method:

   ```
           modelTree = BudgetModelTree::construct(Tree);
           modelTree.buildTree();
   ```

6. Override `selectionChanged()` on the `Tree` control with the following code snippet:

   ```
   void selectionChanged(
       FormTreeItem    _oldItem,
       FormTreeItem    _newItem,
       FormTreeSelect  _how)
   ```

```
{
    BudgetModel    model;
    BudgetModelId  modelId;

    super(_oldItem, _newItem, _how);

    if (_newItem.data())
    {
        select firstOnly model
            where model.RecId == _newItem.data();
        if (model.Type == HeadingSub::SubModel)
        {
            modelId = model.SubModelId;
            select firstOnly model
                where model.ModelId == modelId
                   && model.Type    == HeadingSub::Heading;
        }
        BudgetModel_ds.findRecord(model);
        BudgetModel_ds.refresh();
    }

}
```

7. Override the `delete()` method on the `BudgetModel` data source with the following code snippet:

```
void delete()
{
    super();

    if (BudgetModel.RecId)
    {
        modelTree.buildTree();
    }
}
```

8. Override the `delete()` method on the `SubModel` data source with the following code snippet:

```
void delete()
{
    super();

    if (SubModel.RecId)
    {
        modelTree.buildTree();
    }
}
```

9. Add the following line of code at the bottom of the `write()` method on the `BudgetModel` data source:

   ```
   modelTree.buildTree();
   ```

10. Override the `write()` method on the `SubModel` data source and add the following line of code at the bottom:

    ```
    modelTree.buildTree();
    ```

11. In the AOT, the `BudgetModel` form should look like the following screenshot:

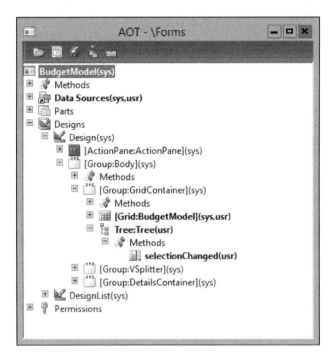

12. To test the `Tree` control, navigate to **Budgeting** | **Setup** | **Basic budgeting** | **Budget models**. Notice how the budget models are presented as a hierarchy, as shown here:

Chapter 2

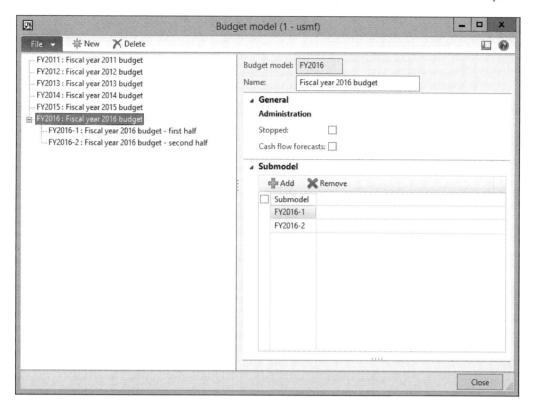

How it works...

This recipe contains a lot of code, so we create a class to hold most of it. This allows you to reuse the code and keep the form less cluttered.

The new class contains a few common methods, such as `new()` and `construct()`, to initialize the class, and two methods, which actually generate the tree.

The first method is `createNode()` and is used to create a single budget model node with its children, if any. It is a recursive method, and it calls itself to generate the children of the current node. It accepts a parent node and a budget model as arguments. In this method, we create the node by calling the `addTreeItem()` method of the `SysFormTreeControl` class. The rest of the code loops through all the submodels and creates subnodes (if there are any) for each of them.

Working with Forms

The second method is `buildTree()`. This is the main method where the `Tree` control is populated with the tree structure. At the top of this method, we delete all the existing nodes (in case we are updating an existing tree) and then lock the `Tree` control to make sure that the user cannot modify it while it's being built. Then, we add nodes by looping through all the parent budget models and calling the previously mentioned `createNode()`. We call the `expandTree()` method of the `SysFormTreeControl` class in order to expand every node. Once the hierarchy is ready, we unlock the `Tree` control.

Next, we modify the **BudgetModel** form by hiding the existing grid section and adding a new `Tree` control. Tree nodes are always generated from the code and the previously mentioned class will do exactly that. On the form, we declare and initialize the `modelTree` object and build the tree in the form's `init()` method.

In order to ensure that the currently selected tree node is displayed on the form on the right-hand side, we override the `Tree` control's `selectionChanged()` event, which is triggered every time a tree node is selected. Here, we locate a corresponding budget model record to make sure it is displayed on the right-hand side once the tree node is selected.

The rest of the code on the form is to ensure that the tree is rebuilt whenever the data is modified.

There's more...

There are a few other things to be considered when working with `Tree` controls. One of them is the performance of the tree and the other one is the drag and drop support in the tree.

Performance
Generating a tree hierarchy might be time consuming, so for bigger trees, it is not beneficial to build the whole tree initially. Instead, it is better to generate only a visible part of the tree which, most of the time, is the first level of nodes, and to generate the rest of the branches only when/if the user expands them. This can be achieved by placing the relevant code into the `expanding()` method of the `Tree` control, which represents an event when a tree node is being expanded. Such an approach ensures that no system resources are used to generate unused tree nodes.

Drag and drop
Besides the hierarchical layout, `Tree` controls also allow users to use the drag and drop functionality. This makes daily operations much quicker and more effective. Let's modify the previous example to support drag and drop. We are going to allow users to move budget submodels to different parents within the tree. In order to do this, we need to make some changes to the `BudgetModelTree` class and the `BudgetModel` form.

Let's perform the following steps:

1. Add the following lines of code to the `BudgetModelTree` class declaration:

   ```
   TreeItemIdx dragItemIdx;
   TreeItemIdx lastItemIdx;
   ```

2. Create the following additional methods in the `BudgetModelTree` class:

   ```
   private boolean canMove()
   {
       BudgetModel model;
       RecId       recId;

       recId = tree.getItem(dragItemIdx).data();

       select firstOnly recId from model
           where model.RecId == recId
               && model.Type  == HeadingSub::SubModel;

       return model.RecId ? true : false;
   }

   private void move(RecId _from, RecId _to)
   {
       BudgetModel modelFrom;
       BudgetModel modelTo;

       select firstOnly ModelId from modelTo
           where modelTo.RecId == _to;

       ttsBegin;

       select firstOnly forupdate modelFrom
           where modelFrom.RecId == _from;

       modelFrom.ModelId = modelTo.ModelId;

       if (modelFrom.validateWrite())
       {
           modelFrom.update();
       }

       ttsCommit;
   }
   ```

Working with Forms

```
void stateDropHilite(TreeItemIdx _idx)
{
    FormTreeItem item;

    if (lastItemIdx)
    {
        item = tree.getItem(lastItemIdx);
        item.stateDropHilited(false);
        tree.setItem(item);
        lastItemIdx = 0;
    }

    if (_idx)
    {
        item = tree.getItem(_idx);
        item.stateDropHilited(true);
        tree.setItem(item);
        lastItemIdx = _idx;
    }
}

int beginDrag(int _x, int _y)
{
    [dragItemIdx] = tree.hitTest(_x, _y);
    return 1;
}

FormDrag dragOver(
    FormControl _dragSource,
    FormDrag    _dragMode,
    int         _x,
    int         _y)
{
    TreeItemIdx currItemIdx;

    if (!this.canMove())
    {
        return FormDrag::None;
    }

    [currItemIdx] = tree.hitTest(_x, _y);

    this.stateDropHilite(currItemIdx);
```

```
        return FormDrag::Move;
}

void drop(
    FormControl  _dragSource,
    FormDrag     _dragMode,
    int          _x,
    int          _y)
{
    TreeItemIdx currItemIdx;

    if (!this.canMove())
    {
        return;
    }

    this.stateDropHilite(0);

    [currItemIdx] = tree.hitTest(_x,_y);

    if (!currItemIdx)
    {
        return;
    }

    this.move(
        tree.getItem(dragItemIdx).data(),
        tree.getItem(currItemIdx).data());

    tree.moveItem(dragItemIdx, currItemIdx);

}
```

3. In the AOT, locate the `BudgetModel` form, find its `Tree` control, and change its following property:

Property	Value
DragDrop	Manual

4. Also, override the following methods of the `Tree` control:

    ```
    int beginDrag(int _x, int _y)
    {
        return modelTree.beginDrag(_x, _y);
    }
    ```

```
            FormDrag dragOver(
                FormControl  _dragSource,
                FormDrag     _dragMode,
                int          _x,
                int          _y)
            {
                return modelTree.dragOver(
                    _dragSource,
                    _dragMode,
                    _x,
                    _y);
            }

            void drop(
                FormControl  _dragSource,
                FormDrag     _dragMode,
                int          _x,
                int          _y)
            {
                modelTree.drop(_dragSource, _dragMode, _x, _y);
            }
```

   5. Now when you navigate to **Budgeting | Setup | Basic Budgeting | Budget models**, you should be able to move budget models within the tree with a mouse.

The main element in the latter modification is the `DragDrop` property of the `Tree` control. It enables the drag and drop functionality in the tree, once we set its value to `Manual`. The next step is to override the drag and drop events on the `Tree` control. Trees can have a number of methods covering various drag and drop events. A good place to start investigating them is the `Tutorial_Form_TreeControl` form in the standard application. In this example, we will cover only three of them, as follows:

- `beginDrag()`: This is executed when dragging begins. Here, we normally store the number of the item that is being dragged for later processing.
- `dragOver()`: This is executed once the dragged item appears over another node. This method is responsible for highlighting nodes when the dragged item is over them. Its return value defines the mouse cursor icon once the item is being dragged.
- `drop()`: This is executed when the mouse button is released, that is, the dragged item is dropped over some node. Here, we normally place the code that does the actual data modifications.

In this example, all the logic is stored in the `BudgetModelTree` class. Each of the mentioned form methods call the corresponding method in the class. This is to reduce the amount of code placed on the form and in order to allow the code to be reused on multiple forms. We add the following methods to the class:

- `canMove()`: This checks whether the currently selected node can be dragged. Although there might be more conditions, for this demonstration, we only disallow the dragging of the top nodes.
- `move()`: This is where the actual movement of the budget model is performed, that is, the submodel is assigned to another parent.
- `stateDropHilite()`: This is responsible for highlighting and removing the highlighting from relevant items. Using `stateDropHilited()`, we highlight the current item and remove the highlight from the previously highlighted one. This ensures that as we move the dragged item over the tree, items are highlighted once the dragged item is over them and the highlight is removed once the dragged item leaves them. This method is called later from several places to ensure that node highlighting works correctly.
- `beginDrag()`: This stores the item currently being dragged into a variable.
- `dragOver()`: This first checks whether the currently selected item can be moved. If not, then it returns `FormDrag::None`, which changes the mouse cursor to the forbidden sign. Otherwise, the cursor is changed to an icon that represents node movement. This method also calls `stateDropHilite()` to ensure the correct node highlighting.
- `drop()`: This also checks whether the item being dropped can be moved. If yes, then it uses `move()` in order to update the data and `moveItem()` to visually change the node's place in the tree. It also calls `stateDropHilite()` to update tree node highlighting.

See also

- The *Preloading images* recipe in *Chapter 3, Working with Data in Forms*
- The *Building a tree lookup* recipe in *Chapter 4, Building Lookups*

Building a checklist

Anyone who has performed a Dynamics AX application installation or upgrade has to be familiar with standard checklists. Normally, a checklist is a list of menu items displayed in a logical sequence. Each item represents either mandatory or optional actions to be executed by the user in order to complete the whole procedure. In custom Dynamics AX implementations, checklists can be used as a convenient way to configure nonstandard settings. Checklists can also be implemented as a part of third-party modules for their initial setup.

Working with Forms

In this recipe, we will create a checklist for user friendly ledger budget setup. The checklist will consist of two mandatory items and one optional item.

How to do it...

Carry out the following steps in order to complete this recipe:

1. Open the AOT and create a new interface called `SysCheckListInterfaceBudget`:

    ```
    interface SysCheckListInterfaceBudget
    extends   SysCheckListInterface
    {
    }
    ```

2. Create a new class for the first checklist item with the following code snippet:

    ```
    class SysCheckListItem_BudgetModel
    extends SysCheckListItem
    implements SysCheckListInterfaceBudget
    {
    }

    str getCheckListGroup()
    {
        return "Setup";
    }

    str getHelpLink()
    {
        #define.TopicId('Dynamics://DynamicsHelp/Topic?Id=' +
            '84030522-0057-412c-bfc7-dbeb4d40e5a1')
        return #TopicId;
    }

    MenuItemName getMenuItemName()
    {
        return menuitemDisplayStr(BudgetModel);
    }

    MenuItemType getMenuItemType()
    {
        return MenuItemType::Display;
    }
    ```

```
    str label()
    {
        return "Models";
    }
```

3. Create another class for the second checklist item with the following code snippet:

```
    class SysCheckListItem_BudgetCode
    extends SysCheckListItem
    implements SysCheckListInterfaceBudget
    {
    }

    void new()
    {
        super();
        this.placeAfter(classNum(SysCheckListItem_BudgetModel));
    }

    str getCheckListGroup()
    {
        return "Setup";
    }

    str getHelpLink()
    {
        #define.TopicId('Dynamics://DynamicsHelp/Topic?Id=' +
            'd42c3c30-d3b3-4d71-aa86-396516a3c8ee')
        return #TopicId;
    }

    MenuItemName getMenuItemName()
    {
        return menuitemDisplayStr(BudgetTransactionCode);
    }

    MenuItemType getMenuItemType()
    {
        return MenuItemType::Display;
    }

    str label()
    {
        return "Codes";
    }
```

Working with Forms

4. Create one more class for the last checklist item with the following code snippet:

```
class SysCheckListItem_Budget
extends SysCheckListItem
implements SysCheckListInterfaceBudget
{
}

void new()
{
    super();

    this.addDependency(classNum(SysCheckListItem_BudgetModel));
    this.addDependency(classNum(SysCheckListItem_BudgetCode));
    this.placeAfter(classNum(SysCheckListItem_BudgetCode));
    this.indeterminate(true);
}

str getCheckListGroup()
{
    return "Create budgets";
}

str getHelpLink()
{
    #define.TopicId('Dynamics://DynamicsHelp/Topic?Id=' +
        '846e3e47-acc3-4a86-bbd3-678a62d2953f')
    return #TopicId;
}

MenuItemName getMenuItemName()
{
    return menuitemDisplayStr(BudgetTransactionListPage);
}

MenuItemType getMenuItemType()
{
    return MenuItemType::Display;
}

str label()
{
    return "Budget register entries";
}
```

5. Now, create a class for the checklist itself, as shown here:

```
class SysCheckList_Budget extends SysCheckList
{
    container log;
}

protected str getCheckListCaption()
{
    return "Budget checklist";
}

protected str getHtmlHeader()
{
    return "Budget checklist";
}

protected ClassId getInterfaceId()
{
    return classNum(SysCheckListInterfaceBudget);
}

void save(
    IdentifierName    _name,
    ClassDescription  _description = "")
{
    if (!conFind(log, _name))
    {
        log = conIns(log, conLen(log)+1, _name);
    }
}

boolean find(
    IdentifierName    _name,
    ClassDescription  _description = "")
{
    return conFind(log, _name) ? true : false;
}

protected boolean isRunnable()
{
    return true;
}
```

Working with Forms

```
        static void main(Args _args)
        {
            SysCheckList::runCheckListSpecific(
                classNum(SysCheckList_Budget),
                true);
        }
```

6. Find the `SysCheckList` class in the AOT and add the following code snippet at the bottom of its `checkListItemsHook()` method, just before the closing square bracket of the returning container. The method should look similar to this:

```
    protected static container checkListItemsHook()
    {
        return [
                classNum(RetailStoreSetup_CreateStoreDatabase),
                ...
                ,classNum(SysCheckListItem_Budget)
                ,classNum(SysCheckListItem_BudgetCode)
                ,classNum(SysCheckListItem_BudgetModel)
                ];
    }
```

7. In the same `SysCheckList` class, replace its `checkListsHook()` method with the following code snippet:

```
    protected static container checkListsHook()
    {
        return [classNum(SysCheckList_Budget)];
    }
```

8. Open the `BudgetModel` form in the AOT and override its `close()` method with the following code snippet:

```
    void close()
    {
        super();

        SysCheckList::finished(
            classNum(SysCheckListItem_BudgetModel));
    }
```

9. Open the `BudgetTransactionCode` form in the AOT and override its `close()` method with the following code snippet:

```
    void close()
    {
        super();
```

```
      SysCheckList::finished(
          classNum(SysCheckListItem_BudgetCode));
}
```

10. In the AOT, create a new action menu item with the following properties:

Property	Value
Name	SysCheckList_Budget
Label	Budget checklist
ObjectType	Class
Object	SysCheckList_Budget

11. To test the checklist, run the `SysCheckList_Budget` menu item from the AOT. On the right-hand side of the Dynamics AX window, you will see something similar to what is shown in the following screenshot:

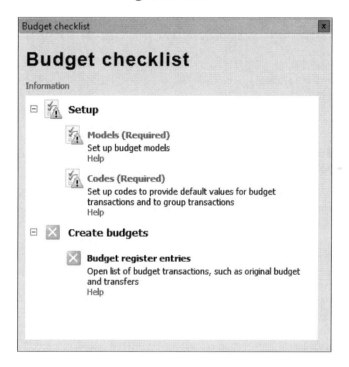

12. Click on the listed items to start and complete the relevant actions. Notice how the status icons change upon the completion of each task, as shown here:

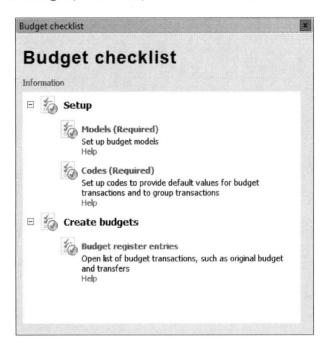

How it works...

The main principle when creating a checklist is that we have to create a main class, which represents the checklist itself, and a number of checklist item classes representing each item in the checklist. The main class has to extend the SysCheckList class, and the items must extend the SysCheckListItem class. The relationships between the main class and the checklist item classes are made by the use of an interface; that is, each checklist item class implements the interface, and the main class holds a reference to that interface.

In this example, we create a new interface called SysCheckListInterfaceBudget and specify it in the getInterfaceId() method of the main checklist class, SysCheckList_Budget. Next, we implement the interface in three SysCheckListItem classes, which correspond to **Models**, **Codes**, and **Budget register entries** items in the checklist.

Each SysCheckListItem class contains a set of inherited methods, which allow you to define a number of different parameters for individual items, as follows:

- All the initialization code can be added to the new() methods. In this example, we use placeAfter() to determine the position of the item in the list relative to other items, indeterminate() to make an item optional, and addDependency() to make an item inactive until another specified item is completed.

- The `getCheckListGroup()` methods define the dependency on a specific group. The budget checklist has two groups: **Setup** and **Create budgets**.
- The `getHelpLink()` methods are responsible for placing relevant help links.
- The `getMenuItemName()` and `getMenuItemType()` methods contain a name and the type of menu item, which is executed on user request. Here, we have the **Budget models**, **Budget codes**, and **Budget register entries** menu items in each class.
- Finally, custom labels can be set in the `label()` methods.

Once the items are ready, we create the main checklist class named `SysCheckList_Budget`, which extends the standard `SysCheckList` class. Next, we override some of the methods to add custom functionality to the checklist, as follows:

- The `getCheckListCaption()` method sets the title of the checklist.
- The `getHtmlHeader()` method is used to add some descriptive text.
- As mentioned before, `getInterfaceId()` is the place where we specify the name of the interface which is used for the checklist item classes.
- The `save()` and `find()` methods are used to store and retrieve, respectively, the status of each item in the list. In this example, we store statuses in the local variable named `log` to make sure that statuses are reset every time we run the checklist.
- The `main()` static method runs the class. Here, we use `runCheckListSpecific()` of the `SysCheckList` class to start the checklist.

The display menu item we have created points to the checklist class and may be used to add the checklist to any menu.

When building checklists, it is necessary to add them and their items to the global checklist and the checklist item list. The `SysCheckList` class contains two methods—`checkLists()` and `checkListItems()`—where all the system checklists and their items are registered. The same class provides two more methods, `checkListsHook()` and `checkListItemsHook()`, where custom checklists should be added. As a part of this example, we add our budget checklist and its items to the `SysCheckList` class.

Final modifications have to be done on each form called by the checklist. We call the `finished()` method of the `SysCheckList` class, within the `close()` method of each form, to update the corresponding checklist item. This means that the checklist item status will be set as completed when the user closes the form. Obviously, this will not ensure that each checklist item was completed successfully but still it gives some level of control. This code does not affect the normal use of the form when it is opened from the regular menu. Normally, more logic is added here if the completion of a specific item is not that straightforward.

Working with Forms

There's more...

In this example, the checklist's statuses are maintained only while the checklist is running. This means that every time the checklist is closed, the statuses are lost and are set to their initial states if the checklist is started again.

However, it is possible to store the statuses permanently in the `SysSetupLog` table just by replacing `save()` and `find()` in `SysCheckList_Budget` with the following code snippet:

```
boolean find(
    IdentifierName    _name,
    ClassDescription  _description = "")
{
    return (SysSetupLog::find(_name, _description).RecId != 0);
}

void save(
    IdentifierName    _name,
    ClassDescription  _description = "")
{
    SysSetupLog::save(_name, _description);
}
```

In this case, every time the checklist starts, the system will pick up its last status from the `SysSetupLog` table and allow the user to continue with the checklist.

Adding the View details link

Dynamics AX has a very useful feature that allows the user on any form to view related record information with just a few mouse clicks. The feature is called **View details** and is available in the right-click context menu on some controls. It is based on table relationships and is available for those controls whose data fields have foreign key relationships with other tables.

Because of the data structure's integrity, the **View details** feature works most of the time. However, when it comes to complex table relations, it does not work correctly or does not work at all. Another example of when this feature does not work automatically is when the `display` or `edit` methods are used on a form. In these and many other cases, the **View details** feature has to be implemented manually.

In this recipe, to demonstrate how it works, we will modify the **General journal** form in the **General ledger** module and add the **View details** feature to the **Description** control, allowing users to jump from the right-click context menu to the **Journal names** form.

How to do it...

Carry out the following steps in order to complete this recipe:

1. Open the `LedgerJournalTable` form in the AOT and override the `jumpRef()` method of the `Name` field in the `LedgerJournalTable` data source with the following code snippet:

```
void jumpRef()
{
    LedgerJournalName   name;
    Args                args;
    MenuFunction        mf;

    name = LedgerJournalName::find(
        LedgerJournalTable.JournalName);

    if (!name)
    {
        return;
    }

    args = new Args();
    args.caller(element);
    args.record(name);

    mf = new MenuFunction(
        menuitemDisplayStr(LedgerJournalSetup),
        MenuItemType::Display);
    mf.run(args);
}
```

Working with Forms

2. Navigate to **General ledger | Journals | General journal**, select any of the existing records, and right-click on the **Description** column. Notice that the **View details** option, which will open the **Journal names** form, is available now, as shown here:

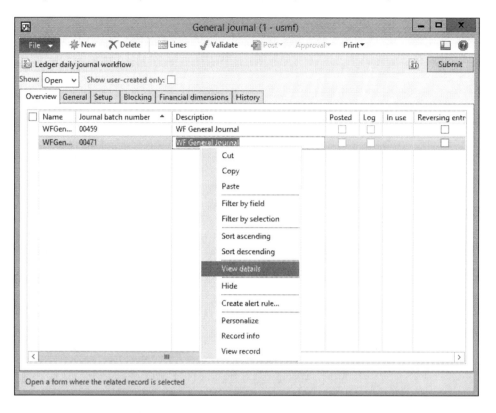

How it works...

Normally, the **View details** feature is controlled by the relationships between the underlying tables. If there are no relationships or the form control is not bound to a table field, then this option is not available. However, we can force this option to appear by overriding the control's `jumpRef()` method.

In this method, we add code that opens the relevant form. This can be done by declaring, instantiating, and running a `FormRun` object, but an easier way to do this is to simply run the relevant menu item from the code. In this recipe, the code in `jumpRef()` does exactly that.

In the code, first we check whether a valid journal name record is found. If yes, we run the `LedgerJournalSetup` menu item with an `Args` object that holds the journal name record and the current form object as a caller. The rest is done automatically by the system, that is, the **Journal names** form is opened with the currently selected journal name.

3
Working with Data in Forms

In this chapter, we will cover the following recipes:

- Using a number sequence handler
- Creating a custom filter control
- Creating a custom instant search filter
- Building a selected/available list
- Preloading images
- Creating a wizard
- Processing multiple records
- Coloring records
- Adding an image to records

Introduction

This chapter basically supplements the previous one and explains about data organization in the forms. It shows how to add custom filters to forms to allow users to filter data and create record lists for quick data manipulation.

This chapter also discusses how the displaying of data can be enhanced by adding icons to record lists and trees and how normal images can be stored along with the data.

Working with Data in Forms

A couple of recipes will show you how to create wizards for guiding users through complex tasks. This chapter will also show several approaches to capture user-selected records on forms for further processing and ways to distinguish specific records by coloring them.

Using a number sequence handler

As already discussed in the *Creating a new number sequence* recipe in *Chapter 1, Processing Data*, number sequences are widely used throughout the system as a part of the standard application. Dynamics AX also provides a special number sequence handler class to be used in forms. It is called `NumberSeqFormHandler`, and its purpose is to simplify the usage of record numbering on the user interface. Some of the standard Dynamics AX forms, such as **Customers** or **Vendors**, already have this feature implemented.

This recipe shows you how to use the number sequence handler class. Although in this demonstration we will use an existing form, the same approach will be applied when creating brand-new forms.

For demonstration purposes, we will use the existing **Customer groups** form located in **Accounts receivable | Setup | Customers** and change the **Customer group** field from manual to automatic numbering. We will use the number sequence created earlier in the *Creating a new number sequence* recipe in *Chapter 1, Processing Data*.

How to do it...

Carry out the following steps in order to complete this recipe:

1. In the AOT, open the `CustGroup` form and add the following code snippet to its class declaration:

   ```
   NumberSeqFormHandler numberSeqFormHandler;
   ```

2. Also, create a new method called `numberSeqFormHandler()` in the same form:

   ```
   NumberSeqFormHandler numberSeqFormHandler()
   {
       if (!numberSeqFormHandler)
       {
           numberSeqFormHandler = NumberSeqFormHandler::newForm(
               CustParameters::numRefCustGroupId().NumberSequenceId,
               element,
               CustGroup_ds,
               fieldNum(CustGroup,CustGroup));
       }
       return numberSeqFormHandler;
   }
   ```

3. In the same form, override the `CustGroup` data source's `create()` method with the following code snippet:

```
void create(boolean _append = false)
{
    element.numberSeqFormHandler(
        ).formMethodDataSourceCreatePre();

    super(_append);

    element.numberSeqFormHandler(
        ).formMethodDataSourceCreate();
}
```

4. Then, override its `delete()` method with the following code snippet:

```
void delete()
{
    ttsBegin;

    element.numberSeqFormHandler().formMethodDataSourceDelete();

    super();

    ttsCommit;
}
```

5. Then, override the data source's `write()` method with the following code snippet:

```
void write()
{
    ttsBegin;

    super();

    element.numberSeqFormHandler().formMethodDataSourceWrite();

    ttsCommit;
}
```

6. Similarly, override its `validateWrite()` method with the following code snippet:

```
boolean validateWrite()
{
    boolean ret;

    ret = super();

    ret = element.numberSeqFormHandler(
        ).formMethodDataSourceValidateWrite(ret) && ret;

    return ret;
}
```

Working with Data in Forms

7. In the same data source, override its `linkActive()` method with the following code snippet:

   ```
   void linkActive()
   {
       element.numberSeqFormHandler(
           ).formMethodDataSourceLinkActive();

       super();
   }
   ```

8. Finally, override the form's `close()` method with the following code snippet:

   ```
   void close()
   {
       if (numberSeqFormHandler)
       {
           numberSeqFormHandler.formMethodClose();
       }

       super();
   }
   ```

9. In order to test the numbering, navigate to **Accounts receivable | Setup | Customers | Customer groups** and try to create several new records—the **Customer group** value will be generated automatically:

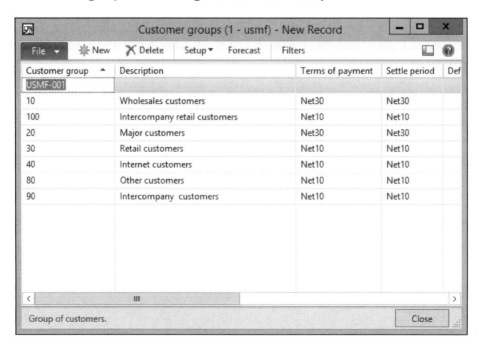

How it works...

First, we declare an object of type `NumberSeqFormHandler` in the form's class declaration. Then, we create a new corresponding form method called `numberSeqFormHandler()`, which instantiates the object if it is not instantiated yet and returns it. This method allows us to hold the handler creation code in one place and reuse it many times within the form.

In this method, we use the `newForm()` constructor of the `NumberSeqFormHandler` class to create the `numberSeqFormHandler` object. It accepts the following arguments:

- The number sequence code, which was created in the *Creating a new number sequence* recipe in *Chapter 1, Processing Data*, and which ensures a proper format of the customer group numbering. Here, we call the `numRefCustGroupId()` helper method from the `CustParameters` table to find which number sequence code will be used when creating a new customer group record.
- The `FormRun` object, which represents the form itself.
- The form data source, where we need to apply the number sequence handler.
- The field ID into which the number sequence will be populated.

Finally, we add the various `NumberSeqFormHandler` methods to the corresponding methods on the form's data source to ensure proper handling of the numbering when various events are triggered.

See also

- The *Creating a new number sequence* recipe in *Chapter 1, Processing Data*

Creating a custom filter control

Filtering in forms in Dynamics AX is implemented in a variety of ways. As a part of the standard application, Dynamics AX provides various filtering options, such as **Filter By Selection**, **Filter By Grid**, or **Advanced Filter/Sort** that allows you to modify the underlying query of the currently displayed form. In addition to the standard filters, the Dynamics AX list pages normally allow quick filtering on most commonly used fields. Besides that, some of the existing forms have even more advanced filtering options, which allow users to quickly define complex search criteria.

Although the latter option needs additional programming, it is more user-friendly than standard filtering and is a very common request in most of the Dynamics AX implementations.

In this recipe, we will learn how to add custom filters to a form. We will use the **Main accounts** form as a basis and add a few custom filters, which will allow users to search for accounts based on their name and type.

Working with Data in Forms

How to do it...

Carry out the following steps in order to complete this recipe:

1. In the AOT, locate the `MainAccountListPage` form and change the following property for its `Filter` group:

Property	Value
Columns	2

2. In the same group, add a new `StringEdit` control with the following properties:

Property	Value
Name	FilterName
AutoDeclaration	Yes
ExtendedDataType	AccountName

3. Add a new `ComboBox` control to the same group with the following properties:

Property	Value
Name	FilterType
AutoDeclaration	Yes
EnumType	DimensionLedgerAccountType
Selection	10

4. Override the `modified()` methods for both the newly created controls with the following code snippet:

   ```
   boolean modified()
   {
       boolean ret;

       ret = super();

       if (ret)
       {
           MainAccount_ds.executeQuery();
       }

       return ret;
   }
   ```

5. After all modifications, in the AOT, the `MainAccountListPage` form will look similar to the following screenshot:

6. In the same form, update the `executeQuery()` method of the `MainAccount` data source as follows:

```
public void executeQuery()
{
    QueryBuildRange qbrName;
    QueryBuildRange qbrType;

    MainAccount::updateBalances();

    qbrName = SysQuery::findOrCreateRange(
        MainAccount_q.dataSourceTable(tableNum(MainAccount)),
        fieldNum(MainAccount,Name));

    qbrType = SysQuery::findOrCreateRange(
        MainAccount_q.dataSourceTable(tableNum(MainAccount)),
        fieldNum(MainAccount,Type));
```

Working with Data in Forms

```
        if (FilterName.text())
        {
            qbrName.value(SysQuery::valueLike(queryValue(
                FilterName.text())));
        }
        else
        {
            qbrName.value(SysQuery::valueUnlimited());
        }

        if (FilterType.selection() ==
            DimensionLedgerAccountType::Blank)
        {
            qbrType.value(SysQuery::valueUnlimited());
        }
        else
        {
            qbrType.value(queryValue(FilterType.selection()));
        }

        super();
    }
```

7. In order to test the filters, navigate to **General ledger | Common | Main accounts** and change the values in the newly created filters—the account list will change reflecting the selected criteria:

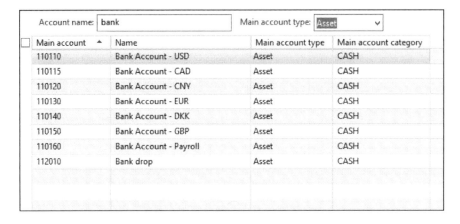

8. Click on the **Advanced Filter/Sort** button in the toolbar to inspect how the criteria was applied in the underlying query (note that although changing the filter values here will affect the search results, the earlier created filter controls will not reflect those changes):

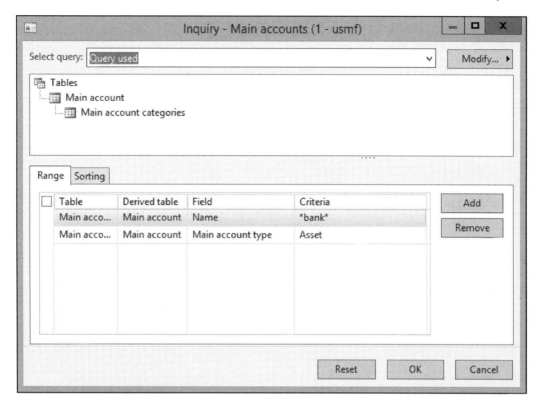

How it works...

We start by changing the Columns property of the existing empty Filter group control to make sure all our controls are placed from the left to the right in one line.

We add two new controls that represent the **Account name** and **Main account type** filters and enable them to be automatically declared for later usage in the code. We also override their modified() event methods to ensure that the MainAccount data source's query is re-executed whenever the controls' value change.

All the code is placed in the executeQuery() method of the form's data source. The code has to be placed before super() to make sure the query is modified before fetching the data.

Here, we declare and create two new QueryBuildRange objects, which represent the ranges on the query. We use the findOrCreateRange() method of the SysQuery application class to get the range object. This method is very useful and important, as it allows you to reuse previously created ranges.

Working with Data in Forms

Next, we set the ranges' values. If the filter controls are blank, we use the `valueUnlimited()` method of the `SysQuery` application class to clear the ranges. If the user types some text into the filter controls, we pass those values to the query ranges. The global `queryValue()` function—which is actually a shortcut to `SysQuery::value()`—ensures that only safe characters are passed to the range. The `SysQuery::valueLike()` method adds the * character around the account name value to make sure that the search is done based on partial text.

Note that the `SysQuery` helper class is very useful when working with queries, as it does all kinds of input data conversions to make sure they can be safely used. Here is a brief summary of few other useful methods in the `SysQuery` class:

- `valueUnlimited()`: This method returns a string representing an unlimited query range value, that is, no range at all.
- `value()`: This method converts an argument into a safe string. The global `queryValue()` method is a shortcut for this.
- `valueNot()`: This method converts an argument into a safe string and adds an inversion sign in front of it.

See also

- The *Building a query object* recipe in *Chapter 1, Processing Data*

Creating a custom instant search filter

The standard form filters and majority of customized form filters in Dynamics AX are only applied once the user presses some button or key. It is acceptable in most cases, especially if multiple criteria are used. However, when the result retrieval speed and usage simplicity has priority over system performance, it is possible to set up the search so the record list is updated instantly when the user starts typing.

In this recipe, to demonstrate the instant search, we will modify the **Main accounts** form. We will add a custom **Account name** filter, which will update the account list automatically when the user starts typing.

How to do it...

Carry out the following steps in order to complete this recipe:

1. In the AOT, open the `MainAccountListPage` form and add a new `StringEdit` control with the following properties to the existing `Filter` group:

Property	Value
Name	FilterName
AutoDeclaration	Yes
ExtendedDataType	AccountName

2. Override the control's `textChange()` method with the following code snippet:

    ```
    void textChange()
    {
        super();

        MainAccount_ds.executeQuery();
    }
    ```

3. On the same control, override the control's `enter()` method with the following code snippet:

    ```
    void enter()
    {
        super();
        this.setSelection(
            strLen(this.text()),
            strLen(this.text()));
    }
    ```

4. Update the `executeQuery()` method of the `MainAccount` data source as follows:

    ```
    public void executeQuery()
    {
        QueryBuildRange qbrName;

        MainAccount::updateBalances();

        qbrName = SysQuery::findOrCreateRange(
            this.queryBuildDataSource(),
            fieldNum(MainAccount,Name));

        qbrName.value(
            FilterName.text() ?
    ```

Working with Data in Forms

```
            SysQuery::valueLike(queryValue(FilterName.text())) :
            SysQuery::valueUnlimited());

    super();
}
```

5. In order to test the search, navigate to **General ledger | Common | Main accounts** and start typing into the **Account name** filter. Note how the account list is being filtered automatically:

Main account	Name	Main account type	Main account category
110180	Petty Cash	Asset	CASH
112100	Deposits - Cash	Asset	CASH
119999	TOTAL CASH & CASH EQUIVALE...	Total	
403300	Customer Cash Discounts Taken	Revenue	SALESRETDIS
520200	Vendor Cash Discounts Taken	Expense	OTHERINC
520201	Cash Discounts Received	Expense	OTHERINC
618150	Cash Discrepancies	Expense	OTHEREXP

Account name: cash

How it works...

Firstly, we add a new control, which represents the **Account name** filter. Normally, the user's typing triggers the `textChange()` event method on the active control every time a character is entered. So, we override this method and add the code to re-execute the form's query whenever a new character is typed in.

Next, we have to correct the cursor's behavior. Currently, once the user types in the first character, the search is executed and the system moves the focus out of this control and then moves back into the control selecting all the typed text. If the user continues typing, the existing text will be overwritten with the new character and the loop will continue.

In order to get around this, we have to override the control's `enter()` event method. This method is called every time the control receives a focus whether it was done by a user's mouse, key, or by the system. Here, we call the `setSelection()` method. Normally, the purpose of this method is to mark a control's text or a part of it as selected. Its first argument specifies the beginning of the selection and the second one specifies the end. In this recipe, we are using this method in a slightly different way.

Chapter 3

We pass the length of the typed text as a first argument, which means the selection starts at the end of the text. We pass the same value as a second argument, which means that selection ends at the end of the text. It does not make any sense from the selection point of view, but it ensures that the cursor always stays at the end of the typed text allowing the user to continue typing.

The last thing to do is to add some code to the `executeQuery()` method to change the query before it is executed. Modifying the query was discussed in detail in the *Creating a custom filter control* recipe. The only thing to note here is that we use the `SysQuery::valueLike()` helper method which adds * to the beginning and the end of the search string to make the search by a partial string.

Note that the system's performance might be affected as the data search is executed every time the user types in a character. It is not recommended to use this approach for large tables.

See also

- The *Creating a custom filter control* recipe

Building a selected/available list

Frequent users might note that some of the Dynamics AX forms contain two sections placed next to each other and allow moving items from one side to the other. Normally, the right section contains a list of available values and the left one contains the values that have been chosen by the user. Buttons in the middle allow moving data from one side to another. Double-click and drag-and-drop mouse events are also supported. Such design improves the user's experience as data manipulation becomes more user-friendly. Some of the examples in the standard application can be found at **General ledger | Setup | Financial dimensions | Financial dimension sets** or **System administration | Common | Users | User groups**.

This functionality is based on the `SysListPanelRelationTable` application class. Developers only need to create its instance with the required parameters and the rest is done automatically.

This recipe will show the basic principle of how to create selected/available lists. We will add an option for assigning customers to buyer groups in the **Buyer groups** form in the **Inventory management** module.

Working with Data in Forms

How to do it...

Carry out the following steps in order to complete this recipe:

1. In the AOT, create a new table named `InventBuyerGroupList`. We will not change any of its properties as this table is for demonstration only.
2. Add a new field to the table with the following properties (click on **Yes** if asked to add a new relation to the table):

Property	Value
Type	String
Name	GroupId
ExtendedDataType	ItemBuyerGroupId

3. Add another field to the table with the following properties:

Property	Value
Type	String
Name	CustAccount
ExtendedDataType	CustAccount

4. In the AOT, open the `InventBuyerGroup` form and change its design's property as follows:

Property	Value
Style	Auto

5. Add a new `Tab` control with the following properties to the design's bottom:

Property	Value
Name	Tab
Width	Column width
Height	Column height

6. Add a new `TabPage` control with the following properties to the newly created tab:

Property	Value
Name	BuyerGroups
Caption	Buyer groups

7. Add another `TabPage` control with the following properties to the newly created tab:

Property	Value
Name	Customers
Caption	Customers

8. Move the existing `Grid` control into the first tab page and hide the existing `Body` group by setting its property:

Property	Value
Visible	No

9. The form will look similar to the following screenshot:

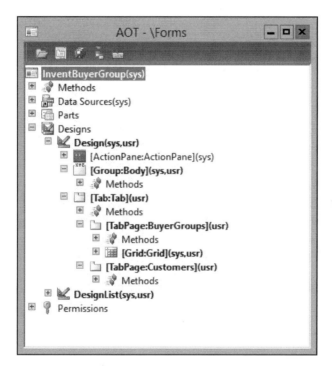

10. Add the following line to the form's class declaration:

    ```
    SysListPanelRelationTable sysListPanel;
    ```

11. Override the form's `init()` method with the following code snippet:

    ```
    void init()
    {
        container columns;
        #ResAppl
    ```

```
        columns = [fieldNum(CustTable, AccountNum)];


        sysListPanel = SysListPanelRelationTable::newForm(
            element,
            element.controlId(
                formControlStr(InventBuyerGroup,Customers)),
            "Selected",
            "Available",
            #ImageCustomer,
            tableNum(InventBuyerGroupList),
            fieldNum(InventBuyerGroupList,CustAccount),
            fieldNum(InventBuyerGroupList,GroupId),
            tableNum(CustTable),
            fieldNum(CustTable,AccountNum),
            columns);

        super();

        sysListPanel.init();

    }
```

12. Override the `pageActivated()` method on the newly created `Customers` tab page with the following code snippet:

    ```
    void pageActivated()
    {
        sysListPanel.parmRelationRangeValue(
            InventBuyerGroup.Group);

        sysListPanel.parmRelationRangeRecId(
            InventBuyerGroup.RecId);

        sysListPanel.fill();

        super();
    }
    ```

13. In order to test the list, navigate to **Inventory management | Setup | Inventory | Buyer groups** and select any group. Then, go to the **Customers** tab page and use the buttons provided to move records from one side to the other. You can also double-click or drag-and-drop with your mouse:

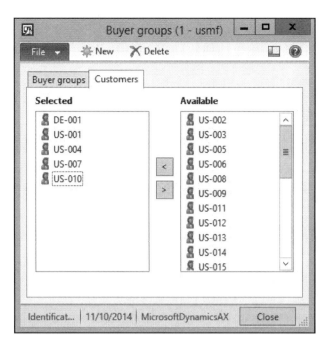

How it works...

In this recipe, the `InventBuyerGroupList` table is used as a many-to-many relationship table between the buyer groups and the customers.

In terms of form design, the only thing that needs to be added is a new tab page. The rest is created dynamically by the `SysListPanelRelationTable` application class.

In the form's class declaration, we declare a new variable based on the `SysListPanelRelationTable` class and instantiate it in the form's `init()` method using its `newForm()` constructor. The method accepts the following parameters:

- The `FormRun` object representing the form itself.
- The name of the tab page.
- The label of the left section.
- The label of the right section.
- The number of the image that is shown next to each record in the lists.
- The relationship table number.
- The field number in the relationship table representing the child record. In our case, it is the customer account number—`CustAccount`.

Working with Data in Forms

- The field number in the relationship table representing the parent table. In this case, it is the buyer group number—`GroupId`.
- The number of the table that is displayed in the lists.
- A container of the field numbers displayed in each column.

We also have to initialize the list by calling it's member method `init()` in the form's `init()` method right after the `super()` method.

The list's controls are created dynamically when the **Customers** tab page is opened. In order to accommodate that, we add the list's creation code to the `pageActivated()` event method of the newly created tab page. In this way, we ensure that the list is populated whenever a new buyer group is selected.

There's more...

The `SysListPanelRelationTable` class can only display fields from a single table. Alternatively, there is another application class named `SysListPanelRelationTableCallback`, which allows you to create more complex lists.

In order to demonstrate its capabilities, we will expand the previous example by displaying the customer name next to the account number. The customer name is stored in another table and can be retrieved by using the `name()` method on the `CustTable` table.

First, in the form's class declaration, we have to change the list declaration to the following code line:

```
SysListPanelRelationTableCallback sysListPanel;
```

Next, we create two new methods—one for the left list and another one for the right list—that generate and return data containers to be displayed in each section. The methods will be placed on the `InventBuyerGroupList` table. In order to improve the performance, these methods will be executed on the server tier (note the server modifier):

```
static server container selectedCustomers(
    ItemBuyerGroupId _groupId)
{
    container            ret;
    container            data;
    CustTable            custTable;
    InventBuyerGroupList groupList;

    while select custTable
        order by AccountNum
        exists join groupList
```

```
            where groupList.CustAccount == custTable.AccountNum
                && groupList.GroupId     == _groupId
    {
        data = [custTable.AccountNum,
                custTable.AccountNum,
                custTable.name()];

        ret += [data];
    }

    return ret;
}

static server container availableCustomers(
    ItemBuyerGroupId _groupId)
{
    container            ret;
    container            data;
    CustTable            custTable;
    InventBuyerGroupList groupList;

    while select custTable
        order by AccountNum
        notExists join firstOnly groupList
            where groupList.CustAccount == custTable.AccountNum
                && groupList.GroupId     == _groupId
    {
        data = [custTable.AccountNum,
                custTable.AccountNum,
                custTable.name()];

        ret += [data];
    }

    return ret;
}
```

Each of the methods returns a container of containers. The outer container holds all the items in the list. The inner container represents one item in the section and it contains three elements—the first is an identification number of the element and the next two are the values displayed in the lists.

Working with Data in Forms

Next, we create two new methods with the same names on the `InventBuyerGroup` form itself. These methods are required to be present on the form by the `SysListPanelRelationTableCallback` class. These methods are nothing else but wrappers to the previously created methods:

```
private container selectedCustomers()
{
    return InventBuyerGroupList::selectedCustomers(
        InventBuyerGroup.Group);
}

private container availableCustomers()
{
    return InventBuyerGroupList::availableCustomers(
        InventBuyerGroup.Group);
}
```

In this way, we are reducing the number of calls between the client and server tiers while generating the lists.

Finally, we replace the form's `init()` method with the following code snippet:

```
void init()
{
    container columns;
    #ResAppl

    columns = [0, 0];

    sysListPanel = SysListPanelRelationTableCallback::newForm(
        element,
        element.controlId(
            formControlStr(InventBuyerGroup,Customers)),
        "Selected",
        "Available",
        #ImageCustomer,
        tableNum(InventBuyerGroupList),
        fieldNum(InventBuyerGroupList,CustAccount),
        fieldNum(InventBuyerGroupList,GroupId),
        tableNum(CustTable),
        fieldNum(CustTable,AccountNum),
        columns,
        0,
        '',
        '',
```

```
        identifierStr(selectedCustomers),
        identifierStr(availableCustomers));

    super();

    sysListPanel.init();

}
```

This time, we used the `newForm()` constructor of the `SysListPanelRelationTableCallback` class, which is very similar to the previous one, but accepts the names of methods as arguments, which will be used to populate the data in the right and left sections.

Note that the `columns` container that previously held a list of fields now contains two zeros. By doing that, we simply define that there will be two columns in each list. Since the lists actually are generated outside the `SysListPanelRelationTableCallback` class, we do not need to specify the field numbers of the columns anymore.

Now, when you run the **Buyer groups** form, both the sections contain a new **Customer name** column:

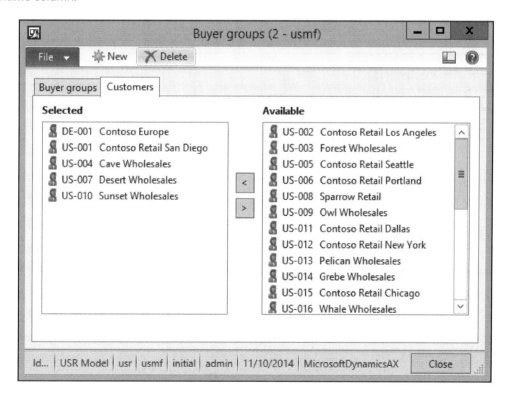

Working with Data in Forms

Preloading images

Some of the Dynamics AX controls such as trees or lists, in most cases, have small icon images in front of the text. These icons make the user interface look better and can represent a type, status, availability, or any other property of the current item in the control.

Images are binary data and their processing may be resource demanding. The Dynamics AX application provides a way of handling images to increase application performance. Normally, on those forms with lists or trees, all required images are preloaded during the forms' initialization. This reduces the image-loading time when the image is actually displayed to the user.

For this purpose, Dynamics AX contains a set of `ImageListAppl` derivative classes, which holds a specific set of image data required in specific circumstances. For example, the `ImageListAppl_Proj` class in the **Project management and accounting** module preloads project-related images representing project types during the project tree initialization. So, virtually no time is consumed for displaying the images later, when the user starts browsing the project tree control.

In this recipe, we will create a new image list class for image preloading. As a base, we will use the list created in the *Building a selected/available list* recipe. We will enhance that list by showing different icons for customers, which are marked as on hold.

How to do it...

Carry out the following steps in order to complete this recipe:

1. In the AOT, create a new class named `ImageListAppl_Cust` with the following code snippet:

    ```
    class ImageListAppl_Cust extends ImageListAppl
    {
    }

    protected void build()
    {
        super();
        this.add(#ImageCustomer);
        this.add(#ImageWarning);
    }
    ```

2. Then, find the `SysListPanelRelationTableCallback` class and modify its `newForm()` method by adding one more argument to the end of its argument list:

    ```
    ImageListAppl _imageListAppl = null
    ```

3. In the same method, add the following line of code right before `sysListPanel.build()`:

    ```
    sysListPanel.parmImageList(_imageListAppl);
    ```

4. In the AOT, find the `InventBuyerGroup` form and add the following line of code to its class declaration:

    ```
    #ResAppl
    ```

5. On the same form, replace its existing methods with the following code snippet:

    ```
    void init()
    {
        container columns;
        ImageListAppl_Cust imageListAppl;

        columns = [0, 0];

        imageListAppl = new ImageListAppl_Cust(
            Imagelist::smallIconWidth(),
            Imagelist::smallIconHeight());

        sysListPanel = SysListPanelRelationTableCallback::newForm(
            element,
            element.controlId(
                formControlStr(InventBuyerGroup,Customers)),
            "Selected",
            "Available",
            0,
            tableNum(InventBuyerGroupList),
            fieldNum(InventBuyerGroupList,CustAccount),
            fieldNum(InventBuyerGroupList,GroupId),
            tableNum(CustTable),
            fieldNum(CustTable,AccountNum),
            columns,
            0,
            '',
            '',
            identifierStr(selectedCustomers),
            identifierStr(availableCustomers),
            0,
            imageListAppl);

        super();

        sysListPanel.init();

    }
    ```

```
private container selectedCustomers()
{
    container            ret;
    container            data;
    CustTable            custTable;
    InventBuyerGroupList groupList;

    while select custTable
        exists join groupList
            where groupList.CustAccount == custTable.AccountNum
               && groupList.GroupId     == InventBuyerGroup.Group
    {
        data = [custTable.AccountNum,
                (custTable.Blocked==CustVendorBlocked::No ?
                    #ImageCustomer :
                    #ImageWarning),
                custTable.AccountNum,
                custTable.name()];

        ret = conIns(ret, conLen(ret)+1, data);
    }

    return ret;
}

private container availableCustomers()
{
    container            ret;
    container            data;
    CustTable            custTable;
    InventBuyerGroupList groupList;

    while select custTable
        notExists join firstOnly groupList
            where groupList.CustAccount == custTable.AccountNum
               && groupList.GroupId     == InventBuyerGroup.Group
    {
        data = [custTable.AccountNum,
                (custTable.Blocked==CustVendorBlocked::No ?
                    #ImageCustomer :
                    #ImageWarning),
                custTable.AccountNum,
                custTable.name()];

        ret = conIns(ret, conLen(ret)+1, data);
    }

    return ret;
}
```

Chapter 3

6. In order to test the results, navigate to **Inventory management | Setup | Inventory | Buyer groups**, go to the **Customers** tab page, and note that customers on hold are now marked with a different icon:

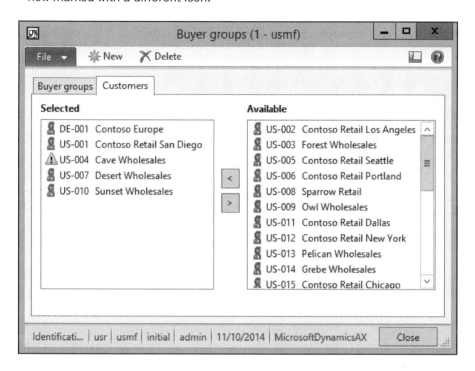

How it works...

The first task in this recipe is to create a class that handles the required set of images. We use two different images—one for normal customers and one for customers on hold.

Dynamics AX has lots of image resources, which can be used for any given scenario. The resources can be found in the Development Workspace by navigating to **Tools | Embedded resources**. Each of the images has a number associated with it, and most of those numbers are already associated with descriptive textual representations in the `#ResAppl` macro library, which is located in the AOT under the Macros node. In this example, we have chosen a few images from the resource library and added them into the `build()` method of the new `ImageListAppl_Cust` class.

The second step is to modify the `SysListPanelRelationTableCallback` class to make sure its `newForm()` method accepts `ImageListAppl` as an argument and passes it to the class using the `parmImageList()` method. A new method can be created here, but it is not a good idea to copy so much code, especially when our changes are very small and do not affect the standard method's behavior as the parameter is set to `null` by default.

Working with Data in Forms

The final step is to modify the form. First, we instantiate a new `imageListAppl` object based on our class and pass it to the modified `newForm()` method of the `SysListPanelRelationTableCallback` class as a last argument. In this way, we ensure that all the images defined in `imageListAppl` will be stored and reused from cache instead of loading them every time from the original source. Then, we modify the form's `selectedItems()` method and the `availableItems()` methods to include image resource numbers in the returned data. We use the `#ImageCustomer` macro for normal customers and `#ImageWarning` for customers on hold. Note that the inner container structure, when using the `SysListPanelRelationTableCallback` class, is different—the second element is an image resource number.

There's more...

As mentioned earlier, images can be used on tree controls too. In this section, we will enhance the tree created in the *Using a Tree control* recipe in *Chapter 2, Working with Forms*. We will add small icons in front of each node.

First in the AOT, we create a new class called `ImageListAppl_LedgerBudget` with the following code snippet:

```
class ImageListAppl_LedgerBudget extends ImageListAppl
{
}

protected void build()
{
    super();
    this.add(#ImageFolder);
    this.add(#ImageLedgerBudget);
}
```

As in the previous example, the class extends `ImageListAppl` and is responsible for preloading the images to be used on the tree. We will only use two different images— a folder icon for parent ledger budget models and a budget icon for submodels.

Next, we need to modify the `BudgetModelTree` class created earlier in the book. Let's add the following line of code to the bottom of its class declaration:

```
ImageListAppl imageListAppl;
```

Add the following lines of code to the `buildTree()` method right after the variable declaration section:

```
imageListAppl = new ImageListAppl_LedgerBudget();
tree.setImagelist(imageListAppl.imageList());
```

Chapter 3

This creates an instance of the `ImageListAppl_LedgerBudget` class and passes it to the `Tree` control.

Replace the `createNode()` method with the following code snippet:

```
private TreeItemIdx createNode(
    TreeItemIdx     _parentIdx,
    BudgetModelId   _modelId,
    RecId           _recId)
{
    TreeItemIdx itemIdx;
    BudgetModel model;
    BudgetModel submodel;
    ImageRes    imageRes;
    #ResAppl

    if (_parentIdx == FormTreeAdd::Root)
    {
        imageRes = imageListAppl.image(#ImageFolder);
    }
    else
    {
        imageRes = imageListAppl.image(#ImageLedgerBudget);
    }

    model = BudgetModel::find(HeadingSub::Heading, _modelId);

    itemIdx = SysFormTreeControl::addTreeItem(
        tree,
        _modelId + ' : ' + model.Txt,
        _parentIdx,
        _recId,
        imageRes,
        true);

    if (modelId == _modelId)
    {
        tree.select(itemIdx);
    }

    while select submodel
        where submodel.ModelId == _modelId &&
              submodel.Type    == HeadingSub::SubModel
    {
```

Working with Data in Forms

```
            this.createNode(
                itemIdx,
                submodel.SubModelId,
                submodel.RecId);
        }

        return itemIdx;
    }
```

At the top of this method, we check whether the current node is a parent node. If yes, we set its image as the folder icon. If not, we set it as the budget model icon. Then, we pass the image to the `addTreeItem()` method.

In order to test the tree icons, navigate to **Budgeting | Setup | Basic budgeting | Budget models** and note how the tree has changed:

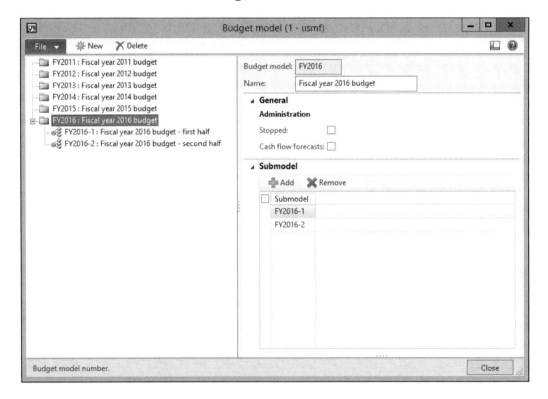

See also

- The *Using a Tree control* recipe in *Chapter 2, Working with Forms*

Chapter 3

Creating a wizard

Wizards in Dynamics AX are used to help a user perform a specific task. Some examples of standard Dynamics AX wizards are **Report Wizard, Class Wizard**, **Number Sequence Wizard**, and so on.

Normally, a wizard is presented to a user as a form with a series of steps. During the wizard run, all the user's inputs are collected and committed to the database when the user presses the **Finish** button on the last page.

In this recipe, we will create a new wizard, which helps creating new main accounts. First, we will use the standard Dynamics AX Wizard to create a framework, and then we will add some additional controls manually.

How to do it...

Carry out the following steps in order to complete this recipe:

1. In the Development Workspace, navigate to **Tools | Wizards | Wizard Wizard**.
2. Click on **Next** on the first page:

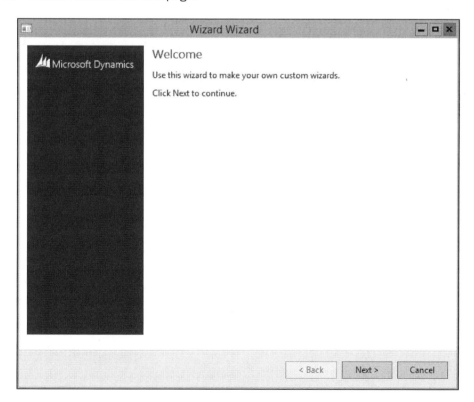

3. Select **Standard Wizard** and click on **Next**:

Chapter 3

4. Specify `MainAccount` in the name field and click on **Next**:

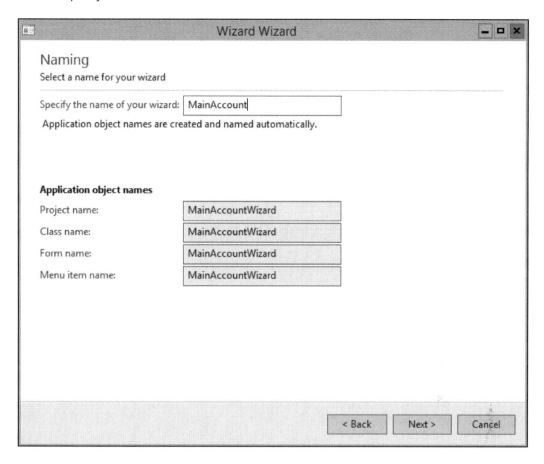

5. Accept the default number of steps and click on **Next**:

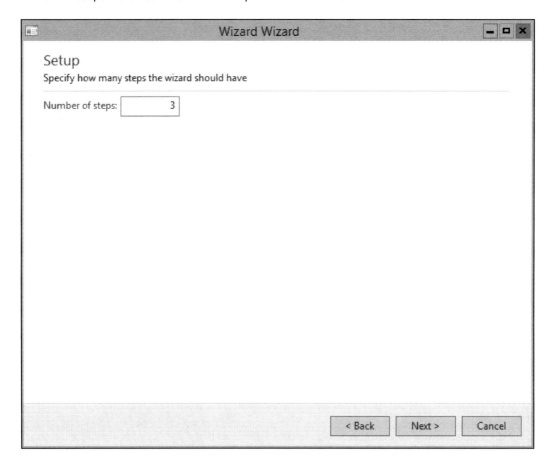

6. On the last page, click on **Finish** to complete the wizard:

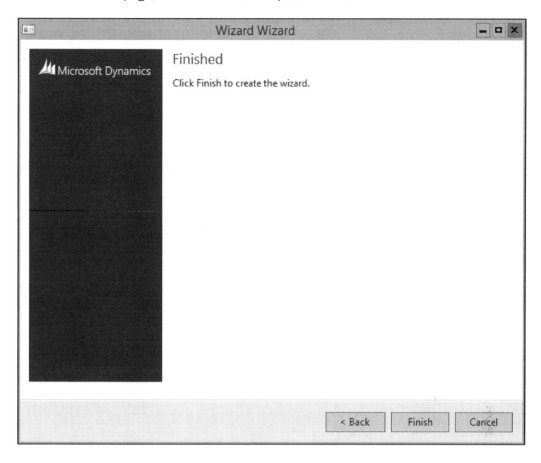

Working with Data in Forms

7. The wizard creates an AOT development project with three new objects in it: a form, a class, and a menu item, as shown in the following screenshot:

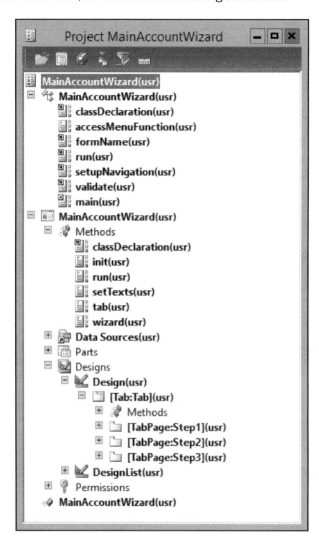

8. Create a new macro library named `MainAccountWizard` with the following line of code:

   ```
   #define.tabStep2(2)
   ```

9. Modify the `MainAccountWizard` class by adding the following lines of code to its class declaration:

   ```
   MainAccount mainAccount;
   #MainAccountWizard
   ```

10. Add the following line of code to the existing `setupNavigation()` method in the same class:

    ```
    nextEnabled[#tabStep2] = false;
    ```

11. Override the `finish()` method of the class with the following code snippet:

    ```
    protected void finish()
    {
        mainAccount.initValue();
        mainAccount.LedgerChartOfAccounts =
            LedgerChartOfAccounts::current();
        mainAccount.MainAccountId = formRun.accountNum();
        mainAccount.Name = formRun.accountName();
        mainAccount.Type = formRun.accountType();

        super();
    }
    ```

12. Replace the `validate()` method of the same class with the following code snippet:

    ```
    boolean validate()
    {
        return mainAccount.validateWrite();
    }
    ```

13. Replace the `run()` method of the same class with the following code snippet:

    ```
    void run()
    {
        mainAccount.insert();

        info(strFmt(
            "Ledger account '%1' was successfully created",
            mainAccount.MainAccountId));
    }
    ```

14. In the `MainAccountWizard` form, add the following line of code to its class declaration:

    ```
    #MainAccountWizard
    ```

15. Change the form's design property:

Property	Value
Caption	Main account wizard

Working with Data in Forms

16. Modify the properties of the `Step1` tab page, as follows:

Property	Value
Caption	Welcome

17. Add a new `StaticText` control in this tab page with the following properties:

Property	Value
Name	WelcomeTxt
Text	This wizard helps you to create a new main account.

18. Modify the properties of the `Step2` tab page:

Property	Value
Caption	Account setup
HelpText	Specify account number, name, and type.

19. Add a new `StringEdit` control in this tab page with the following properties:

Property	Value
Name	AccountNum
AutoDeclaration	Yes
Label	Main account
ExtendedDataType	AccountNum

20. Add one more `StringEdit` control in this tab page with the following properties:

Property	Value
Name	AccountName
AutoDeclaration	Yes
ExtendedDataType	AccountName

21. Add a new `ComboBox` control in this tab page with the following properties:

Property	Value
Name	AccountType
AutoDeclaration	Yes
EnumType	DimensionLedgerAccountType

22. Modify the properties of the `Step3` tab page, as follows:

Property	Value
Caption	Finish

23. Add a new `StaticText` control on this tab page with the following properties:

Property	Value
Name	FinishTxt
Text	This wizard is now ready to create new main account.

24. Create the following four methods at the top level of the form:

    ```
    MainAccountNum accountNum()
    {
        return AccountNum.text();
    }


    AccountName accountName()
    {
        return AccountName.text();
    }


    DimensionLedgerAccountType accountType()
    {
        return AccountType.selection();
    }


    void setNext()
    {
        sysWizard.nextEnabled(
            this.accountNum() && this.accountName(),
            #tabStep2,
            false);
    }
    ```

25. Now, override the `textChange()` method on the `AccountNum` and `AccountName` controls with the following code:

    ```
    void textChange()
    {
        super();
        element.setNext();
    }
    ```

Working with Data in Forms

After all modifications, the form will look as follows:

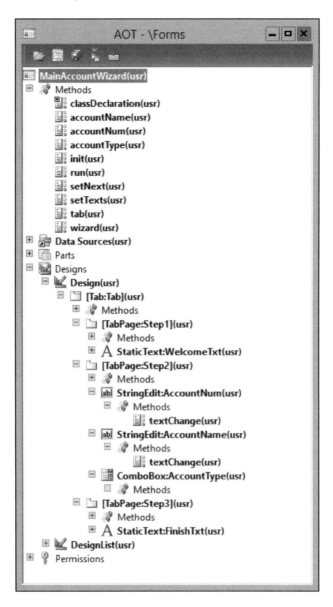

26. In order to test the newly created wizard, run the **MainAccountWizard** menu item, and the wizard will appear. On the first page, click on **Next**:

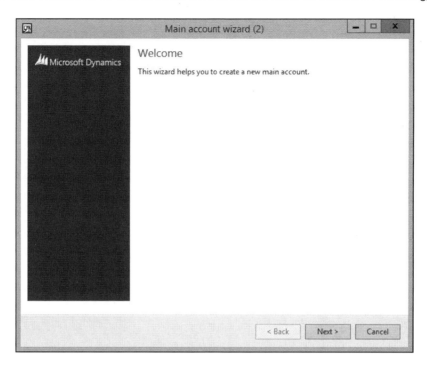

27. On the second page, specify **Main account**, **Account name**, and **Main account type**:

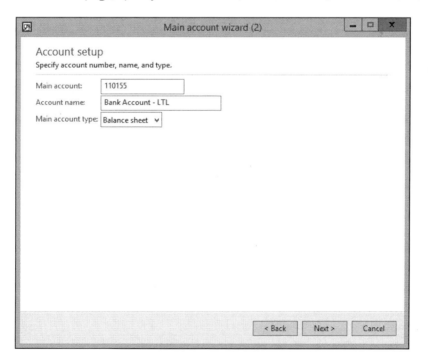

Working with Data in Forms

28. On the last page, click on **Finish** to complete the wizard:

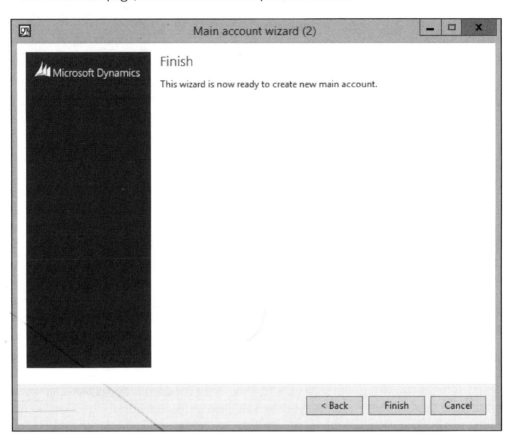

29. The **Infolog** window will display a message that a new account was created successfully:

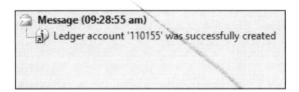

How it works...

The Dynamics AX Wizard creates three AOT objects for us:

- The `MainAccountWizard` class, which contains all the logic required to run the wizard

- The `MainAccountWizard` form, which is the wizard layout
- Finally, the `MainAccountWizard` display menu item, which is used to start the wizard and can be added to a menu

The generated objects are just a starting point for our custom wizard. It already has three pages as we specified during the creation, but we still have to add new user input controls and custom code in order to implement our requirements.

We start with defining a new `#tabStep2` macro, which holds the number of the second tab page. We are going to refer to this page several times, so it is good practice to define its number in one place.

In the `MainAccountWizard` class, we override its `setupNavigation()` method, which is used for defining initial button states. We use this method to disable the **Next** button on the second page by default. The `nextEnabled` variable is an array holding the initial enabled or disabled state for each tab page.

The overridden `finish()` method is called when the user clicks on the **Finish** button. Here, we initialize the record and and assign the user's input values to the corresponding field values.

In the `validate()` method, we check the account that will be created. This method is called right after the user clicks on the **Finish** button at the end of the wizard and before the main code is executed in the `run()` method. Here, we simply call the `validateWrite()` method for the record, from the main account table.

The last thing to do in the class is to place the main wizard code—insert the record and display a message—in the `run()` method.

In the `MainAccountWizard` form's design, we modify properties of each tab page and add text to explain to the user the purpose of each step. Note that the `HelpText` property value on the second tab page appears as a step description right below the step title during runtime. This is done automatically by the `SysWizard` class.

Finally, on the second tab page, we place three controls for user input. Later on, we create three methods, which return the controls' values: account number, name, and type values, respectively. We also override the `textChange()` event methods on the controls to determine and update the runtime state of the **Next** button. These methods call the `setNext()` method, which actually controls the behavior of the **Next** button. In our case, we enable the **Next** button as soon as all input controls have values.

Working with Data in Forms

Processing multiple records

In Dynamics AX, by default, most of the functions available on forms are related to a currently selected single record. It is also possible to process several selected records at once, although some modification is required.

In this recipe, we will explore how a selection of multiple records can be processed on a form. For this demonstration, we will add a button to the action pane on the **Main account** list page to show multiple selected accounts in the **Infolog** window.

How to do it...

Carry out the following steps in order to complete this recipe:

1. In the AOT, open the `MainAccountListPage` form and create a new method with the following code snippet:

    ```
    void processSelected()
    {
        MultiSelectionHelper helper =
            MultiSelectionHelper::construct();

        helper.parmDatasource(MainAccount_ds);

        tmpMainAccount = helper.getFirst();

        while (tmpMainAccount)
        {
            info(strFmt(
                "You've selected '%1'",
                tmpMainAccount.MainAccountId));
            tmpMainAccount = helper.getNext();
        }
    }
    ```

2. Add a new `Button` control anywhere in the form's action pane with the following properties:

Property	Value
Name	ProcessSelected
Text	Process
MultiSelect	Yes

― Chapter 3

3. Override the button's `clicked()` event method with the following code snippet:

   ```
   void clicked()
   {
       super();
       element.processSelected();
   }
   ```

4. In order to test the record selection, navigate to **General ledger | Common | Main accounts**, select several records, and click on the new **Process** button. The selected items will be displayed in the **Infolog** window:

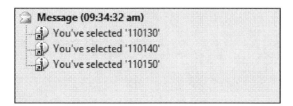

How it works...

The key element in this recipe is the `processSelected()` method, where we utilize the `MultiSelectionHelper` application class to handle user selections.

Firstly, we create a new instance of the `MultiSelectionHelper` class, and then specify which data source will be used to track user selections.

Next, get the first marked record, and then we go through all the other marked records (if any) and process them one by one. In this demonstration, we simply show them on the screen.

The last thing to do is to add the `ProcessSelected` button to the form and call `processSelected()` from its `clicked()` method. Note that the button's `MultiSelect` property is set to `Yes` to ensure it is still enabled when multiple records are marked.

Coloring records

One of Dynamics AX's exciting features, which can enhance user experiences, is the ability to color individual records. Some users might find the system more intuitive and user-friendly through this modification.

For example, emphasizing the importance of disabled records, by highlighting the terminated employees or stopped customers in red, allows users to identify relevant records at a glance. Another example is to show processed records, such as posted journals or invoiced sales orders in green.

Working with Data in Forms

In this recipe, we will learn how to change a record's color. We will modify the existing **Users** form located in **System administration** | **Common** | **Users** and show disabled users in red.

How to do it...

Carry out the following steps in order to complete this recipe:

1. In the AOT, open the `SysUserInfoPage` form and override the `displayOption()` method in its `UserInfo` data source with the following code snippet:

    ```
    void displayOption(
        Common _record,
        FormRowDisplayOption _options)
    {
        if (!_record.(fieldNum(UserInfo,Enable)))
        {
            _options.backColor(WinAPI::RGB2int(255,100,100));
        }

        super(_record, _options);
    }
    ```

2. In order to test the coloring, navigate to **System administration** | **Common** | **Users** | **Users** and note how disabled users are displayed now in a different color:

Account type	Alias	Network domain	User ID ▲	User name	Company	Enabled	External
Active Directory user	AarenE	contoso.com	AarenE	Aaren Ekelund	usmf	✓	☐
Active Directory user	AaronP	contoso.com	AaronP	Aaron Painter	DAT	✓	☐
Active Directory user	AdinaH	contoso.com	AdinaH	Adina Hagege	usmf	☐	☐
Active Directory user	Administra...	Contoso.com	admin	administrator	usmf	✓	☐
Active Directory user	AdminBRMF	contoso.com	AdminBRM	AdminBRMF	brmf	☐	☐
Active Directory user	admininmf	contoso.com	admininm	admininmf	inmf	☐	☐
Active Directory user	AdrianL	contoso.com	AdrianL	Adrian Lannin	usmf	✓	☐
Active Directory user	Ahmed	contoso.com	Ahmed	Ahmed Barnett	usmf	✓	☐
Active Directory user	AlexanderE	contoso.com	Alexande	Alexander Eggerer	usmf	✓	☐
Active Directory user	AlexD	contoso.com	AlexD	Alex Darrow	USRT	✓	☐
Active Directory user	ALICIA	contoso.com	ALICIA	Alicia Thornber	usmf	✓	☐
Active Directory user	AliciaA	contoso.com	AliciaA	Alicia Andersen	usmf	✓	☐
Active Directory user	ALICIABR	contoso.com	ALICIABR	Alicia Thornber Br	BRMF	✓	☐
Active Directory user	ALICIAINMF	contoso.com	ALICIAIN	Alicia Thornber INMF	inmf	✓	☐
Active Directory user	AmritanshR	contoso.com	Amritans	Amritansh Raghav	usmf	✓	☐
Active Directory user	AnahitaB	contoso.com	AnahitaB	Anahita Bahrami	usmf	✓	☐
Active Directory user	AndersL	contoso.com	AndersL	Anders Langvad-Niel...	usmf	✓	☐
Active Directory user	AndersM	contoso.com	AndersM	Anders Madsen	usmf	✓	☐
Active Directory user	AndreaD	contoso.com	AndreaD	Andrea Dunker	usmf	✓	☐
Active Directory user	AndrewD	contoso.com	AndrewD	Andrew Dixon	usmf	✓	☐

How it works...

The `displayOption()` method on any form's data source can be used to change some of the visual options. Before displaying each record, this method is called by the system with two arguments—the first is the current record and the second is a `FormRowDisplayOption` object—whose properties can be used to change a record's visual settings just before it appears on the screen. In this example, we check if the current user is disabled, and if it is, we change the background property to light red by calling the `backColor()` method with the color code.

In this example, we used the `_record.(fieldNum(UserInfo,Enable))` expression to address the `Enable` field on the `UserInfo` table. This type of expression is normally used when we know the type of record, but it is declared as a generic `Common` type.

For demonstration purposes, we specified the color directly in the code, but it is a good practice if the color code comes from some configuration table. See the *Creating a color picker lookup* recipe in *Chapter 4, Building Lookups*, to learn how to allow the user to choose and store the color selection.

See also

- The *Creating a color picker lookup* recipe in *Chapter 4, Building Lookups*

Adding an image to records

Company-specific images in Dynamics AX can be stored along with the data in the database tables. They can be used for different purposes, such as a company logo that is displayed on every printed document, employee photos, inventory pictures, and so on.

Images are binary objects and can be stored in the container table fields. In order to make the system perform better, it is always recommended to store the images in a separate table so that it does not affect the retrieval speed of main data.

One of the most convenient ways to attach images to any record is to use the **Document handling** feature of Dynamics AX. It does not require any change in the application. However, the **Document handling** feature is a very generic way of attaching files to any record and might not be suitable for specific circumstances.

Another way of attaching images to records can be to utilize the standard application objects, though minor application changes are required. For example, the company logo in the **Legal entities** form, located at **Organization administration | Setup | Organization**, is one of the places where the images are stored that way.

In this recipe, we will explore the latter option. As an example, we will add the ability to store an image for each customer. We will also add a new **Image** button on the **Customers** list page allowing to attach or remove images from the customers.

Working with Data in Forms

How to do it...

Carry out the following steps in order to complete this recipe:

1. Open the `CustTableListPage` form in the AOT. Add a new `MenuItemButton` control to the bottom of the `MaintainGroup` button group, which is located at `ActionPane | HomeTab`, with the following properties:

Property	Value
Name	Image
Text	Image
ButtonDisplay	Text & Image above
NormalImage	10598
ImageLocation	EmbeddedResource
DataSource	CustTable
MenuItemType	Display
MenuItemName	CompanyImage

2. Navigate to **Accounts receivable | Common | Customers | All customers** and note the new **Image** button in the action pane:

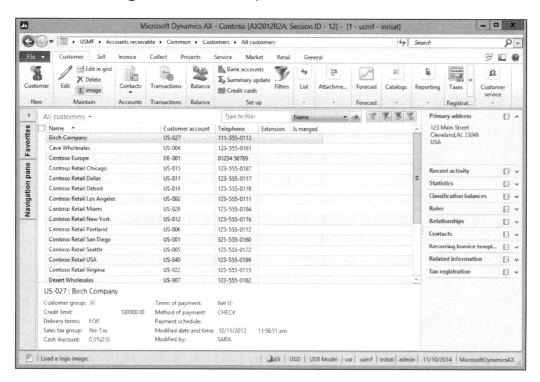

154

3. Click on the button, and then use the **Change** button to upload a new image for the selected item:

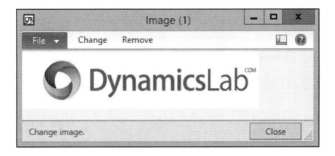

The **Remove** button can be used to delete an existing image.

How it works...

In this demonstration, there are only three standard Dynamics AX objects used:

- The `CompanyImage` table, which holds image data and information about the record to which the image is attached. The separate table allows you to easily hook image functionality to any other existing table without modifying that table or decreasing its performance.
- The `CompanyImage` form, which shows an image and allows you to modify it.
- The display menu item `CompanyImage`, which allows you to open the form.

We added the menu item to the `CustTableListPage` form and modified some of its visual properties. This ensures that it looks consistent with the rest of the action pane. We also changed its `DataSource` property to the `CustTable` data source. This makes sure that the image is stored against that record.

There's more...

The following two topics will explain how a stored image can be displayed as a new tab page on the main form and how it can be saved back to a file.

Displaying an image as part of a form

In this section, we will extend the recipe by displaying the stored image on a new tab page on the **Customers** form.

Firstly, we need to add a new tab page to the end of the `CustTable` form's `TabHeader` control, which is located inside another tab page called `TabPageDetails`. This is where our image will be displayed.

Working with Data in Forms

Set the properties of the new tab page:

Property	Value
Name	TabImage
AutoDeclaration	Yes
Height	Column height
Caption	Image

Add a new `Window` control to the tab page. This control will be used for displaying the image. Set its properties as follows:

Property	Value
Name	CustImage
AutoDeclaration	Yes
Width	Column width
Height	Column height
AlignControl	No

Setting the `Height` and `Width` properties to `Column height` and `Column width`, respectively, will ensure that the image control occupies all the available space. The image does not have a label, so we exclude it from the form's label alignment by setting the `AlignControl` property to `No`.

Next, let's create a new method at the top level of the `CustTable` form:

```
void loadImage()
{
    Image           img;
    CompanyImage    companyImage;

    companyImage = CompanyImage::find(
        CustTable.dataAreaId,
        CustTable.TableId,
        CustTable.RecId);

    if (companyImage.Image)
    {
        img = new Image();
        img.setData(companyImage.Image);
        CustImage.image(img);
    }
    else
    {
        CustImage.image(null);
    }
}
```

This method finds a `CompanyImage` record first, which is attached to the current record, and then displays the binary data using the `CustImage` control. If no image is attached, the `Window` control is cleared to display an empty space.

Next, we add the following line of code to the bottom of the `selectionChanged()` method of the `CustTable` data source to ensure that the image is loaded for a currently selected record:

```
element.loadImage();
```

In the AOT, the form will look similar to the following screenshot:

Working with Data in Forms

Now, navigate to **Account receivable** | **Common** | **Customers** | **All customers**, select previously used customers, and click on the **Edit** button in the action pane. On the **Customers** form, note the new tab page with the image displayed:

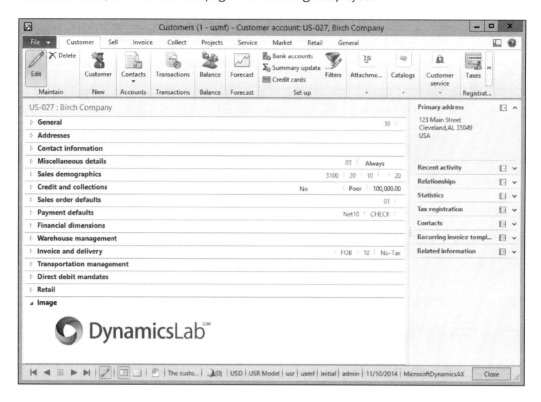

Saving a stored image as a file

This section will describe how the stored image can be restored back to a file. This is quite a common case when the original image file is lost. We will enhance the standard `Image` form by adding a new **Save as** button, which allows us to save the stored image to a file.

Let's find the `CompanyImage` form in the AOT and add a new `Button` control to the form's `ButtonGroup`, which is located in the first tab of the `ActionPane` control. Set the button's properties as follows:

Property	Value
Name	SaveAs
Text	Save as

Create a new method at the top level of the form:

```
void saveImage()
{
    Image      img;
    Filename   name;
    str        type;
    #File

    if (!imageContainer)
    {
        return;
    }

    img = new Image();
    img.setData(imageContainer);

    type = '.'+strLwr(enum2value(img.saveType()));
    name = WinAPI::getSaveFileName(
        element.hWnd(),
        [WinAPI::fileType(type),#AllFilesName+type],
        '',
        '');

    if (name)
    {
        img.saveImage(name);
    }
}
```

This method will present the user with the **Save as** dialog, allowing them to choose the desired filename to save the current image. Note that the `imageContainer` form variable holds image data. If it is empty, it means there is no image attached, and we do not run any of the code. We also determine the loaded file type to make sure our **Save as** dialog shows only files of that particular type, for example, JPG.

Override the button's `clicked()` method with the following code snippet to make sure that the `saveImage()` method is executed once the user clicks on the button:

```
void clicked()
{
    super();
    element.saveImage();
}
```

Working with Data in Forms

In the AOT, the form will look similar to the following screenshot:

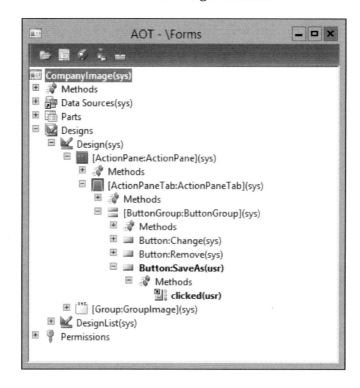

Now, when you open the image form, a new **Save as** button is available:

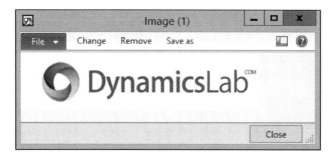

Use this button to save the stored image to a file:

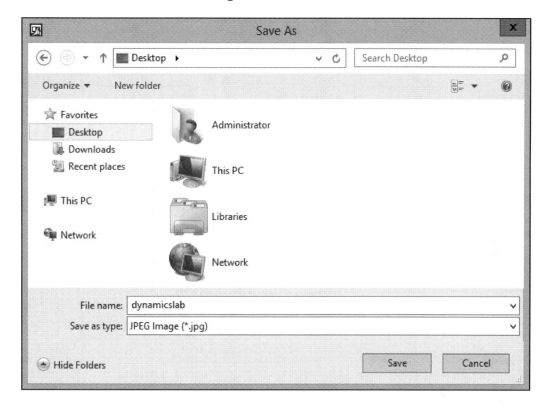

Note that the `CompanyImage` form is used system wide and the new button is available across the whole system now.

4
Building Lookups

In this chapter, we will cover the following recipes:

- Creating an automatic lookup
- Creating a lookup dynamically
- Using a form to build a lookup
- Building a tree lookup
- Displaying a list of custom options
- Displaying custom options in another way
- Building a lookup based on the record description
- Building the browse for folder lookup
- Building a lookup to select a file
- Creating a color picker lookup

Introduction

Lookups are the standard way to display a list of possible selection values to the user, while editing or creating database records. Normally, standard lookups are created automatically by the system and are based on the extended data types and table setup. It is also possible to override the standard functionality by creating your own lookups from the code or using the Dynamics AX forms.

In this chapter, we will cover various lookup types, such as file selector, color picker, or tree lookup, as well as the different approaches to create them.

Building Lookups

Creating an automatic lookup

Simple lookups in Dynamics AX can be created in seconds without any programming knowledge. They are based on table relations and appear automatically. No additional modifications are required.

This recipe will show you how to create a very basic automatic lookup using table relations. To demonstrate this, we will add a new **Method of payment** column to the existing **Customer group** form.

How to do it...

1. Open the `CustGroup` table in the AOT and create a new field with the following properties:

Property	Value
Type	String
Name	PaymMode
ExtendedDataType	CustPaymMode

2. Add the newly created field to the end of the `Overview` field group of the table.

3. Open the **EDT relations migration tool** form located in **Tools | Code upgrade**. Find the `CustGroup` table on the left (refresh relation data, if required). In the **EDT relations** section, change the value in the **Migration action** field to `Migrate`, where **Field name** is set to `PaymMode` as follows:

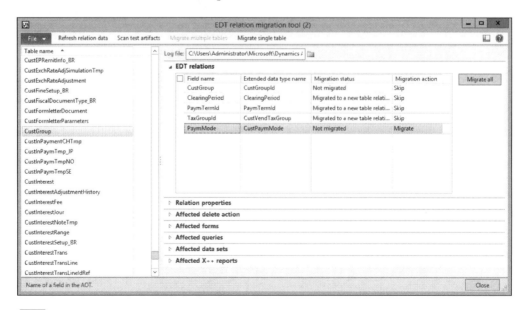

164

4. Click on the **Migrate single table** button to migrate the relation. The message in the **Infolog** window will inform us that the migration was successful.
5. To check the results, navigate to **Accounts receivable** | **Setup** | **Customers** | **Customer groups** and note the newly created **Method of payment** column with the lookup:

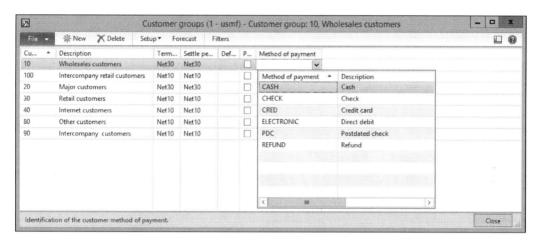

How it works...

The newly created `PaymMode` field is based on the `CustPaymMode` extended data type and therefore it automatically inherits its relation. To follow the best practices, all relations must be present on tables, so we run the **EDT relation migration tool** to copy the relation from the extended data type to the table. We also add the newly created field to the table's `Overview` group to make sure that the field automatically appears on the **Customer group** form. This relation ensures that the field has an automatic lookup.

There's more...

The automatically generated lookup, in the preceding example, has only two columns—**Method of payment** and **Description**. Dynamics AX allows us to add more columns or change the existing columns with minimum effort by changing various properties. Lookup columns can be controlled at several different places:

- Relation fields, on either an extended data type or a table, are always shown on lookups as columns.
- Fields defined in the table's `TitleField1` and `TitleField2` properties are also displayed as lookup columns.
- The first field of every table's index is displayed as a column.

Building Lookups

> ▶ The index fields and the `TitleField1` and `TitleField2` properties are in effect only when the `AutoLookup` field group of a table is empty. Otherwise, the fields defined in the `AutoLookup` group are displayed as lookup columns along with the relation columns.
>
> ▶ Duplicate columns are shown only once.

Now, to demonstrate how the `AutoLookup` group can affect the lookup's columns, let's modify the previous example by adding an additional field to this group. Let's add the `PaymSumBy` field to the `AutoLookup` group on the `CustPaymModeTable` table in the middle between the `PaymMode` and `Name` fields. Now, the lookup has one more column labeled **Period**:

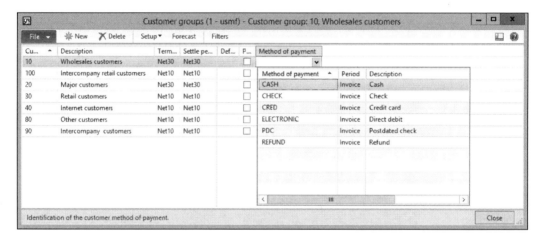

It is also possible to add display methods to the lookup's column list. We can extend our example by adding the `paymAccountName()` display method to the `AutoLookup` group on the `CustPaymModeTable` table right after `PaymSumBy`. This is the result:

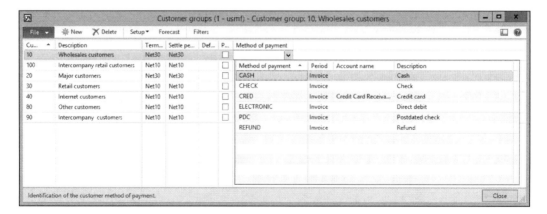

Creating a lookup dynamically

Automatic lookups, mentioned in the previous recipe, are widely used across the system and are very useful in simple scenarios. When it comes to showing different fields from different data sources, applying various static or dynamic filters, some coding is required. Dynamics AX is flexible enough that the developer can create custom lookups, either using the AOT forms or by running them dynamically from the X++ code.

This recipe will show how to dynamically build a runtime lookup from the code. In this demonstration, we will modify the **Vendor account** lookup on the **Customers** form to allow users to select only those vendors that use the same currency as the currently selected customer.

How to do it...

1. Open the `VendTable` table in the AOT and create a new method:

```
public static void lookupVendorByCurrency(
    FormControl    _callingControl,
    CurrencyCode   _currency)
{
    Query                   query;
    QueryBuildDataSource    qbds;
    QueryBuildRange         qbr;
    SysTableLookup          lookup;

    query = new Query();

    qbds = query.addDataSource(tableNum(VendTable));

    qbr = qbds.addRange(fieldNum(VendTable,Currency));

    qbr.value(queryvalue(_currency));

    lookup = SysTableLookup::newParameters(
        tableNum(VendTable),
        _callingControl,
        true);

    lookup.parmQuery(query);

    lookup.addLookupField(
        fieldNum(VendTable, AccountNum),
        true);
```

Building Lookups

```
        lookup.addLookupField(fieldNum(VendTable,Party));

        lookup.addLookupField(fieldNum(VendTable,Currency));

        lookup.performFormLookup();
    }
```

2. In the AOT, open the `CustTable` form and find its data source named `CustTable`. Then, in the data source, locate the `VendAccount` field and override its `lookup()` method with the following code snippet:

```
public void lookup(FormControl _formControl, str _filterStr)
{
    VendTable::lookupVendorByCurrency(
        _formControl,
        CustTable.Currency);
}
```

3. To test this, navigate to **Accounts receivable** | **Common** | **Customers** | **All customers**, select any of the customers, and click on **Edit** in the action pane. Once the **Customers** form is displayed, expand the **Vendor account** lookup located in the **Miscellaneous details** tab page, under the **Remittance** group. The modified lookup now has an additional column named **Currency**, and vendors in the list will match the customer's currency:

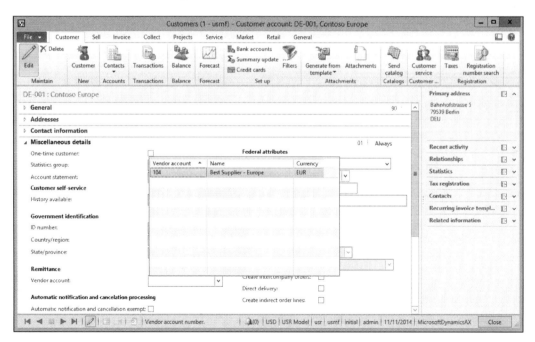

168

How it works...

First, on the `VendTable` table, we create a new method that generates the lookup. This is the most convenient place for such a method, taking into consideration that it may be reused in other places.

In this method, we first create a new query, which will determine the data displayed in the lookup. In this query, we add a new data source based on the `VendTable` table and define a new range based on the `Currency` field.

Next, we create the actual lookup object and and pass the query object to it using its `parmQuery()` method. The `lookup` object is created using the `newParameters()` constructor of the `SysTableLookup` class. It accepts the following three parameters:

- The table ID, which is going to be displayed in the lookup.
- A reference to the calling control on the form.
- An optional `boolean` value, which specifies that the value in the form control should be preselected in the lookup. The default is `true`.

We use the `addLookupField()` method to add three columns—**Vendor account**, **Name**, and **Currency**. This method accepts the following parameters:

- The ID of the field that will be displayed as a column.
- An optional `boolean` parameter that defines which column will be used as a return value to the caller control upon user selection. Only one column can be marked as a return value. In our case, it is vendor account.

Finally, we run the lookup by calling the `performFormLookup()` method.

The last thing to do is to add some code to the `lookup()` method of the **VendAccount** field of the **CustTable** data source in the **CustTable** form. By replacing its `super()` method with our custom code, we override the standard automatically generated lookup with the custom one.

Using a form to build a lookup

For the most complex scenarios, Dynamics AX offers the possibility to create and use a form as a lookup. The form lookups support various features like tab pages, event handling, complex logic, and so on.

In this recipe, we will demonstrate how to create a lookup using a form. As an example, we will modify the standard customer account lookup to display only the customers who are not placed on hold for invoicing and delivery.

Building Lookups

How to do it...

1. In the AOT, create a new form named `CustLookup`. Add a new data source with the following properties:

Property	Value
Name	CustTable
Table	CustTable
Index	AccountIdx
AllowCheck	No
AllowEdit	No
AllowCreate	No
AllowDelete	No
OnlyFetchActive	Yes

2. Change the properties of the form's design as follows:

Property	Value
Frame	Border
WindowType	Popup

3. Add a new grid control to the form's design with the following properties:

Property	Value
Name	Customers
ShowRowLabels	No
DataSource	CustTable

4. Add a new `StringEdit` control to the grid with the following properties:

Property	Value
Name	AccountNum
AutoDeclaration	Yes
DataSource	CustTable
DataField	AccountNum

5. Add a new `ReferenceGroup` control to the grid with the following properties, right after `AccountNum`:

Property	Value
Name	Name
DataSource	CustTable

Property	Value
ReferenceField	Party

6. Add one more `StringEdit` control to the grid with the following properties, right after the `Name`:

Property	Value
Name	Phone
DataSource	CustTable
DataMethod	phone

7. Add a new `ComboBox` control with the following properties to the end of the grid:

Property	Value
Name	Blocked
DataSource	CustTable
DataField	Blocked

8. Override the form's `init()` method with the following code snippet:

```
public void init()
{
    super();
    element.selectMode(AccountNum);
}
```

9. Override the form's `run()` method with the following code snippet:

```
public void run()
{
    FormStringControl callingControl;
    boolean           filterLookup;

    callingControl = SysTableLookup::getCallerStringControl(
        element.args());

    filterLookup = SysTableLookup::filterLookupPreRun(
        callingControl,
        AccountNum,
        CustTable_ds);

    super();

    SysTableLookup::filterLookupPostRun(
        filterLookup,
        callingControl.text(),
        AccountNum,
        CustTable_ds);
}
```

10. Finally, override the `init()` method of the `CustTable` data source with the following code snippet:

```
public void init()
{
    Query                 query;
    QueryBuildDataSource  qbds;
    QueryBuildRange       qbr;

    query = new Query();

    qbds = query.addDataSource(tableNum(CustTable));

    qbr = qbds.addRange(fieldNum(CustTable,Blocked));

    qbr.value(queryvalue(CustVendorBlocked::No));

    this.query(query);
}
```

11. The form in the AOT will look similar to the following screenshot:

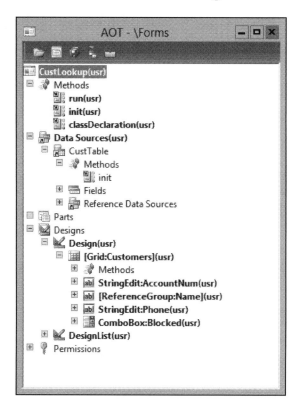

12. Locate the `CustAccount` extended data type in the AOT and change its property as follows:

Property	Value
FormHelp	CustLookup

13. To test the results, navigate to **Sales and marketing | Common | Sales orders | All sales orders** and start creating a new sales order. Note that now the **Customer account** lookup is different, and it includes active customers only:

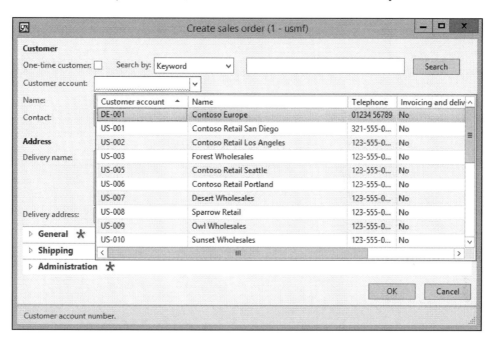

How it works...

Automatically generated lookups have a limited set of features and are not suitable in more complex scenarios. In this recipe, we are creating a brand new form-based lookup, which will replace the existing customer account lookup. The name of the newly created form is `CustLookup` and it contains the `Lookup` text at the end to make sure it can be easily distinguished from other forms in the AOT.

In the form, we add a new data source and change its properties. We do not allow any data updating by setting the `AllowEdit`, `AllowCreate`, and `AllowDelete` properties to `No`. Security checks will be disabled by setting `AllowCheck` to `No`. To increase the performance, we set `OnlyFetchActive` to `Yes`, which will reduce the size of the database result set to the fields that are visible on the form only. We also set the data source index to define the initial data sorting.

Building Lookups

Next, in order to make our form lookup look exactly like a standard lookup, we have to adjust its layout. Therefore, we set its `Frame` and `WindowType` properties to `Border` and `Popup`, respectively. This removes form borders and makes the form very similar to a standard lookup. Then, we add a new grid control with four controls inside, which are bound to the relevant `CustTable` table fields and methods. We set the `ShowRowLabels` property of the grid to `No` to hide the grid's row labels.

After this, we have to define which form control will be used to return a value from the lookup to the calling form control. We need to specify the form control manually in the form's `init()` method, by calling `element.selectMode()`, with the name of the control as an argument.

In the form's `run()` method, we add some filtering, which allows the user to use the asterisk (*) symbol to search for records in the lookup. For example, if the user types `1*` into the `Customer account` control, the lookup will open automatically with all customer accounts starting with 1. To achieve this, we use the `filterLookupPreRun()` and `filterLookupPostRun()` methods of the standard `SysTableLookup` class. Both these methods require a reference to the calling control, which can be obtained by calling the `getCallerStringControl()` method of the same `SysTableLookup` class. The first method reads the user input and returns `true` if a search is being performed, otherwise, it returns `false`. It must be called before the `super()` method in the form's `run()` method, and it accepts four arguments:

- The calling control on the parent form
- The returning control on the lookup form
- The main data source on the lookup form
- An optional list of other data sources on the lookup form, which are used in the search

The `filterLookupPostRun()` method must be called after the `super()` method in the form's `run()` method, and it also accepts four arguments:

- The result from the previously called `filterLookupPreRun()` method
- The user text specified in the calling control
- The returning control on the lookup form
- The lookup's data source

The code in the `CustTable` data source's `init()` method replaces the data source query created by its `super()` method with the custom one. Basically, here, we create a new `Query` object and change its range to include only active customers.

The `FormHelp` property of the `CustAccount` extended data type will make sure that this form is opened every time the user opens the **Customer account** lookup.

See also

- The *Building a query object* recipe in *Chapter 1, Processing Data*

Chapter 4

Building a tree lookup

The `Tree` controls are a user-friendly way of displaying a hierarchy of related records, such as a company's organizational structure, inventory bill of materials, projects with their subprojects, and so on. These hierarchies can also be displayed in the custom lookups, allowing users to browse and select the required value in a more convenient way.

The *Using a Tree control* recipe in *Chapter 2, Working with Forms*, explained how to present the budget model hierarchy as a tree in the **Budget model** form. In this recipe, we will reuse the previously created `BudgetModelTree` class and demonstrate how to build a budget model tree lookup.

How to do it...

1. In the AOT, create a new form named `BudgetModelLookup`. Set its design's properties as follows:

Property	Value
Frame	Border
WindowType	Popup

2. Add a new `Tree` control to the design with the following properties:

Property	Value
Name	ModelTree
Width	250

3. Add the following line of code to the form's class declaration:

   `BudgetModelTree budgetModelTree;`

4. Override the form's `init()` method with the following code snippet:

   ```
   public void init()
   {
       FormStringControl callingControl;

       callingControl = SysTableLookup::getCallerStringControl(
           this.args());

       super();

       budgetModelTree = BudgetModelTree::construct(
           ModelTree,
   ```

Building Lookups

```
            callingControl.text());

        budgetModelTree.buildTree();
    }
```

5. Override the `mouseDblClick()` and `mouseUp()` methods of the `ModelTree` control with the following code snippet:

```
public int mouseDblClick(
    int _x,
    int _y,
    int _button,
    boolean _ctrl,
    boolean _shift)
{
    int          ret;
    FormTreeItem formTreeItem;
    BudgetModel  budgetModel;

    ret = super(_x, _y, _button, _ctrl, _shift);

    formTreeItem = this.getItem(this.getSelection());

    select firstOnly SubModelId from budgetModel
        where budgetModel.RecId == formTreeItem.data();

    element.closeSelect(budgetModel.SubModelId);

    return ret;
}

public int mouseUp(
    int _x,
    int _y,
    int _button,
    boolean _ctrl,
    boolean _shift)
{
    int ret;

    ret = super(_x, _y, _button, _ctrl, _shift);

    return 1;
}
```

6. The form will look similar to the following screenshot:

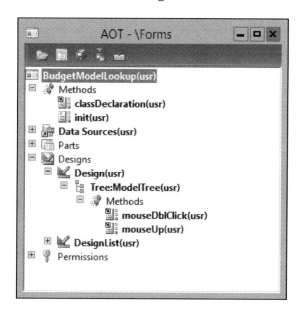

7. In the AOT, open the `BudgetModel` table and change its `lookupBudgetModel()` method with the following code snippet:

```
public static void lookupBudgetModel(
    FormStringControl _ctrl,
    boolean _showStopped = false)
{
    Args    args;
    Object  formRun;

    args = new Args();
    args.name(formStr(BudgetModelLookup));
    args.caller(_ctrl);

    formRun = classfactory.formRunClass(args);
    formRun.init();

    _ctrl.performFormLookup(formRun);
}
```

Building Lookups

8. To see the results, navigate to **Budgeting | Common | Budget register entries | All budget register entries**. Start creating a new entry by clicking on the **Budget register entry** button in the action pane and expanding the **Budget model** lookup:

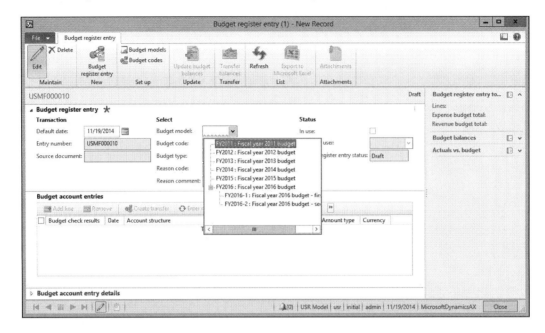

How it works...

First, we create a new form named `BudgetModelLookup`, which we will use as a custom lookup. We set its design's `Frame` and `WindowType` to `Border` and `Popup` respectively, to change the layout of the form so that it looks like a lookup. We also add a new `Tree` control and set its width.

In the form's class declaration, we define the `BudgetModelTree` class, which we have already created in the *Using a Tree control* recipe in *Chapter 2, Working with Forms*.

The code in the form's `init()` method builds the tree. Here, we create a new object of the `BudgetModelTree` type by calling the `construct()` constructor, which accepts two arguments:

- The `Tree` control, which represents the actual tree.
- The `Budget` model, which is going to be preselected initially. Normally, it's a value in the calling control, which can be detected using the `getCallerStringControl()` method of the `SysTableLookup` application class.

The code in `mouseDblClick()` returns the user-selected value from the tree node back to the calling control and closes the lookup.

Chapter 4

Finally, the `mouseUp()` method has to be overridden to return 1 to make sure that the lookup does not close while the user expands or collapses the tree nodes.

See also

- The *Using a Tree control* recipe in *Chapter 2, Working with Forms*

Displaying a list of custom options

Besides normal lookups, Dynamics AX provides a number of other ways to present the available data for user selection. It doesn't necessarily have to be a record from the database; it can be a list of "hardcoded" options or some external data. Normally, such lists are much smaller as opposed to those of the data-driven lookups and are used for very specific tasks.

In this recipe, we will create a lookup of several predefined options. We will use a job for this demonstration.

How to do it...

1. In the AOT, create a new job named `PickList`:

    ```
    static void PickList(Args _args)
    {
        Map choices;
        str ret;

        choices = new Map(
            Types::Integer,
            Types::String);

        choices.insert(1, "Axapta 3.0");
        choices.insert(2, "Dynamics AX 4.0");
        choices.insert(3, "Dynamics AX 2009");
        choices.insert(4, "Dynamics AX 2012");
        choices.insert(5, "Dynamics AX 2012 R2");
        choices.insert(6, "Dynamics AX 2012 R3");

        ret = pickList(choices, "", "Choose version");

        if (ret)
        {
            info(strFmt("You've selected option No. %1", ret));
        }
    }
    ```

Building Lookups

2. Run the job to view the results:

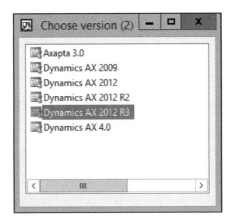

3. Double-click on one of the options to show the selected option in the **Infolog** window:

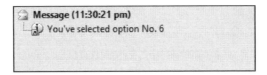

How it works...

The key element in this recipe is the global `pickList()` function. Lookups created using this function are based on values stored in a map. In our example, we define and initialize a new map. Then, we insert a few key-value pairs and pass the map to the `pickList()` function. This function accepts three parameters:

- A map that contains lookup values
- A column header, which is not used here
- A lookup title

The function that displays values from the map returns the corresponding key, once the option is selected.

There's more...

The global `pickList()` function can basically display any list of values. Besides that, Dynamics AX also provides a number of other global lookup functions, which can be used in more specific scenarios. Here are a few of them:

- `pickDataArea()`: This shows a list of Dynamics AX companies.

- `pickUserGroups()`: This shows a list of user groups in the system.
- `pickUser()`: This shows a list of Dynamics AX users.
- `pickTable()`: This shows all Dynamics AX tables.
- `pickField()`: This shows table fields. The table number has to be specified as an argument for the function.
- `pickClass()`: This shows a list of Dynamics AX classes.

Displaying custom options in another way

The global system functions, such as `pickList()` and `pickUser()`, allow developers to build various lookups displaying a list of custom options. Besides that, the standard Dynamics AX application contains a few more useful functions, allowing the user to build more complex lookups of custom options.

One of the functions is called `selectSingle()`, and it presents the user with a list of options. It also displays a checkbox next to each option that allows users to select the option. To demonstrate this, we will create a new job that shows the usage of this function.

How to do it...

1. In the AOT, create a new job named `SysListSelectSingle`:

```
static void SysListSelectSingle(Args _args)
{
    container choices;
    container headers;
    container selection;
    container selected;
    boolean   ok;

    choices = [
        ["3.0\nAxapta 3.0", 1, false],
        ["4.0\nDynamics AX 4.0", 2, false],
        ["2009\nDynamics AX 2009", 3, false],
        ["2012\nDynamics AX 2012", 4, false],
        ["2012R2\nDynamics AX 2012 R2", 5, false],
        ["2012R3\nDynamics AX 2012 R3", 6, true]];

    headers = ["Version", "Description"];

    selection = selectSingle(
        "Choose version",
```

```
            "Please select Dynamics AX version",
            choices,
            headers);

    [ok, selected] = selection;

    if (ok && conLen(selected))
    {
        info(strFmt(
            "You've selected option No. %1",
            conPeek(selected,1)));
    }
}
```

2. Run the job to display the options:

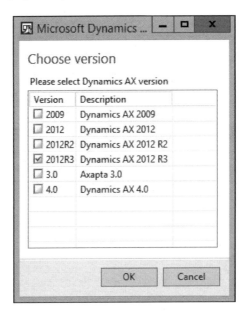

3. Select any of the options, click on the **OK** button, and note that your choice is displayed in the **Infolog** window

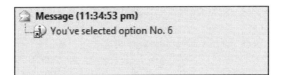

How it works...

We start with defining the `choices` variable and setting its value. The variable is a container of containers, where each container inside the parent container is made of three elements and represents one selectable option in the list:

- The first element is text displayed on the lookup. By default, in the lookup, only one column is displayed, but it is possible to define more columns, simply by separating the texts using the new line symbol.
- The second element is a number of an item in the list. This value is returned from the lookup.
- The third value specifies whether the option is marked by default.

Now, when the list values are ready, we call the `selectSingle()` function to build the actual lookup. This function accepts five arguments:

- The window title
- The lookup description
- A container of list values
- A container representing column headings
- An optional reference to a caller object

The `singleSelect()` function returns a container of two elements:

- `true` or `false` depending on whether the lookup was closed using the **OK** button or not
- The numeric value of the selected option

There's more...

You may notice that the lookup, which was created using the `singleSelect()` method, allows the choosing of only one option from the list. There is another similar function named `selectMultiple()`, which is exactly the same except that the user can select multiple options from the list. The following code snippet demonstrates its usage:

```
static void SysListSelectMultiple(Args _args)
{
    container choices;
    container headers;
    container selection;
    container selected;
    boolean   ok;
    int       i;
```

Building Lookups

```
        choices = [
            ["3.0\nAxapta 3.0", 1, false],
            ["4.0\nDynamics AX 4.0", 2, false],
            ["2009\nDynamics AX 2009", 3, true],
            ["2012\nDynamics AX 2012", 4, false],
            ["2012R2\nDynamics AX 2012 R2", 5, false],
            ["2012R3\nDynamics AX 2012 R3", 6, true]];

        headers = ["Version", "Description"];

        selection = selectMultiple(
            "Choose version",
            "Please select Dynamics AX version",
            choices,
            headers);

        [ok, selected] = selection;

        if (ok && conLen(selected) > 0)
        {
            for (i = 1; i <= conLen(selected); i++)
            {
                info(strFmt(
                    "You've selected option No. %1",
                    conPeek(selected,i)));
            }
        }
    }
```

Now, in the lookup, it is possible to select multiple options:

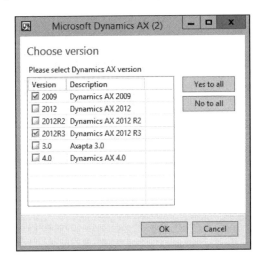

Note that, in this case, the returned value is a container holding the selected options.

Building a lookup based on the record description

Normally, data lookups in Dynamics AX display a list of records where the first column always contains a value, which is returned to the calling form control. The first column in the lookup normally contains a unique record identification value, which is used to build relations between tables. For example, the **Customer** lookup displays the customer account number, the customer name, and some other fields; the **Inventory item** lookup displays the item number, the item name, and other fields.

In some cases, the record identifier can be not so informative. For example, it is much more convenient to display a person's name versus its number. In the standard application, you can find a number of places where the contact person is displayed as a person's name, even though the actual table relation is based on the contact person's ID.

In this recipe, we will create such a lookup. We will replace the **Vendor group selection** lookup on the **Vendors** form to show group description, instead of group ID.

How to do it...

1. In the AOT, create a new String extended data type with the following properties:

Property	Value
Name	VendGroupDescriptionExt
Label	Group
Extends	Description

2. Open the VendTable table and create a new method with the following code snippet:

   ```
   public edit VendGroupDescriptionExt editVendGroup(
       boolean                  _set,
       VendGroupDescriptionExt  _group)
   {
       VendGroup vendGroup;

       if (_set)
       {
           if (_group)
           {
               if (VendGroup::exist(_group))
               {
                   this.VendGroup = _group;
               }
   ```

```
            else
            {
                select firstOnly VendGroup from vendGroup
                    where vendGroup.Name == _group;
                this.VendGroup = vendGroup.VendGroup;
            }
        }
        else
        {
            this.VendGroup = '';
        }
    }

    return VendGroup::name(this.VendGroup);
}
```

3. In the AOT, find the `VendTable` form, locate the `Posting group` control inside **MainTab | TabPageDetails | Tab | TabGeneral | UpperGroup | Identification**, and modify its properties as follows:

Property	Value
DataGroup	

4. In the same form, in the `Posting` group, modify the `Posting_VendGroup` control as follows:

Property	Value
DataField	
DataMethod	editVendGroup

5. Override the `lookup()` method of the `Posting_VendGroup` control with the following code snippet:

```
public void lookup()
{
    this.performTypeLookup(extendedTypeNum(VendGroupId));
}
```

6. To check the results, navigate to **Accounts payable | Common | Vendors | All vendors**, select any record, and click on the **Edit** button in the action pane. In the opened form, check the newly created lookup on the **Group** control, located in the **General** tab page:

Chapter 4

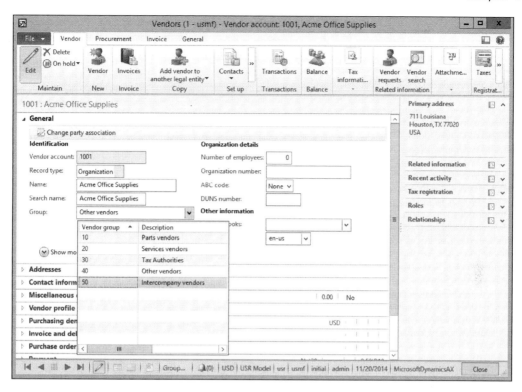

How it works...

First, we create a new extended data type, which we will use as the basis for the vendor **Group** selection control. The type extends the existing `Description` extended data type as it has to be of the same size as the vendor group name. It will also have the same label as `VendGroupId` because it is going to replace the existing **Group** control on the form and their labels has to match.

Next, we create a new `edit` method, which is used to show the group description instead of the group ID on the form. It also allows changing the control's value.

The `edit` method is created on the `VendTable` table—the most convenient place—and it uses the newly created extended data type. This ensures that the label of the user control stays the same. The method accepts two arguments as this is a mandatory requirement for the `edit` methods. The first argument defines whether the control was modified by the user, and, if yes, the second argument holds the modified value. In this recipe, the second value can be either group ID or group description. The value will be group ID if the user selects this value from the lookup. It will be group description if the user decides to manually type the value into the control. We use the `VendGroupDescriptionExt` extended data type, which is bigger in size and fits for both the group ID and group description values.

Building Lookups

Next, we need to modify the `VendTable` form. We change the existing vendor group ID control to use the newly created `edit` method. By doing this, we make the control unbound and therefore lose the standard lookup functionality. To correct this, we override the `lookup()` method on the control. Here, we use the `performTypeLookup()` method to restore the lookup functionality.

There's more...

In the previous example, you may notice that the lookup does not find the currently selected group. This is because the system tries to search for group ID by group description. This section will show you how to correct this issue.

First, we have to create a new form named `VendGroupLookup` that acts as a lookup. Add a new data source to the form, with the following properties:

Property	Value
Name	VendGroup
Table	VendGroup
Index	GroupIdx
AllowCheck	No
AllowEdit	No
AllowCreate	No
AllowDelete	No
OnlyFetchActive	Yes

Change the properties of the form's design as follows:

Property	Value
Frame	Border
WindowType	Popup

Add a new `Grid` control to the form's design with the following properties:

Property	Value
Name	VendGroups
ShowRowLabels	No
DataSource	VendGroup
DataGroup	Overview

Several new controls will appear in the grid automatically. Change the properties of the `VendGroups_VendGroup` control as follows:

Property	Value
AutoDeclaration	Yes

Override the form's `init()` and `run()` methods with the following code snippet, respectively:

```
public void init()
{
    super();
    element.selectMode(VendGroups_VendGroup);
}

public void run()
{
    VendGroupId groupId;

    groupId = element.args().lookupValue();

    super();

    VendGroup_ds.findValue(
        fieldNum(VendGroup,VendGroup), groupId);
}
```

The key element here is the `findValue()` method in the form's `run()` method. It places the cursor on the currently selected vendor group record. The group ID is retrieved from the arguments object using the `lookupValue()` method.

Building Lookups

In the AOT, the form will look similar to the following screenshot:

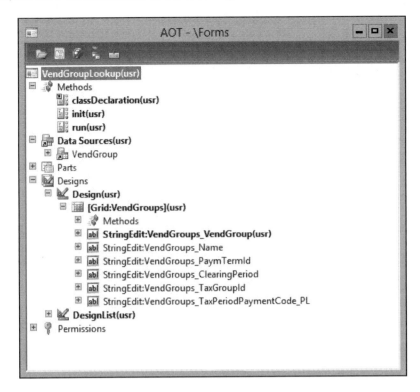

Next, we need to create a new static method on the `VendGroup` table, which opens the new lookup form:

```
public static void lookupVendorGroupForm(
    FormStringControl _callingControl,
    VendGroupId       _groupId)
{
    FormRun formRun;
    Args    args;

    args = new Args();
    args.name(formStr(VendGroupLookup));
    args.lookupValue(_groupId);

    formRun = classFactory.formRunClass(args);
    formRun.init();

    _callingControl.performFormLookup(formRun);
}
```

Chapter 4

Here, we use the `formRunClass()` method of the global `classFactory` object. Note that here we pass the group ID to the form through the `Args` object.

The final touch is to change the code in the `lookup()` method of the `VendGroups_VendGroup` control on the `VendTable` form:

```
public void lookup()
{
    VendGroup::lookupVendorGroupForm(this, VendTable.VendGroup);
}
```

Now, when you open the **Vendors** form, the current vendor group in the **Group** lookup is preselected correctly:

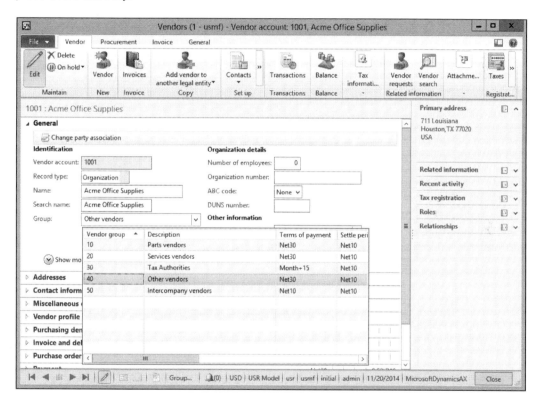

Building the browse for folder lookup

Folder browsing lookups can be used when the user is required to specify a local or network folder for storing or retrieving external files. Such lookups are generated outside Dynamics AX using Windows API.

In this recipe, we will learn how to create a lookup for folder browsing. As an example, we will create a new field and control named **Documents** on the **General ledger parameters** form, which will allow us to store a folder path.

How to do it...

1. In the AOT, open the `LedgerParameters` table and create a new field with the following properties:

Property	Value
Type	String
Name	DocumentPath
Label	Documents
ExtendedDataType	FilePath

2. Add the newly created field to the bottom of the table's `General` field group.

3. In the AOT, open the `LedgerParameters` form and create a new method with the following code snippet at the top level of the form:

    ```
    public str filePathLookupTitle()
    {
        return "Select document folder";
    }
    ```

4. To test the results, navigate to **General ledger | Setup | General ledger parameters** and note the newly created **Documents** control, which allows us to select a folder:

Chapter 4

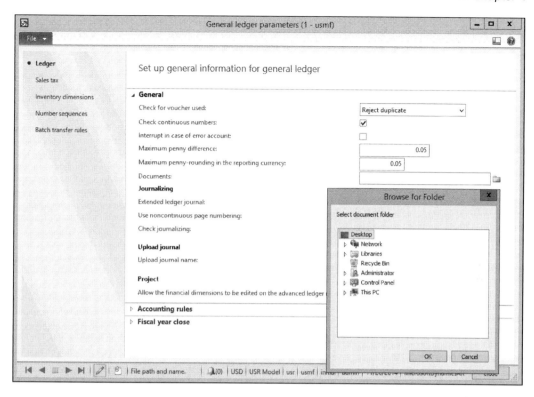

How it works...

The folder browsing lookup form is bound to the `FilePath` extended data type, and it appears automatically for every control that is based on that type. In this recipe, we create a new field, which extends `FilePath` and consequently inherits the lookup. We also add the newly created field to the field group, for it to appear on the form automatically.

We also create a new form method named `filePathLookupTitle()`, which is required by the folder browsing lookup. This method holds a description displayed on the lookup window. The system will show an error if this method is not present on the caller form.

There's more...

In this section, we will explore other enhancements to the previous example. Firstly, we will build exactly the same lookup, but use a slightly different technique. Secondly, we will enable the **Make New Folder** button on the lookup, allowing users to create new folders.

Manual folder browsing lookup

The lookup created in this recipe has a few programming limitations. Firstly, the lookup requires the `filePathLookupTitle()` method to be present on a caller form. The name of this method has to be exactly like this and cannot be changed.

Another reason is that a single form cannot have two or more folder browsing lookups unless they share the same description. Every lookup calls the same `filePathLookupTitle()` method and will obviously have the same description.

Internally, the browsing for folder lookup is generated with the help of the `browseForPath()` method of the `WinAPI` class. This method invokes the standard Windows folder browsing dialog box, and we can call this method directly, without using the extended data type.

Let's modify our previous example by deleting the `filePathLookupTitle()` method from the `LedgerParameters` form and overriding the `lookup()` method of the `DocumentPath` field in the `LedgerParameters` form data source with the following code snippet:

```
public void lookup(FormControl _formControl, str _filterStr)
{
    FilePath path;

    path = WinAPI::browseForPath(
        element.hWnd(),
        "Select document folder extended");

    LedgerParameters.DocumentPath = path;
    LedgerParameters_ds.refresh();
}
```

Now, if you open the lookup, you may note that it looks exactly the same as before, apart from its description. The description is defined in the `lookup()` method, and is only used for this particular lookup. Using this technique, we can create more than one folder browsing lookup on the same form without adding additional methods to the form itself.

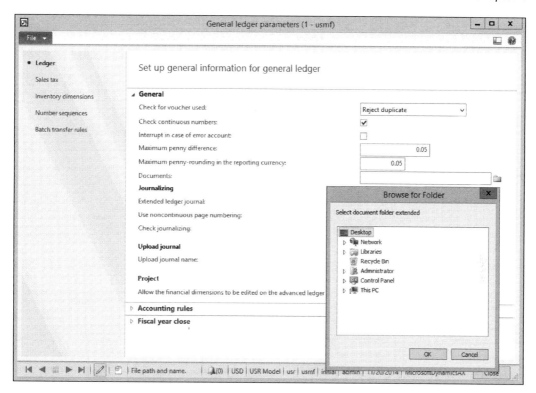

Adding a Make New Folder button

The previously mentioned `WinAPI` class has one more method named `browseForFolderDialog()`. Besides folder browsing, it also allows for creating a new one. The method accepts three optional arguments:

- The lookup description.
- The folder path selected initially.
- The `boolean` value, where `true` shows and `false` hides the **Make New Folder** button. The button is shown by default if this argument is omitted.

Let's replace the `lookup()` method of the `DocumentPath` field in the `LedgerParameters` form data source with the following code snippet:

```
public void lookup(FormControl _formControl, str _filterStr)
{
    FilePath path;

    path = WinAPI::browseForFolderDialog(
        "Select document folder extended",
```

Building Lookups

```
            LedgerParameters.DocumentPath,
            true);

        LedgerParameters.DocumentPath = path;
        LedgerParameters_ds.refresh();
}
```

Now, the folder browsing lookup has a new **Make New Folder** button, which allows the user to create a new folder straight away, without leaving the lookup:

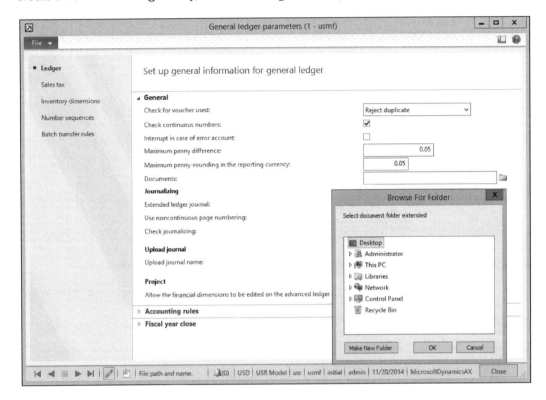

Building a lookup to select a file

In Dynamics AX, file reading or saving is a very common operation. Normally, for non-automated operations, the system prompts the user for file input.

This recipe will demonstrate how the user can be presented with the file browse dialog box in order to choose the files in a convenient way. As an example, we will create a new control called **Terms & conditions** in the **Form setup** form in **Procurement and sourcing** module, which allows storing a path to the text document.

How to do it...

1. In the AOT, open the `VendFormLetterParameters` table and create a new field with the following properties:

Property	Value
Type	String
Name	TermsAndConditions
Label	Terms & conditions
ExtendedDataType	FilenameOpen

2. Then, add the field to the bottom of the table's `PurchaseOrder` field group.

3. Next, open the `PurchFormLetterParameters` form and create the following four methods:

   ```
   public str fileNameLookupTitle()
   {
       return "Select Terms & conditions document";
   }

   public str fileNameLookupInitialPath()
   {
       container file;

       file = fileNameSplit(
           VendFormletterParameters.TermsAndConditions);

       return conPeek(file ,1);
   }

   public str fileNameLookupFilename()
   {
       Filename    path;
       Filename    name;
       Filename    type;

       [path, name, type] = fileNameSplit(
           VendFormletterParameters.TermsAndConditions);

       return name + type;
   }
   ```

Building Lookups

```
public container fileNameLookupFilter()
{
    #File
    return [WinAPI::fileType(#txt), #AllFilesName+#txt];
}
```

4. As a result, we will be able to select and store a text file in the **Procurement and sourcing** | **Setup** | **Forms** | **Form setup** form in the **Terms & conditions** field under the **Purchase order** tab page:

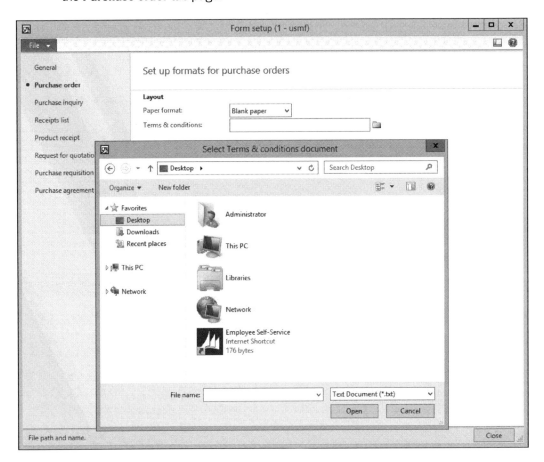

How it works...

In this recipe, we first create a new field to store the file location. We use the `FilenameOpen` extended data type, which is bound to the file selection dialog box. The newly created field automatically inherits the dialog box. We also add this field to the field group in the table to ensure that it is displayed on the form automatically.

The following four form methods are called by the lookup and must be present on the caller form:

- The `fileNameLookupTitle()` method contains a text to be displayed as the lookup title.

- The `fileNameLookupInitialPath()` method defines the initial folder. In our example, if there is a value in the **Terms & conditions** field, then this method strips the filename part, and returns the directory path to the lookup to be used as a starting point. Here, we use the global `fileNameSplit()` function to process the stored file path.

- The `fileNameLookupFilename()` method detects the current value in the field and extracts the filename to be displayed on the lookup. We use the global `fileNameSplit()` function again to separate the given directory path into three parts: directory path, filename, and file extension. For example, if the current **Terms & conditions** value is `C:\Documents\terms.txt`, then once the user clicks on the lookup button, the method returns only the filename `terms.txt` (file name + file extension) separated from the rest of the directory path.

- The `fileNameLookupFilter()` method is responsible for the displaying of a list of allowed file extensions. It returns a container of allowed extensions in pairs of two. The first, third, fifth, and the other odd values hold the name of the file extension and the second, fourth, sixth, and the other even values contain the extension itself. In this example, only the text files are allowed, so the method returns two values in the container. The first value is a string, `Text Document`, and the second one is `*.txt`. In order to avoid literals in the X++ code, we use these `#File` macro definitions: `#txt` and `#AllFileName`. These contain the `.txt` and `*` strings, respectively, and are concatenated by the lookup to present the user with `Text Document (*.txt)` as a file extension filter. The `fileType()` method of the `WinAPI` class converts file extensions to their textual representation.

There's more...

Although the file browsing dialog box created in this recipe is technically correct, it still has some limitations. Firstly, it requires creating a number of methods on the caller form. Secondly, it will not work with multiple file lookups on the same form. A slightly different approach can be used to avoid these issues and keep the lookup's appearance unchanged.

Let's modify the previous example by removing all four methods from the form itself and overriding the `lookup()` method on the on the `TermsAndConditions` field on the `VendFormletterParameters` data source with the following code snippet:

```
public void lookup(FormControl _formControl, str _filterStr)
{
    FilenameOpen file;
    Filename     path;
```

Building Lookups

```
        Filename    name;
        Filename    type;
        #File

        [path, name, type] = fileNameSplit(
            VendFormLetterParameters.TermsAndConditions);

        file = WinAPI::getOpenFileName(
            element.hWnd(),
            [WinAPI::fileType(#txt), #AllFilesName+#txt],
            path,
            "Select Terms & conditions document",
            "",
            name + type);

        if (file)
        {
            VendFormLetterParameters.TermsAndConditions = file;
            VendFormLetterParameters_ds.refresh();
        }
    }
```

The file browsing dialog box is in the `getOpenFileName()` method of the `WinAPI` class, which in turn opens the Windows file browsing dialog. The method accepts a number of arguments:

- A handler to the calling window.
- A container of allowed file extensions. This is exactly what the `fileNameLookupFilter()` method returns in the previous example.
- The file path selected initially.
- The lookup's title.
- The default filename.

Creating a color picker lookup

In Dynamics AX, the color selection dialog boxes are used in various places, allowing the user to select and store a color code in a table field. Then the stored color code can be used in various places to color data records, change form backgrounds, set colors for various controls, and so on.

In this recipe, we will create a color lookup. For demonstration purposes, we will add an option to set a color for each legal entity in the system.

How to do it...

1. In the AOT, open the `CompanyInfo` table and create a new field with the following properties:

Property	Value
Type	Integer
Name	CompanyColor
ExtendedDataType	CCColor

2. Open the `OMLegalEntity` form, locate the `TopPanel` group in **Body | Content | Tab | General**, and add a new `IntEdit` control with the following properties to the bottom of the group:

Property	Value
Name	CompanyColor
AutoDeclaration	Yes
LookupButton	Always
ShowZero	No
ColorScheme	RGB
Label	Company color

3. In the same form, create a new method with the following code snippet in the `CompanyInfo` data source:

   ```
   public edit CCColor editCompanyColor(
       boolean     _set,
       CompanyInfo _companyInfo,
       CCColor     _color)
   {
       if (_companyInfo.CompanyColor)
       {
           CompanyColor.backgroundColor(
               _companyInfo.CompanyColor);
       }
       else
       {
           CompanyColor.backgroundColor(
               WinAPI::RGB2int(255,255,255));
       }

       CompanyColor.foregroundColor(
           CompanyColor.backgroundColor());
   ```

Building Lookups

```
        return 0;
}
```

4. Update the properties of the newly created `CompanyColor` control as follows:

Property	Value
DataSource	CompanyInfo
DataMethod	editCompanyColor

5. On the same control, override its `lookup()` method with the following code snippet:

```
public void lookup()
{
    int        red;
    int        green;
    int        blue;
    container  color;

    [red, green, blue] = WinApi::RGBint2Con(
        CompanyColor.backgroundColor());

    color = WinAPI::chooseColor(
        element.hWnd(),
        red,
        green,
        blue,
        null,
        true);

    if (color)
    {
        [red, green, blue] = color;
        CompanyInfo.CompanyColor = WinAPI::RGB2int(
            red,
            green,
            blue);

        CompanyColor.backgroundColor(
            CompanyInfo.CompanyColor);
    }
}
```

Chapter 4

6. To test the results, navigate to **Organization administration | Setup | Organization | Legal entities** and note the newly created **Company color** control with the color lookup:

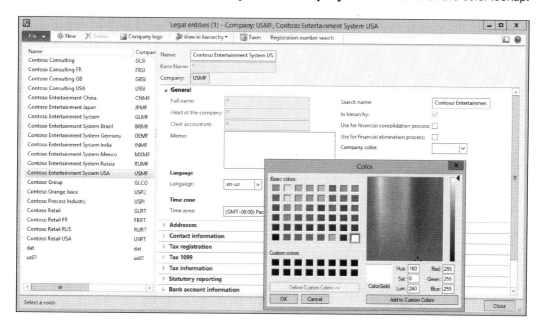

How it works...

Dynamics AX does not have a special control to select colors. Therefore, we have to create a fake control, which is presented to the user as a color selection.

Colors in Dynamics AX are stored as integers, so we first create a new `Integer` field on the `CompanyInfo` table. On the form, we create a new control, which will display the color. The created control does not have any automatic lookup and therefore it does not have the lookup button next to it. We have to force the button to appear by setting the control's `LookupButton` property to `Always`. We also need to set the `ColorScheme` property to `RGB` to make sure the control allows us to set its color using the red-green-blue code.

Next, we create a new edit method, which is then set on the created control as a data method. This method is responsible for changing the control's background to match the stored color. This gives an impression to the user that the chosen color was saved. The background is set to white if no value is present. The method always returns the value 0 because we do not want to show the actual color code in it. The control's `ShowZero` property is set to `No` to ensure that even the returned 0 is not displayed. In this way, we create a control that looks like a real color selection control.

Building Lookups

The last thing to do is to override the control's `lookup()` method with the code that invokes the color selection dialog box. Here, we use the `RGBint2Con()` method of the `WinAPI` class to convert the current control's background color into a red-green-blue component set. This set is then passed to the `chooseColor()` method of the same `WinAPI` class to make sure that the currently set color is selected on the lookup initially. The `chooseColor()` method is the `main` method, which invokes the lookup. It accepts the following arguments:

- The current window handle
- The red color component
- The green color component
- The blue color component
- A binary object representing up to 16 custom colors
- A `boolean` value, which defines whether the full or short version of the lookup is displayed initially

This method returns a container of red, green, and blue color components, which has to be converted back to a numeric value in order to store it in the table field.

There's more...

You probably have noticed that the fifth argument in the preceding example is set to `null`. This is because we did not use custom colors. This feature is not that important, but it might be used in some circumstances.

To demonstrate how it can be used, let's modify the `lookup()` method with the following code snippet in order to implement the custom colors:

```
public void lookup()
{
    int         red;
    int         green;
    int         blue;
    container   color;
    Binary      customColors;

    customColors = new Binary(64);

    customColors.byte(0,255);
    customColors.byte(1,255);
    customColors.byte(2,0);

    customColors.byte(4,0);
    customColors.byte(5,255);
```

```
        customColors.byte(6,0);

        customColors.byte(8,255);
        customColors.byte(9,0);
        customColors.byte(10,0);

        [red, green, blue] = WinApi::RGBint2Con(
            CompanyColor.backgroundColor());

        color = WinAPI::chooseColor(
            element.hWnd(),
            red,
            green,
            blue,
            customColors,
            true);

        if (color)
        {
            [red, green, blue] = color;
            CompanyInfo.CompanyColor = WinAPI::RGB2int(
                red,
                green,
                blue);

            CompanyColor.backgroundColor(
                CompanyInfo.CompanyColor);
        }
    }
```

Here, we define the `customColors` variable as a Binary object to store the initial set of custom colors. The object structure contains 64 elements to store the color codes. The set of red, green, and blue components for each color is stored in three subsequent elements in the object, followed by an empty element. In our code, we store yellow (red = 255, green = 255, and blue = 0) in the elements from 0 to 2, green (red = 0, green, = 255, blue = 0) in the elements from 4 to 6, and red (red = 255, green = 0, blue = 0) in the elements from 8 to 10. This system allows you to create up to 16 custom colors.

Building Lookups

After implementing those changes, the color selection dialog box now looks slightly different, as shown in the following screenshot:

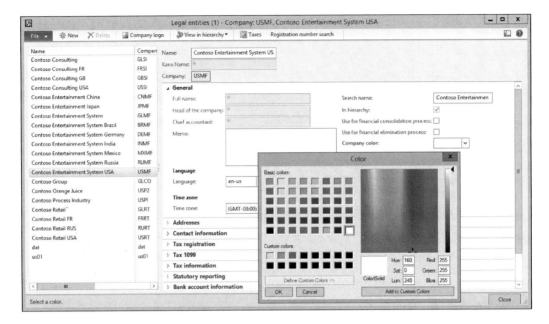

The custom colors can also be modified by the user and be saved in a table field or cache for later use by storing the whole binary `customColors` object.

5
Processing Business Tasks

In this chapter, we will cover the following recipes:

- Using a segmented entry control
- Creating a general journal
- Posting a general journal
- Processing a project journal
- Creating and posting a ledger voucher
- Changing an automatic transaction text
- Creating a purchase order
- Posting a purchase order
- Creating a sales order
- Posting a sales order
- Creating an electronic payment format

Introduction

In Dynamics AX, various business operations, such as creating financial journals, posting sales orders, and generating vendor payments are performed from the user interface by the user on a periodic basis. For developers, it is very important to understand how it works internally so that the knowledge can be used to design and implement new custom business logic.

Processing Business Tasks

This chapter will explain how various Dynamics AX business operations can be performed from the code. We will discuss how to create and post various journals. This chapter also explains how to work with the ledger voucher object and how to enhance the setup of the automatically generated transaction texts. Posting purchase and sales orders, and creating electronic payments are also discussed here.

Using a segmented entry control

In Dynamics AX, segmented entry control can simplify the task of entering complex account and dimension combinations. The control consists of a dynamic number of elements named segments. The number of segments may vary depending on the setup, and their lookup values may depend on the values specified in other segments in the same control. The segmented entry control always uses the controller class, which handles the entry and display of the control.

In this recipe, we will show you how a segmented entry control can be added to a form. In this demonstration, we will add a new **Ledger account** control to the **General ledger parameters** form, assuming that the control can be used as a default ledger account for various functions. The example does not make much sense in practice, but it is perfectly suitable to demonstrate the usage of the segmented entry control.

How to do it...

Carry out the following steps in order to complete this recipe:

1. In the AOT, locate the `LedgerParameters` table and create a new field with the following properties (click on **Yes** to automatically add a foreign key relationship once you are asked):

Property	Value
Type	`Int64`
Name	`LedgerDimension`
ExtendedDataType	`LedgerDimensionAccount`

2. Add the newly created field to the `General` group in the table.
3. Find the table's relation, named `DimensionAttributeValueCombination`, and change its property, as follows:

Property	Value
`UseDefaultRoleNames`	No

4. In the AOT, find the `LedgerParameters` form and add the following line of code to its class declaration:

   ```
   LedgerDimensionAccountController ledgerDimensionAccountController;
   ```

5. Add the following lines of code at the bottom of the form's `init()` method:

   ```
   ledgerDimensionAccountController =
       LedgerDimensionAccountController::construct(
           LedgerParameters_ds,
           fieldStr(LedgerParameters,LedgerDimension));
   ```

6. In the same form, find the `General_LedgerDimension` segmented entry control by going to **Tab | LedgerTab | LedgerTabBody | LedgerTabFastTab | GeneralTabPage | General**, and override three of its methods with the following code snippet:

   ```
   void loadAutoCompleteData(LoadAutoCompleteDataEventArgs _e)
   {
       super(_e);
       ledgerDimensionAccountController.loadAutoCompleteData(_e);
   }

   void loadSegments()
   {
       super();
       ledgerDimensionAccountController.parmControl(this);
       ledgerDimensionAccountController.loadSegments();
   }

   void segmentValueChanged(SegmentValueChangedEventArgs _e)
   {
       super(_e);
       ledgerDimensionAccountController.segmentValueChanged(_e);
   }
   ```

7. In the same form, in its `LedgerParameters` data source, locate the `LedgerDimension` field and override three of its methods with the following code snippet:

   ```
   Common resolveReference(
       FormReferenceControl _formReferenceControl)
   {
       return ledgerDimensionAccountController.resolveReference();
   }

   void jumpRef()
   ```

Processing Business Tasks

```
{
    super();
    ledgerDimensionAccountController.jumpRef();
}

boolean validate()
{
    boolean ret;

    ret = super();

    ret = ledgerDimensionAccountController.validate() && ret;

    return ret;
}
```

8. To test the results, navigate to **General ledger | Setup | General ledger parameters** and notice the newly created **Ledger account** control, which allows you to select and save the main account and a number of financial dimensions, as shown in the following screenshot:

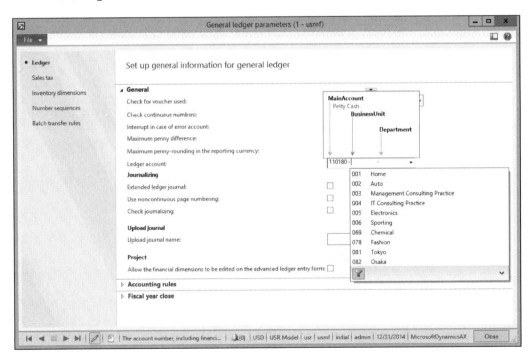

How it works...

We start the recipe by creating a new field in the `LedgerParameters` table. The field extends the `LedgerDimensionAccount` extended data type in order to ensure that the segmented entry control appears automatically once this field is added to the user interface. We also add the newly created field to one of the table's groups in order to make sure that it appears on the form automatically.

Next, we have to modify the `LedgerParameters` form. In its class declaration and the `init()` method, we define and instantiate the `LedgerDimensionAccountController` class, which handles the events raised by the segmented entry control. The combination of the class and the control allows the user to see a dynamic number of segments, based on the system configuration.

Then, we override the following methods of the control:

- `loadAutoCompleteData()`: This retrieves the data for the autocomplete lookup
- `loadSegments()`: This loads the value stored in the table field into the control
- `segmentedValueChanged()`: This updates the controller class when the value of the control is changed by the user

Lastly, we override the following methods in the data source field:

- `resolveReference()`: This finds the ledger account record specified by the user
- `jumpRef()`: This enables the **View details** link in the control's right-click context menu
- `validate()`: This performs user input validation

There's more...

In this section, we will discuss how the input of the segmented entry control can be simulated from the code. It is very useful when migrating or importing data into the system. In the AOT, locate the `DimensionAttributeValueCombination` table and create a new method with the following code snippet:

```
static LedgerDimensionAccount getLedgerDimension(
    MainAccountNum  _mainAccountId,
    container       _dimensions,
    container       _values)
{
    MainAccount             mainAccount;
    DimensionHierarchy      dimHier;
    LedgerStructure         ledgerStruct;
    Map                     dimSpec;
    Name                    dimName;
```

Processing Business Tasks

```
    Name                            dimValue;
    DimensionAttribute              dimAttr;
    DimensionAttributeValue         dimAttrValue;
    List                            dimSources;
    DimensionDefaultingEngine       dimEng;
    int                             i;

    mainAccount = MainAccount::findByMainAccountId(
        _mainAccountId);

    if (!mainAccount.RecId)
    {
        return 0;
    }

    select firstOnly RecId from dimHier
        where dimHier.StructureType ==
            DimensionHierarchyType::AccountStructure
          && dimHier.IsDraft == NoYes::No
        exists join ledgerStruct
            where ledgerStruct.Ledger == Ledger::current()
              && ledgerStruct.DimensionHierarchy == dimHier.RecId;
    if (!dimHier.RecId)
    {
        return 0;
    }

    dimSpec =
        DimensionDefaultingEngine::createEmptyDimensionSpecifiers();

    for (i = 1; i <= conLen(_dimensions); i++)
    {
        dimName = conPeek(_dimensions, i);
        dimValue = conPeek(_values, i);

        dimAttr = DimensionAttribute::findByName(dimName);
        if (!dimAttr.RecId)
        {
            continue;
        }

        dimAttrValue =
            DimensionAttributeValue::findByDimensionAttributeAndValue(
```

```
                dimAttr, dimValue, false, true);
            if (dimAttrValue.IsDeleted)
            {
                continue;
            }

            DimensionDefaultingEngine::insertDimensionSpecifer(
                dimSpec,
                dimAttr.RecId,
                dimValue,
                dimAttrValue.RecId,
                dimAttrValue.HashKey);
        }

        dimSources = new List(Types::Class);
        dimSources.addEnd(dimSpec);

        dimEng = DimensionDefaultingEngine::constructForMainAccountId(
            mainAccount.RecId,
            dimHier.RecId);
        dimEng.applyDimensionSources(dimSources);

        return dimEng.getLedgerDimension();
    }
```

This method can be used to convert a combination of main accounts and a number of financial dimension values into a ledger account. The method accepts the following three arguments:

- The main account number
- A container of dimension names
- A container of dimension values

We start this method by searching for the main account record. We also locate the record of the hierarchy of the current chart of accounts.

Next, we fill an empty map with the dimension values. Before inserting each value, we check whether the dimension and its value are present in the system. To do this, we use the methods in the `DimensionAttribute` and `DimensionAttributeValue` tables.

We end the method by creating a new `DimensionDefaultingEngine` object and passing the list of dimensions and their values to it. Now, when everything is ready, the `getLedgerDimension()` method of `DimensionDefaultingEngine` returns the ledger account number.

Processing Business Tasks

See also

- The *Creating a general journal* recipe
- The *Creating and posting a ledger voucher* recipe

Creating a general journal

Journals in Dynamics AX are manual worksheets that can be posted into the system. One of the frequently used journals for financial operations is the **General journal**. It allows processing of any type of posting: ledger account transfers, fixed asset operations, customer/vendor payments, bank operations, project expenses, and so on. Journals, such as the **Fixed assets journal**, **Payment journal** in **Accounts receivable** or in **Accounts payable**, and many others, are optimized for specific business tasks, but they basically do the same job.

In this recipe, we will demonstrate how to create a new general journal record from the code. The journal will hold a single line for debiting one ledger account and crediting another one. For demonstration purposes, we will specify all the input values in the code.

How to do it...

Carry out the following steps in order to complete this recipe:

1. In the AOT, create a new class named `LedgerJournalTransData` with the following code snippet:

    ```
    class LedgerJournalTransData extends JournalTransData
    {
    }

    void create(
        boolean _doInsert = false,
        boolean _initVoucherList = true)
    {
        lastLineNum++;

        journalTrans.LineNum = lastLineNum;

        if (journalTableData.journalVoucherNum())
        {
            this.initVoucher(
    ```

```
                lastVoucher,
                false,
                _initVoucherList);
        }

        this.addTotal(false, false);

        if (_doInsert)
        {
            journalTrans.doInsert();
        }
        else
        {
            journalTrans.insert();
        }

        if (journalTableData.journalVoucherNum())
        {
            lastVoucher = journalTrans.Voucher;
        }
    }
```

2. Open the `LedgerJournalStatic` class and replace its `newJournalTransData()` method with the following code snippet:

    ```
    JournalTransData newJournalTransData(
        JournalTransMap _journalTrans,
        JournalTableData _journalTableData)
    {
        return new LedgerJournalTransData(
            _journalTrans,
            _journalTableData);
    }
    ```

3. Double-check whether the `getLedgerDimension()` method exists in the `DimensionAttributeValueCombination` table. If not, create the method as described in the first recipe of this chapter.

4. Create a new job named `LedgerJournalCreate` with the following code snippet:

    ```
    static void LedgerJournalCreate(Args _args)
    {
        LedgerJournalTable      jourTable;
        LedgerJournalTrans      jourTrans;
    ```

```
LedgerJournalTableData    jourTableData;
LedgerJournalTransData    jourTransData;
LedgerJournalStatic       jourStatic;
DimensionDynamicAccount   ledgerDim;
DimensionDynamicAccount   offsetLedgerDim;

ttsBegin;

ledgerDim =
    DimensionAttributeValueCombination::getLedgerDimension(
        '110180',
        ['BusinessUnit', 'Department'],
        ['005', '024']);

offsetLedgerDim =
    DimensionAttributeValueCombination::getLedgerDimension(
        '170150',
        [' BusinessUnit', 'Department'],
        ['005', '024']);

jourTableData = JournalTableData::newTable(jourTable);

jourTable.JournalNum = jourTableData.nextJournalId();
jourTable.JournalType = LedgerJournalType::Daily;
jourTable.JournalName = 'GenJrn';

jourTableData.initFromJournalName(
    LedgerJournalName::find(jourTable.JournalName));

jourStatic = jourTableData.journalStatic();

jourTransData = jourStatic.newJournalTransData(
    jourTrans,
    jourTableData);

jourTransData.initFromJournalTable();

jourTrans.CurrencyCode          = 'USD';
jourTrans.initValue();
jourTrans.TransDate             = systemDateGet();
```

Chapter 5

```
        jourTrans.LedgerDimension       = ledgerDim;
        jourTrans.Txt                   = 'General journal demo';
        jourTrans.OffsetLedgerDimension = offsetLedgerDim;
        jourTrans.AmountCurDebit        = 1000;

        jourTransData.create();

        jourTable.insert();

        ttsCommit;

        info(strFmt(
            "Journal '%1' has been created", jourTable.JournalNum));
    }
```

5. Run the job and check the results by navigating to **General ledger | Journals | General journal**, as shown in the following screenshot:

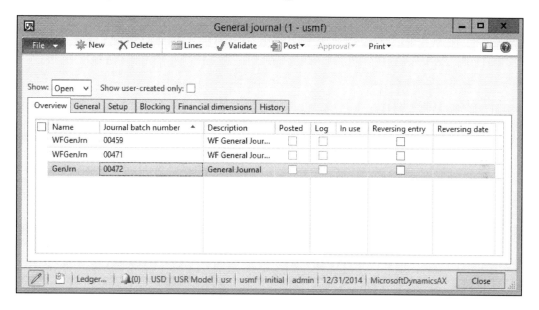

Processing Business Tasks

6. Click on the **Lines** button to open journal lines and notice the created line, as shown here:

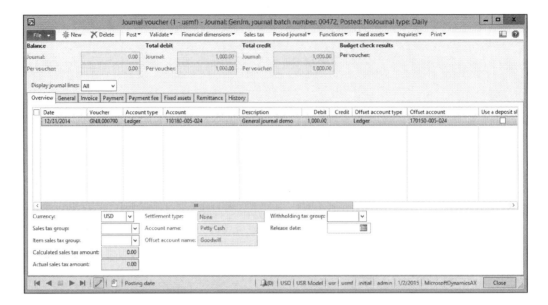

How it works...

We start the recipe by creating the `LedgerJournalTransData` class, which will handle the creation of journal lines. It inherits everything from the `JournalTransData` class, apart from its `create()` method. Actually, this method is a copy of the same method from the `JournalTransData` class, with the exception that it does not contain the code that is not relevant to the ledger journal creation. We also modify the `newJournalTransData()` constructor of the `LedgerJournalStatic` class to use our newly created class.

The journal creation code is placed in a new job. We start the code by initializing ledger accounts. Here, we use the `getLedgerDimension()` method from the previous recipe. This method accepts three parameters: the main account number, a container of dimension names, and a container of dimension values, and returns `RecId` of the ledger account. In this example, the ledger accounts consist of the main account, business unit, and department and their values are `110180-005-024` and `170150-005-024`. Use your own values depending on the data you have.

We also create a new `jourTableData` object that is used for journal record handling. Then, we set the journal number, type, and name and call the `initFromJournalName()` method to initialize some additional values from the journal name settings. At this stage, the journal header record is ready.

Next, we create a journal line. We create a new `jourTransData` object to handle the journal line, and we call its `initFromJournalTable()` method to initialize additional values from the journal header. Then, we set some of the journal line values, such as the currency and transaction date.

Finally, we call the `create()` method on the `jourTransData` object and the `insert()` method on the `jourTable` object to create the journal line and header records, respectively. The journal is now ready to be reviewed.

There's more

The preceding example can be easily modified to create different journals, not just the **General journal**. For instance, the **Payment journal** in the **Accounts payable** module is based on the same tables as the **General journal** and some of its code is the same. So, let's create a new, similar job named `VendPaymJournalCreate` with the following code snippet:

```
static void VendPaymJournalCreate(Args _args)
{
    LedgerJournalTable        jourTable;
    LedgerJournalTrans        jourTrans;
    LedgerJournalTableData    jourTableData;
    LedgerJournalTransData    jourTransData;
    LedgerJournalStatic       jourStatic;
    DimensionDynamicAccount   ledgerDim;
    DimensionDynamicAccount   offsetLedgerDim;

    ttsBegin;

    ledgerDim = DimensionStorage::getDynamicAccount(
        '1001',
        LedgerJournalACType::Vend);

    offsetLedgerDim = DimensionStorage::getDynamicAccount(
        'USMF OPER',
        LedgerJournalACType::Bank);

    jourTableData = JournalTableData::newTable(jourTable);

    jourTable.JournalNum  = jourTableData.nextJournalId();
    jourTable.JournalType = LedgerJournalType::Payment;
    jourTable.JournalName = 'VendPay';
```

```
        jourTableData.initFromJournalName(
            LedgerJournalName::find(jourTable.JournalName));

        jourStatic      = jourTableData.journalStatic();

        jourTransData = jourStatic.newJournalTransData(
            jourTrans,
            jourTableData);

        jourTransData.initFromJournalTable();

        jourTrans.CurrencyCode              = 'USD';
        jourTrans.initValue();
        jourTrans.TransDate                 = systemDateGet();
        jourTrans.AccountType               = LedgerJournalACType::Vend;
        jourTrans.LedgerDimension           = ledgerDim;
        jourTrans.Txt                       = 'Vendor payment journal demo';
        jourTrans.OffsetAccountType         = LedgerJournalACType::Bank;
        jourTrans.OffsetLedgerDimension     = offsetLedgerDim;
        jourTrans.AmountCurDebit            = 1000;

        jourTransData.create();

        jourTable.insert();

        ttsCommit;

        info(strFmt(
            "Journal '%1' has been created", jourTable.JournalNum));
    }
```

Now, the newly created journal can be found by navigating to **Accounts payable | Journals | Payments | Payment journal**, as shown here:

Chapter 5

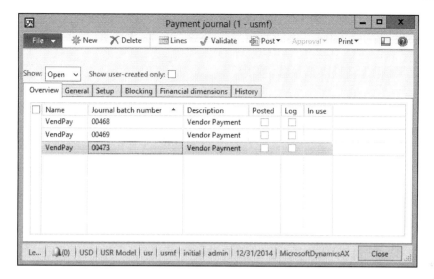

The journal's lines should reflect what we've specified in the code, as shown in the following screenshot:

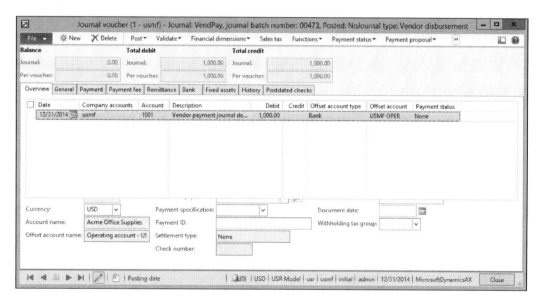

Processing Business Tasks

The code in this section has only slight differences compared to the previous example, as follows:

- The ledger account contains a reference to a vendor account, and the offset ledger account refers to a bank account record
- The journal type is changed to a vendor disbursement, that is, `LedgerJournalType::Payment`
- The journal name is different and is configured for creating payment journals
- The journal line account type is set to `Vendor`, and the offset account type is set to `Bank`

See also

- The *Using a segmented entry control* recipe
- The *Posting a general journal* recipe

Posting a general journal

Journal posting is the next step once the journal has been created. Although most of the time journals are posted from the user interface, it is also possible to perform the same operation from the code.

In this recipe, we will explore how a general journal can be posted from the code. We are going to process an open journal. The journal created in the previous recipe can be used here.

How to do it...

Carry out the following steps in order to complete this recipe:

1. Navigate to **General ledger | Journals | General journal** and find an open journal. Create a new journal if none exists. Note the journal's number.

2. In the AOT, create a new job named `LedgerJournalPost` with the following code snippet (replace the `00472` text with your journal's number):

```
static void LedgerJournalPost(Args _args)
{
    LedgerJournalCheckPost  jourPost;
    LedgerJournalTable      jourTable;

    jourTable = LedgerJournalTable::find('00472');
```

Chapter 5

```
    jourPost = LedgerJournalCheckPost::newLedgerJournalTable(
        jourTable,
        NoYes::Yes);

    jourPost.run();
}
```

3. Run the job and notice the **Infolog** window, confirming that the journal was successfully posted, as shown here:

4. Navigate to **General ledger** | **Journals** | **General journal** and locate the journal in order to make sure that it was posted, as shown in the following screenshot:

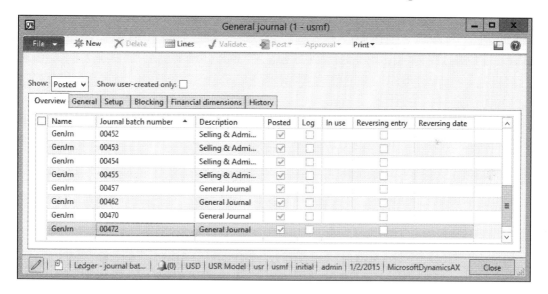

How it works...

In this recipe, we create a new job named `LedgerJournalPost`, which holds all the code and here, we use the `LedgerJournalCheckPost` class, which does all the work. This class ensures that all the necessary validations are performed. It also locks the journal so that no user can access it from the user interface while the posting is being performed.

Processing Business Tasks

In the job, we create the `jourPost` object by calling the `newLedgerJournalTable()` constructor on the `LedgerJournalCheckPost` class. This method accepts two arguments: a journal header record to be processed and `NoYes` parameter, defining whether the journal should be validated and posted or validated only. In this recipe, we use journal `00472` and pass it to the `LedgerJournalCheckPost` class along with the second argument, instructing the method to perform both validation and posting.

See also

- The *Creating a general journal* recipe

Processing a project journal

As with most of the modules in Dynamics AX, the **Project management and accounting** module contain several journals, such as **Hour**, **Expense**, **Fee**, and **Item**. Although they are similar to the **General journal**, they provide a more convenient user interface to work with projects and contain some module-specific features.

In this recipe, we will create and post a project journal from the code. We will process the **Hour** journal, which contains employees' time registrations.

How to do it...

Carry out the following steps in order to complete this recipe:

1. In the AOT, create a new job named `ProjJournalCreate` with the following code snippet (replace the input values in the code to match your data):

    ```
    static void ProjJournalCreate(Args _args)
    {
        ProjJournalTable      jourTable;
        ProjJournalTrans      jourTrans;
        ProjJournalTableData  jourTableData;
        ProjJournalTransData  jourTransData;
        ProjJournalStatic     jourStatic;

        ttsBegin;

        jourTableData = JournalTableData::newTable(jourTable);

        jourTable.JournalId    = jourTableData.nextJournalId();
        jourTable.JournalType  = ProjJournalType::Hour;
    ```

```
    jourTable.JournalNameId = 'Hour';

    jourTableData.initFromJournalName(
        ProjJournalName::find(jourTable.JournalNameId));

    jourStatic = jourTableData.journalStatic();

    jourTransData = jourStatic.newJournalTransData(
        jourTrans,
        jourTableData);

    jourTransData.initFromJournalTable();

    jourTrans.initValue();

    jourTrans.ProjId = '000061';
    jourTrans.initFromProjTable(
        ProjTable::find(jourTrans.ProjId));

    jourTrans.TransDate     = systemDateGet();
    jourTrans.ProjTransDate = jourTrans.TransDate;

    jourTrans.CategoryId = 'Car Audio';
    jourTrans.setHourCostPrice();
    jourTrans.setHourSalesPrice();
    jourTrans.TaxItemGroupId =
        ProjCategory::find(jourTrans.CategoryId).TaxItemGroupId;

    jourTrans.Worker =
        HcmWorker::findByPersonnelNumber('000062').RecId;
    jourTrans.Txt = 'Car audio installtion';
    jourTrans.Qty = 8;

    jourTransData.create();

    jourTable.insert();

    ttsCommit;

    info(strFmt(
        "Journal '%1' has been created", jourTable.JournalId));
}
```

2. Run the job and check the results by navigating to **Project management and accounting | Journals | Hour**, as shown in the following screenshot:

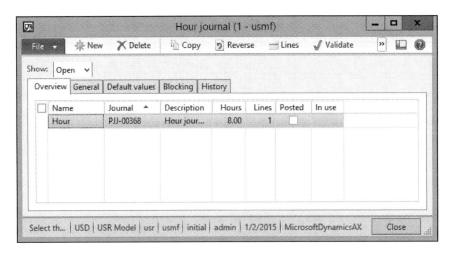

3. Click on the **Lines** button to open journal lines and notice the newly created record, as shown here:

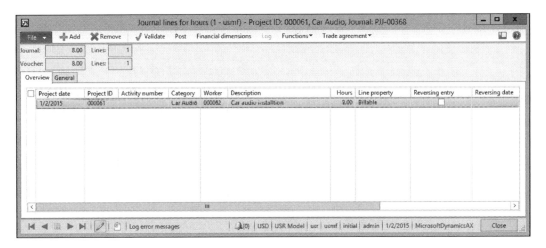

How it works...

In this recipe, we create a new job where we store all the code. In the job, we use the `ProjJournalTableData` and `ProjJournalTransData` classes in a way similar to how we used the `LedgerJournalTableData` and `LedgerJournalTransData` classes in the *Creating a general journal* recipe. Here, we create a new `jourTableData` object used for journal record handling. Then, we initialize the journal number, type, and name of the actual journal record. Next, we call `initFromJournalName()` on the `jourTableData` object in order to initialize some additional values from the journal name settings. At this stage, the journal header record is ready.

Next, we create a journal line. Here, we first create a new `jourTransData` object to handle the journal line. Then, we call its `initFromJournalTable()` method in order to initialize the additional values from the journal header. Finally, we set some of the journal line values, such as transaction and project date, category, and worker number.

Lastly, we call the `create()` method on `jourTransData` and the `insert()` method on `jourTable` to create the journal line and the header records, respectively. The journal is now ready to be reviewed.

There's more...

For further journal processing, we can use the class named `ProjJournalCheckPost` to post project journals from the code. In the AOT, let's create another job named `ProjJournalPost` with the following code snippet (replace `PJJ-00368` with your journal number):

```
static void ProjJournalPost(Args _args)
{
    ProjJournalCheckPost jourPost;

    jourPost = ProjJournalCheckPost::newJournalCheckPost(
        true,
        true,
        JournalCheckPostType::Post,
        tableNum(ProjJournalTable),
        'PJJ-00368');

    jourPost.run();
}
```

Processing Business Tasks

Run the job to post the journal. The **Infolog** window should display the confirmation, as shown here:

In the newly created job, we use the `newJournalCheckPost()` constructor of the `ProjJournalCheckPost` class. The constructor accepts the following arguments:

- A `boolean` value that specifies whether to block the journal while it is being posted. It is good practice to set the value to `true`, as this ensures that no one modifies this journal while it is being posted.
- A `boolean` value that specifies whether to display results in the **Infolog** window.
- The type of action being performed. The possible values for this class are either `Post` or `Check`. The latter one only validates the journal, and the first one validates and posts the journal at once.
- The table ID of the journal being posted.
- The journal number to be posted.

Finally, we call the `run()` method, which posts the journal.

Creating and posting a ledger voucher

In Dynamics AX, all the financial transactions, regardless of where they originated, end up in the **General ledger** module. When it comes to customized functionality, developers should use the Dynamics AX APIs to create the required system entries. No transactions can be created directly in the tables, as this may affect the accuracy of financial data.

In order to ensure data consistency, the system provides numerous APIs for developers to use. One of them is ledger voucher processing. This allows you to post a financial voucher in the **General ledger** module. Vouchers in Dynamics AX are balanced financial entries that represent a single operation. They include two or more ledger transactions. The ledger voucher API ensures that all the required criteria, such as voucher numbers, financial periods, ledger accounts, financial dimensions, balances, and others, are valid.

In this recipe, we will demonstrate how a ledger voucher can be created and posted from the code. We will create a single voucher with two balancing transactions.

How to do it...

Carry out the following steps in order to complete this recipe:

1. Double-check whether the `getLedgerDimension()` method exists in the `DimensionAttributeValueCombination` table. If not, create it as described in the first recipe of this chapter.

2. In the AOT, create a new job named `LedgerVoucherPost` with the following code snippet (replace the values in the code to match your data):

```
static void LedgerVoucherPost(Args _args)
{
    LedgerVoucher              voucher;
    LedgerVoucherObject        voucherObj;
    LedgerVoucherTransObject   voucherTrObj1;
    LedgerVoucherTransObject   voucherTrObj2;
    DimensionDynamicAccount    ledgerDim;
    DimensionDynamicAccount    offsetLedgerDim;
    CurrencyExchangeHelper     currencyExchHelper;
    CompanyInfo                companyInfo;

    ledgerDim =
        DimensionAttributeValueCombination::getLedgerDimension(
            '110180',
            ['BusinessUnit', 'Department'],
            ['005', '024']);

    offsetLedgerDim =
        DimensionAttributeValueCombination::getLedgerDimension(
            '170150',
            ['BusinessUnit', 'Department'],
            ['005', '024']);

    voucher = LedgerVoucher::newLedgerPost(
        DetailSummary::Detail,
        SysModule::Ledger,
        '');

    voucherObj = LedgerVoucherObject::newVoucher('TEST00001');

    companyInfo = CompanyInfo::findDataArea(curext());
```

Processing Business Tasks

```
            currencyExchHelper = CurrencyExchangeHelper::newExchangeDate(
                Ledger::primaryLedger(companyInfo.RecId),
                voucherObj.parmAccountingDate());

            voucher.addVoucher(voucherObj);

            voucherTrObj1 =
                LedgerVoucherTransObject::newTransactionAmountDefault(
                    voucherObj,
                    LedgerPostingType::LedgerJournal,
                    ledgerDim,
                    'USD',
                    1000,
                    currencyExchHelper);

            voucherTrObj2 =
                LedgerVoucherTransObject::newTransactionAmountDefault(
                    voucherObj,
                    LedgerPostingType::LedgerJournal,
                    offsetLedgerDim,
                    'USD',
                    -1000,
                    currencyExchHelper);

            voucher.addTrans(voucherTrObj1);
            voucher.addTrans(voucherTrObj2);

            voucher.end();

            info(strFmt(
                "Voucher '%1' has been posted", voucher.lastVoucher()));
        }
```

3. Run the `LedgerVoucherPost` job to create a new ledger voucher.
4. To check what has been posted, navigate to **General Ledger | Inquiries | Voucher transactions** and type in the voucher number `TEST00001` used in the code, as shown in the following screenshot:

Chapter 5

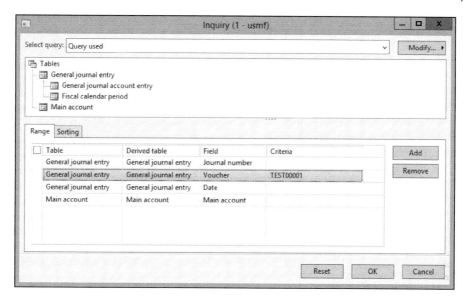

5. Click on **OK** to display the posted voucher:

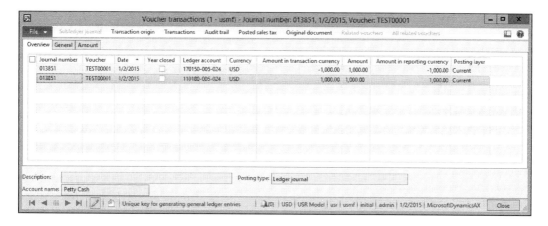

How it works...

In the newly created job, we first define the ledger accounts which will be used for postings. For demonstration purposes, here we have specified it in the code. We use the previously created `getLedgerDimension()` method to simulate the ledger account entry.

Processing Business Tasks

Next, we create a new `LedgerVoucher` object, which represents a collection of vouchers. Here, we call the `newLedgerPost()` constructor of the `LedgerVoucher` class. The `newLedgerPost()` constructor accepts three mandatory and four optional arguments, which are listed as follows:

- Post detailed or summarized ledger transactions.
- The system module from which the transactions originate.
- A number sequence code, which is used to generate the voucher number. In this example, we will set the voucher number manually. So, this argument can be left empty.
- The transaction type that will appear in the transaction log.
- The transaction text.
- A `boolean` value, which specifies whether this voucher should meet the approval requirements.
- A `boolean` value, defining whether the voucher can be posted without a posting type when posting inventory transactions.

Then, we create a new `LedgerVoucherObject` object, which represents a single voucher. We call the `newVoucher()` constructor of the `LedgerVoucherObject` class. It accepts only one mandatory and a number of optional parameters, which are listed as follows:

- The voucher number; normally, this should be generated using a number sequence, but in this example, we set it manually
- The transaction date; the default is the session date
- The system module from which the transactions originate
- The ledger transaction type
- A flag defining whether this is a correcting voucher; the default is `No`
- The posting layer; the default is `Current`
- The document number
- The document date
- The acknowledgement date

The `addVoucher()` method of the `LedgerVoucher` class adds the created voucher object to the voucher

Once the voucher is ready, we create two voucher transactions. The transactions are handled by the `LedgerVoucherTransObject` class. They are created by calling its `newTransactionAmountDefault()` constructor with the following mandatory arguments:

- The ledger voucher object
- The ledger posting type

- The ledger account number
- The currency code
- The amount in the currency
- The currency exchange rate helper

Notice the last argument, which is a currency exchange rate helper, used when operating in currencies other that the main company currency.

We add the created transaction objects to the voucher by calling its `addTrans()` method. At this stage, everything is ready for posting.

Finally, we call the `end()` method on the `LedgerVoucher` object, which posts the transactions to the general ledger.

See also

- The *Using a segmented entry control* recipe

Changing an automatic transaction text

Every financial transaction in Dynamics AX can (and normally should) have a descriptive text. Some texts are entered by users and some can be generated by the system. The latter option holds true for automatically generated transactions where the user cannot interact with the process.

Dynamics AX provides a way to define texts for automatically generated transactions. The setup can be found by navigating to **Organizations administration | Setup | Default descriptions**. Here, the user can create custom transaction texts for various automatic transaction types and languages. The text itself can have a number of placeholders—digits with a percent sign in front of them, which are replaced with actual values during the process. The placeholders can be from `%1` to `%6`, and they can be substituted with the following values:

- `%1`: This is the transaction date
- `%2`: This value depends on a context
- `%3`: This is the voucher number
- `%4` to `%6`: These are custom values and depends on the module

In this recipe, we will demonstrate how the existing automatic transaction text functionality can be modified and extended. One of the places where it is used is the automatic creation of vendor payment journal lines during the vendor payment proposal process. We will modify the system so that the texts of the automatically generated vendor payment lines include the vendor names.

Processing Business Tasks

Getting ready

First, we need to make sure that the vendor payment transaction text is set up properly. Navigate to **Organization administration** | **Setup** | **Default descriptions**, find or create a line with **Description** set to `Vendor - payment, vendor` and change the text to `Vendor payment %2 to %5`, as shown in the following screenshot:

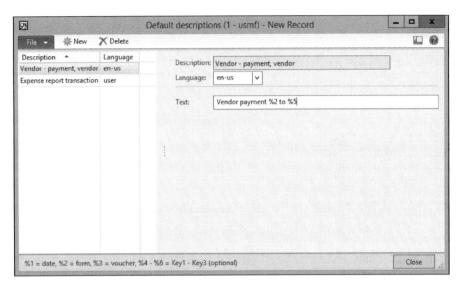

How to do it...

Carry out the following steps in order to complete this recipe:

1. In the AOT, find the `CustVendPaymProposalTransferToJournal` class and add the following lines of code at the bottom of the `getTransactionText()` method, right before its `return` statement:

   ```
   transactionTxt.setKey2(
       _custVendPaymProposalLine.custVendTable().name());
   ```

2. Navigate to **Accounts payable** | **Journals** | **Payments** | **Payment journal** and create a new journal. Click on **Lines**, and then run **Create payment proposal**, which is located in the toolbar under **Payment proposal**. Define the desired criteria or leave the default values and click on **OK**. In the newly opened **Vendor payment proposal** form, click on the **Transfer** button to transfer all the proposed lines to the journal. Notice that the transaction text in each journal line includes the vendor name, as shown in the following screenshot:

Chapter 5

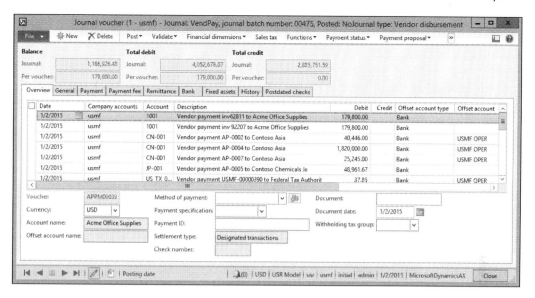

How it works...

The vendor payment proposal uses the `CustVendPaymProposalTransferToJournal` class to create the lines. The same class contains a method named `getTransactionText()`, which is responsible for formatting the text for each line. If we look inside this method, we can see that the `TransactionTxt` class is used for this purpose. This class contains the following methods, which are used to substitute the placeholders from `%1` to `%6` in the defined text:

- `%1: setDate()`
- `%2: setFormLetter()`
- `%3: setVoucher()`
- `%4: setKey1()`
- `%5: setKey2()`
- `%6: setKey3()`

By taking a look at the code, you can see that only the `%4` placeholder is used. So, you can fill the `%5` placeholder with the vendor name. To achieve this, you need to call the `setKey2()` method with the vendor name as an argument. In this way, every journal line created by the automatic vendor payment proposal will contain a vendor name in its description.

There's more...

If more than three custom placeholders are required, it is always possible to add an additional placeholder by creating a new `setKey()` method in the `TransactionTxt` class. For example, if we want to add a %7 placeholder, we have to do the following:

1. Add the following line of code to the class declaration of the `TransactionTxt` class:

    ```
    str 20 key4;
    ```

2. Create a new method with the following code snippet:

    ```
    void setKey4(str 20 _key4)
    {
        key4 = _key4;
    }
    ```

3. Change the last line of the `txt()` method to the following:

    ```
    return strFmt(
        txt,
        date2StrUsr(transDate, DateFlags::FormatAll),
        formLetterNum,
        voucherNum,
        key1,
        key2,
        key3,
        key4);
    ```

4. Now, we can use the `setKey4()` method to substitute the %7 placeholder.

Note that although more placeholders can be added, you should take into consideration the fact that the transaction text field has a finite number of characters and excessive text will simply be truncated.

Creating a purchase order

Purchase orders are used throughout the purchasing process to hold information about the goods or services that a company buys from its suppliers. Normally, purchase orders are created from the user interface, but in automated processes, purchase orders can be also created from the code.

In this recipe, you will learn how to create a purchase order from the code. We will use one of the standard methods provided by the application.

How to do it...

Carry out the following steps in order to complete this recipe:

1. In the AOT, create a new job named `PurchOrderCreate` with the following code snippet: (replace the values in the code to match your data)

    ```
    static void PurchOrderCreate(Args _args)
    {
        NumberSeq  numberSeq;
        PurchTable purchTable;
        PurchLine  purchLine;

        ttsBegin;

        numberSeq = NumberSeq::newGetNum(
            PurchParameters::numRefPurchId());
        numberSeq.used();

        purchTable.PurchId = numberSeq.num();
        purchTable.initValue();
        purchTable.initFromVendTable(VendTable::find('1001'));

        if (!purchTable.validateWrite())
        {
            throw Exception::Error;
        }

        purchTable.insert();

        purchLine.PurchId = purchTable.PurchId;
        purchLine.ItemId  = 'C0004';

        purchLine.createLine(true, true, true, true, true, true);

        ttsCommit;

        info(strFmt(
            "Purchase order '%1' has been created",
            purchTable.PurchId));
    }
    ```

2. Run the job to create a new purchase order.

Processing Business Tasks

3. Navigate to **Procurement and sourcing | Common | Purchase orders | All purchase orders** in order to view the purchase order created, as shown in the following screenshot:

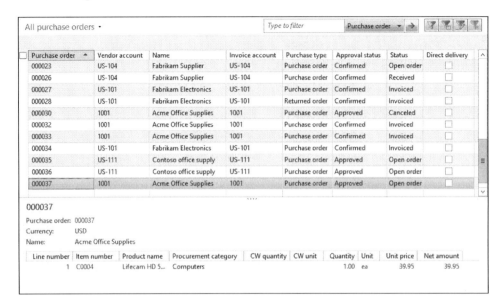

How it works...

In this recipe, we create a new job named `PurchOrderCreate`, which holds all the code. Here, we start by getting the next purchase order number with the help of the `NumberSeq` class. We also call the `initValue()` and `initFromVendTable()` methods to initialize various `purchTable` buffer fields. We insert the purchase order record into the table only if the validation in the `validateWrite()` method is successful.

Next, we create purchase order lines. Here, we assign the previously used purchase order number and then set the item number.

Finally, we call the `createLine()` method of the `PurchLine` table to create a new line. This is a very useful method, allowing you to quickly create purchase order lines. This method accepts a number of optional `boolean` arguments, which are listed as follows:

- Perform data validations; the default is `false`
- Initialize the line record from the `PurchTable` table; the default is `false`
- Initialize the line record from the `InventTable` table; the default is `false`

- Calculate inventory quantity; the default is `false`
- Add miscellaneous charges; the default is `true`
- Use trade agreements to calculate the item price; the default is `false`
- Do not copy the inventory site and warehouse from the purchase order header; the default is `false`
- Use purchase agreements to get the item price; the default is `false`

Posting a purchase order

In Dynamics AX, the purchase order goes through a number of statuses in order to reflect its current position within the purchasing process. The status can be updated either manually by using the user interface or programmatically from the code.

In this recipe, we will demonstrate how a purchase order status can be updated from the code. We will confirm the purchase order created in the previous recipe and print the relevant document on the screen.

How to do it...

Carry out the following steps in order to complete this recipe:

1. In the AOT, create a new job named `PurchOrderPostConfirm` with the following code snippet (replace `000037` with your number):

    ```
    static void PurchOrderPostConfirm(Args _args)
    {
        PurchFormLetter purchFormLetter;
        PurchTable      purchTable;

        purchTable = PurchTable::find('000037');

        purchFormLetter = PurchFormLetter::construct(
            DocumentStatus::PurchaseOrder);

        purchFormLetter.update(
            purchTable,
            '',
            DateTimeUtil::date(DateTimeUtil::utcNow()),
            PurchUpdate::All,
            AccountOrder::None,
            NoYes::No,
            NoYes::Yes);
    }
    ```

2. Run the job to post the specified purchase order and display the **Purchase order** document, as shown in the following screenshot:

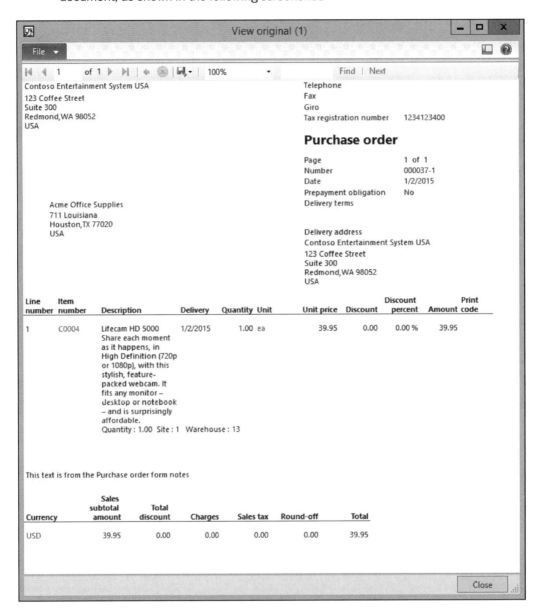

3. Navigate to **Procurement and sourcing** | **Common** | **Purchase orders** | **All purchase orders** and note that the **Approval status** column of the posted order is now different, as shown here:

Chapter 5

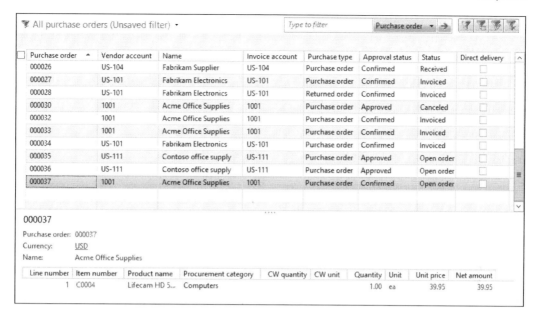

How it works...

In this recipe, we create a new job named `PurchOrderPostConfirm`, which holds all the code.

First, we find a purchase order, which we are going to update. In this recipe, we use the purchase order created in the previous recipe.

Next, we create a new `PurchFormLetter` object using its `construct()` constructor. The constructor accepts an argument of the `DocumentStatus` type, which defines the type of posting to be done. Here, we use `DocumentStatus::PurchaseOrder` as a value, as we want to confirm the purchase order.

The last thing to do is to call the `update()` method of the `PurchFormLetter` object, which does the actual posting. It accepts a number of arguments, which are listed as follows:

- The purchase order header record; in this case, it is the `PurchTable` table.
- An external document number; it's not used in this demonstration, as it is not required when posting a purchase order confirmation.
- The transaction date; the default date is the system's date.
- The quantity to be posted; the default is `PurchUpdate::All`. Other options, such as `PurchUpdate::PackingSlip` or `PurchUpdate::ReceiveNow`, are not relevant when confirming a purchase order.

Processing Business Tasks

- The order summary update; this argument is not used at all. The default is `AccountOrder::None`.
- A `boolean` value defining whether a preview or the actual posting should be done.
- A `boolean` value defining whether the document should be printed.
- A `boolean` value specifying whether printing management should be used. The default value is `false`.
- A `boolean` value defining whether to keep the remaining purchase quantity when posting credit notes; otherwise, it is set to zero.
- A container holding `TmpFrmVirtual` records. This argument is optional and is used only when posting purchase invoices.

There's more...

The same technique can be used to post a purchase packing slip or invoice. Let's modify the previous example so the purchase gets invoiced. Locate the following line of code:

```
purchFormLetter = PurchFormLetter::construct(
    DocumentStatus::PurchaseOrder);
```

Replace the preceding line of code with the following line of code:

```
purchFormLetter = PurchFormLetter::construct(
    DocumentStatus::Invoice);
```

Then, locate another code snippet:

```
purchFormLetter.update(
    purchTable,
    '',
    DateTimeUtil::date(DateTimeUtil::utcNow()),
    PurchUpdate::All,
    AccountOrder::None,
    NoYes::No,
    NoYes::Yes);
```

Replace the preceding code snippet with the following:

```
purchFormLetter.update(
    purchTable,
    '8001',
    DateTimeUtil::date(DateTimeUtil::utcNow()),
    PurchUpdate::All,
    AccountOrder::None,
    NoYes::No,
    NoYes::Yes);
```

Now, when you run the job, the purchase order will be updated to an invoice, and the invoice document will be displayed on the screen, as shown in the following screenshot:

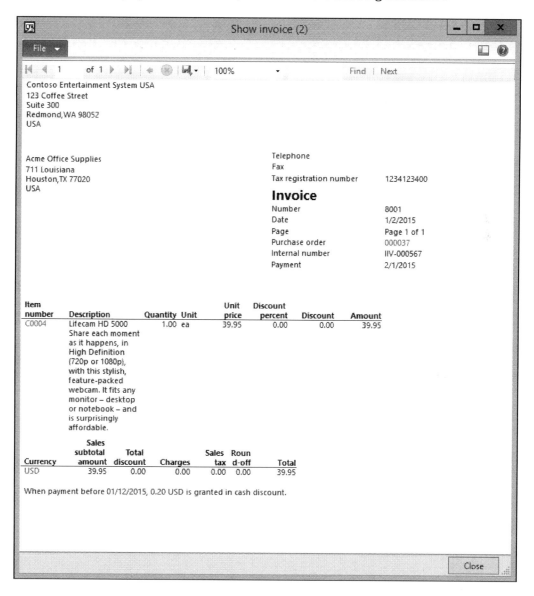

Processing Business Tasks

To check the updated purchase order, navigate to **Procurement and sourcing | Common | Purchase orders | All purchase orders**; notice that its **Status** column is different now, as shown here:

Purchase order	Vendor account	Name	Invoice account	Purchase type	Approval status	Status	Direct delivery
000026	US-104	Fabrikam Supplier	US-104	Purchase order	Confirmed	Received	
000027	US-101	Fabrikam Electronics	US-101	Purchase order	Confirmed	Invoiced	
000028	US-101	Fabrikam Electronics	US-101	Returned order	Confirmed	Invoiced	
000030	1001	Acme Office Supplies	1001	Purchase order	Approved	Canceled	
000032	1001	Acme Office Supplies	1001	Purchase order	Confirmed	Invoiced	
000033	1001	Acme Office Supplies	1001	Purchase order	Confirmed	Invoiced	
000034	US-101	Fabrikam Electronics	US-101	Purchase order	Confirmed	Invoiced	
000035	US-111	Contoso office supply	US-111	Purchase order	Approved	Open order	
000036	US-111	Contoso office supply	US-111	Purchase order	Approved	Open order	
000037	1001	Acme Office Supplies	1001	Purchase order	Confirmed	Invoiced	

000037

Purchase order: 000037
Currency: USD
Name: Acme Office Supplies

Line number	Item number	Product name	Procurement category	CW quantity	CW unit	Quantity	Unit	Unit price	Net amount
1	C0004	Lifecam HD 5...	Computers			1.00	ea	39.95	39.95

Creating a sales order

Sales orders are used throughout the sales process to hold information about the goods or services that a company sells to its customers. Normally, sales orders are created from the user interface, but in automated processes, sales orders can be also created from the code.

In this recipe, you will learn how to create a sales order from the code. We will use a standard method provided by the application.

How to do it...

Carry out the following steps in order to complete this recipe:

1. In the AOT, create a new job named `SalesOrderCreate` with the following code snippet (replace the values in the code to match your data):

    ```
    static void SalesOrderCreate(Args _args)
    {
        NumberSeq   numberSeq;
        SalesTable  salesTable;
    ```

```
    SalesLine    salesLine;

    ttsBegin;

    numberSeq = NumberSeq::newGetNum(
        SalesParameters::numRefSalesId());
    numberSeq.used();

    salesTable.SalesId = numberSeq.num();
    salesTable.initValue();
    salesTable.CustAccount = 'US-017';
    salesTable.initFromCustTable();

    if (!salesTable.validateWrite())
    {
        throw Exception::Error;
    }

    salesTable.insert();

    salesLine.SalesId = salesTable.SalesId;
    salesLine.ItemId  = 'D0001';

    salesLine.createLine(true, true, true, true, true, true);

    ttsCommit;

    info(strFmt(
        "Sales order '%1' has been created", salesTable.SalesId));
}
```

2. Run the job to create a new sales order.

Processing Business Tasks

3. Navigate to **Sales and marketing | Common | Sales orders | All sales orders** in order to view the newly created sales order, as shown in the following screenshot:

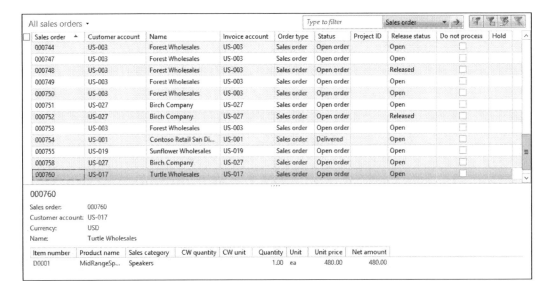

How it works...

In this recipe, we create a new job named `SalesOrderCreate`, which holds all the code. The job starts by generating the next sales order number with the help of the `NumberSeq` class. We also call the `initValue()` and `initFromCustTable()` methods to initialize various `salesTable` buffer fields. Notice that for `initFromCustTable()`, we first set the customer account and call the method afterwards, instead of passing the customer record as an argument. We insert the sales order record into the table only if the validation in the `validateWrite()` method is successful.

Next, we create sales order lines. Here, we assign the previously created sales order number and set the item number.

Finally, we call the `createLine()` method of the `SalesLine` table to create a new line. This is a very useful method, which allows you to quickly create sales order lines. The method accepts a number of optional `boolean` arguments. The following list explains most of them:

- Perform data validations before saving; the default is `false`
- Initialize the line record from the `SalesTable` table; the default is `false`
- Initialize the line record from the `InventTable` table; the default is `false`
- Calculate inventory quantity; the default is `false`
- Add miscellaneous charges; the default is `true`

- Use trade agreements to calculate the item price; the default is `false`
- Reserve the item; the default is `false`
- Ignore customer credit limit; the default is `false`

Posting a sales order

In Dynamics AX, a sales order goes through a number of statuses in order to reflect its current position within the sales process. The status can be updated either manually using the user interface or programmatically from the code.

In this recipe, we will demonstrate how a sales order status can be updated from the code. We will register a packing slip for the sales order created in the previous recipe and print the relevant document on the screen.

How to do it...

Carry out the following steps in order to complete this recipe:

1. In the AOT, create a new job named `SalesOrderPostPackingSlip` with the following code snippet (replace `000760` with your number):

```
static void SalesOrderPostPackingSlip(Args _args)
{
    SalesFormLetter salesFormLetter;
    salesTable      salesTable;

    salesTable = SalesTable::find('000760');

    salesFormLetter = SalesFormLetter::construct(
        DocumentStatus::PackingSlip);

    salesFormLetter.update(
        salesTable,
        DateTimeUtil::date(DateTimeUtil::utcNow()),
        SalesUpdate::All,
        AccountOrder::None,
        NoYes::No,
        NoYes::Yes);
}
```

Processing Business Tasks

2. Run the job to post the specified sales order and display the **Packing slip** document on the screen, as shown here:

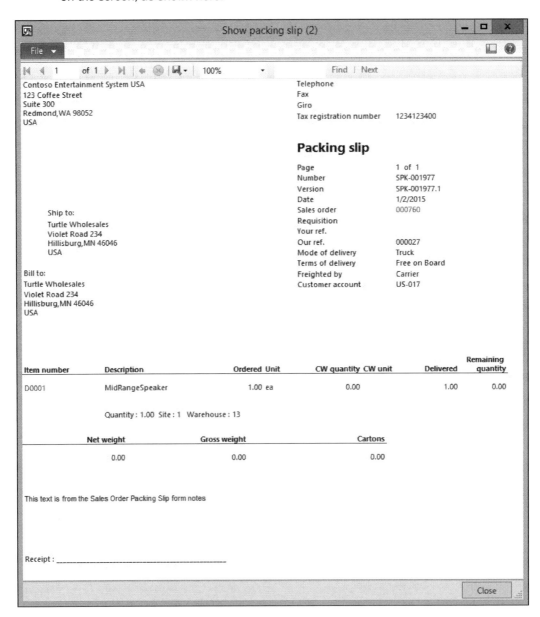

Chapter 5

3. Navigate to **Sales and marketing | Common | Sales orders | All sales orders** and notice the updated sales order status, as shown in the following screenshot:

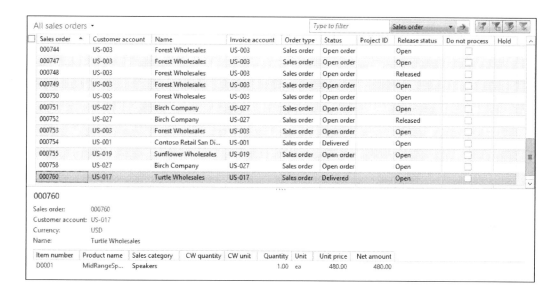

How it works...

In this recipe, we create a new job named `SalesOrderPostPackingSlip`, which holds all the code.

First, we find a sales order, which we are going to update. In this recipe, we use the sales order created in the previous recipe.

Next, we create a new `SalesFormLetter` object using its `construct()` constructor. The constructor accepts an argument of the `DocumentStatus` type, which defines the type of posting to be done. Here, we use `DocumentStatus::PackingSlip` as a value, as we want to register a packing slip.

Finally, we call the `update()` method of `SalesFormLetter`, which does the actual posting. It accepts a number of arguments, as follows:

- The sales order header record, that is, the `SalesTable` table.
- The transaction date; the default is the system date.
- The quantity to be posted; the default is `SalesUpdate::All`.

Processing Business Tasks

- The order summary update; this argument is not used at all. The default is `AccountOrder::None`.
- A `boolean` value defining whether a preview or the actual posting should be done.
- A `boolean` value defining whether the document should be printed.
- A `boolean` value specifying whether printing management should be used; the default is `false`.
- A `boolean` value defining whether to keep the remaining sales quantity when posting credit notes; otherwise, it is set to zero.
- A container holding `TmpFrmVirtual` records; this argument is optional and is used only when posting sales invoices.

There's more...

The `SalesFormLetter` class can also be used to do other types of posting, such as sales order confirmation, picking lists, or invoices. Let's modify the previous example so we could invoice the previously used sales order. Locate the following line of code:

```
salesFormLetter = SalesFormLetter::construct(
    DocumentStatus::PackingSlip);
```

Replace the preceding line of code with the following line of code:

```
salesFormLetter = SalesFormLetter::construct(
    DocumentStatus::Invoice);
```

Now when you run the job, the sales order will be updated to an invoice and the invoice document will be displayed on the screen:

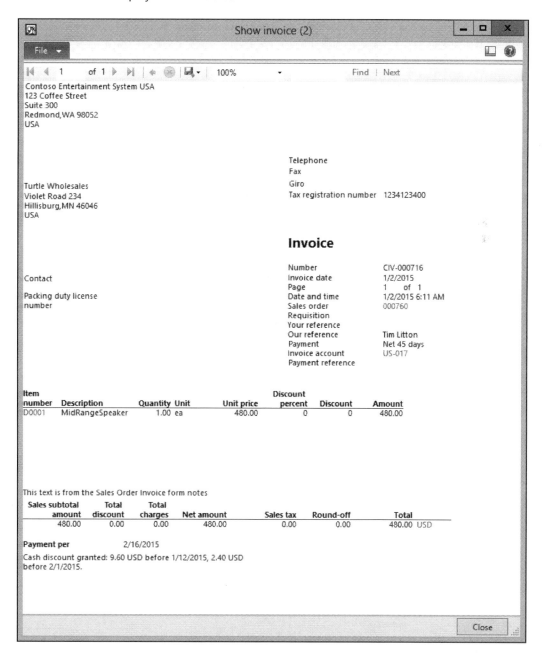

Processing Business Tasks

To check the updated sales order, navigate to **Sales and marketing | Common | Sales orders | All sales orders**; notice that the **Status** column has now changed, as shown here:

Sales order	Customer account	Name	Invoice account	Order type	Status	Project ID	Release status	Do not process	Hold
000744	US-003	Forest Wholesales	US-003	Sales order	Open order		Open		
000747	US-003	Forest Wholesales	US-003	Sales order	Open order		Open		
000748	US-003	Forest Wholesales	US-003	Sales order	Open order		Released		
000749	US-003	Forest Wholesales	US-003	Sales order	Open order		Open		
000750	US-003	Forest Wholesales	US-003	Sales order	Open order		Open		
000751	US-027	Birch Company	US-027	Sales order	Open order		Open		
000752	US-027	Birch Company	US-027	Sales order	Open order		Released		
000753	US-003	Forest Wholesales	US-003	Sales order	Open order		Open		
000754	US-001	Contoso Retail San Di...	US-001	Sales order	Delivered		Open		
000755	US-019	Sunflower Wholesales	US-019	Sales order	Open order		Open		
000758	US-027	Birch Company	US-027	Sales order	Open order		Open		
000760	US-017	Turtle Wholesales	US-017	Sales order	Invoiced		Open		

000760
Sales order: 000760
Customer account: US-017
Currency: USD
Name: Turtle Wholesales

Item number	Product name	Sales category	CW quantity	CW unit	Quantity	Unit	Unit price	Net amount
D0001	MidRangeSp...	Speakers			1.00	ea	480.00	480.00

Creating an electronic payment format

Electronic payments, in general, can save time and reduce paperwork when making or receiving payments within a company. Dynamics AX provides a number of standard out-of-the-box electronic payment formats and also provides an easy way of customizing the existing payment formats or creating new ones.

In this recipe, you will learn how to create a new custom electronic payment format. To demonstrate the principle, we will only output some basic information, and we will concentrate on the approach itself.

How to do it...

Carry out the following steps in order to complete this recipe:

1. In the AOT, create a new class named `VendOutPaymRecord_Test` with the following code snippet:

    ```
    class VendOutPaymRecord_Test extends VendOutPaymRecord
    {
    }
    ```

```
void output()
{
    str            outRecord;
    Name           companyName;
    BankAccount    bankAccount;

    outRecord = strRep(' ', 50);

    companyName = subStr(
        custVendPaym.recieversCompanyName(), 1, 40);
    bankAccount = subStr(
        custVendPaym.recieversBankAccount(), 1, 8);

    outRecord = strPoke(outRecord, companyName, 1);
    outRecord = strPoke(outRecord, bankAccount, 43);

    file.write(outRecord);
}
```

2. Create another class named VendOutPaym_Test with the following code snippet:

```
class VendOutPaym_Test extends VendOutPaym
{
}

PaymInterfaceName interfaceName()
{
    return "Test payment format";
}

ClassId custVendOutPaymRecordRootClassId()
{
    return classNum(VendOutPaymRecord_Test);
}

protected Object dialog()
{
    DialogRunbase dialog;

    dialog = super();

    this.dialogAddFileName(dialog);
```

```
            return dialog;
    }

    boolean validate(Object _calledFrom = null)
    {
        return true;
    }

    void open()
    {
        #LocalCodePage

        file = CustVendOutPaym::newFile(filename, #cp_1252);

        if (!file || file.status() != IO_Status::Ok)
        {
            throw error(
                strFmt("File %1 could not be opened.", filename));
        }

        file.outFieldDelimiter('');
        file.outRecordDelimiter('\r\n');

        file.write('Starting file:');
    }

    void close()
    {
        file.write('Closing file');
    }
```

3. Navigate to **Accounts payable | Setup | Payment | Methods of payment** and create a new record, as follows:

Chapter 5

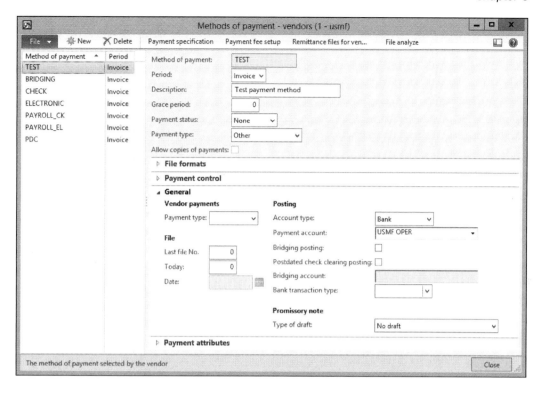

4. Open the **File formats** tab page, click on the **Setup** button, and move your newly created **Test payment format** file format from the pane on the right-hand side to the pane on the left-hand side:

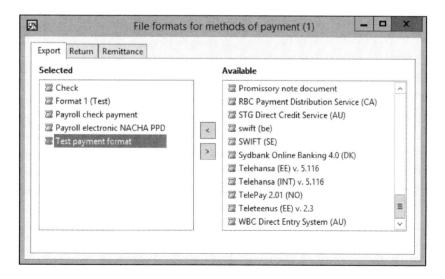

5. Then, go back to the **Methods of payment** form and select **Test payment format** in the **Export format** field as follows:

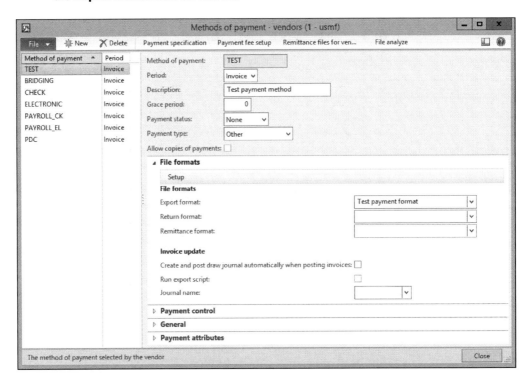

6. Close the **Methods of payment** form. Navigate to **Accounts payable | Journals | Payments | Payment journal** and create a new journal, as shown here:

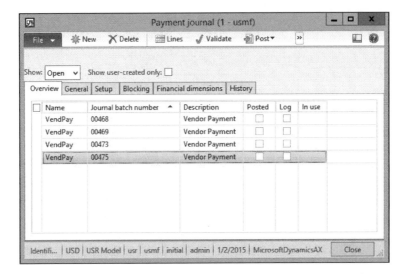

Chapter 5

7. Click on the **Lines** button to open the journal lines. Create a new line and make sure you set **Method of payment** to Test:

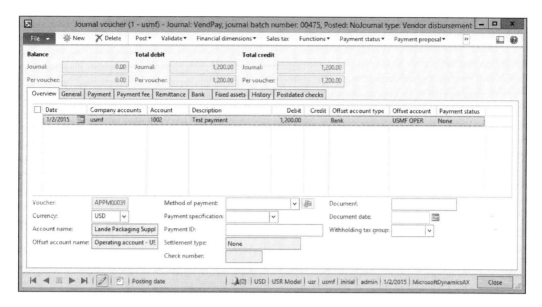

8. Next, navigate to **Functions | Generate payments**. Fill in the dialog fields as displayed in the following screenshot:

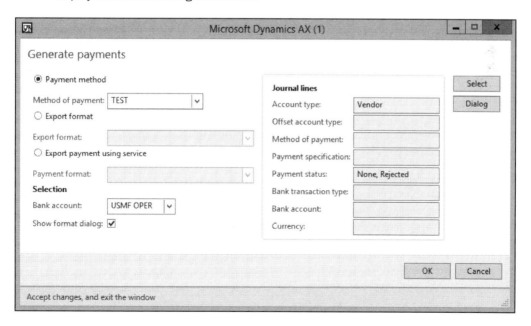

Processing Business Tasks

9. Click on **OK** and select the exported file's name:

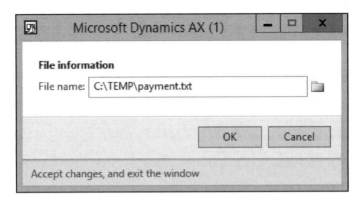

10. Click on **OK** to complete the process; notice that the journal line's **Payment status** changed from **None** to **Sent**, which means that the payment file was generated successfully, as shown in the following screenshot:

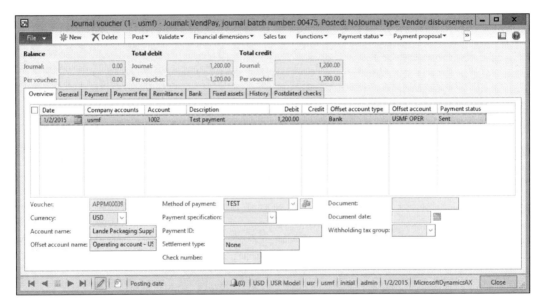

11. Open the created file with any text editor (for example, Notepad) to check its contents, as shown here:

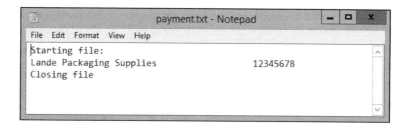

How it works...

In this recipe, we create two new classes, which are normally required for generating custom vendor payments. Electronic payments are presented as text files to be sent to the bank. The first class is the `VendOutPaymRecord_Test` class, which is responsible for formatting the payment lines, and the second one is the `VendOutPaym_Test` class, which generates the header and footer sections and creates the payment file itself.

The `VendOutPaymRecord_Test` class extends `VendOutPaymRecord` and inherits all the common functionality. We only need to override its `output()` method to define our own logic in order to format the payment lines. The `output()` method is called once for each payment line.

Inside the `output()` method, we use the `outRecord` variable, which we initially fill in with 50 blank characters using the global `strRep()` function, and then insert all the necessary information into the predefined positions within the variable as per format requirements. Normally, here we should insert all the required information, such as dates, account numbers, amounts, references, and so on. However, to keep this demonstration to a minimum, we only insert the company name and the bank account number.

In the same method, we use another variable named `custVendPaym` of the `CustVendPaym` type, which already holds all the information we need. In this example, to get the company name and the bank account number, we call `recieversCompanyName()` and `recieversBankAccount()`, respectively. We trim the returned values using the global `subStr()` function, and insert them into the first and 43rd positions of the `outRecord` variable using the global `strPoke()` function.

Finally, at the bottom of the `output()` method, we add the formatted text to the end of the payment file.

Another class that we create is `VendOutPaym_Test`. It extends the `VendOutPaym` class and also inherits all the common functionality. We only need to override some of the methods that are specific to our format.

The `interfaceName()` method returns a name of the payment format. Normally, this text is displayed in the user interface when configuring payments.

The `custVendOutPaymRecordRootClassId()` method returns an ID of the class, which generates payment lines. It is used internally to identify which class to use when formatting the lines. In our case, it is `VendOutPaymRecord_Test`.

The `dialog()` method is used only if we need to add something to the user screen when generating payments. Our payment is a text file, so we need to ask a user to specify the filename. We do this by calling the `dialogAddFileName()` method, which is a member method of the parent class. It will automatically add a file selection control and we won't have to worry about things, such as a label or how to get its value from the user input. There are numerous other standard controls, which can be added to the dialog by calling various `dialogAdd...()` methods. Additional controls can also be added here using `addField()` or similar methods of the dialog object directly.

The `validate()` method is one of the methods that has to be implemented in each custom class. Normally, user input validation should go here. Our example does not have any validation, so we simply return true.

In the `open()` method, we initialize the `file` variable for further processing. Here, we use the `newFile()` constructor of the `CustVendOutPaym` class to create a new instance of the variable. After some standard validations, we set the field and the row delimiters by calling the `outFieldDelimiter()` and `outRecordDelimiter()` methods of the `CustVendOutPaym` class respectively. In this example, the values in each line should not be separated by any symbol, so we call the `outFieldDelimiter()` method with an empty string. We call the `outRecordDelimiter()` method with the new line symbol to define that every line ends with a line break. Note that the last line of this method writes a text to the file's header. Here, we place some simple text so that we can recognize it later when viewing the generated file.

The last one is the `close()` method, which is used to perform additional actions before the file is closed. Here, we specify some text to be displayed in the footer of the generated file.

Now, this new payment format is ready for use. After some setup, we can start creating the vendor payment journals with this type of payment. Note the file generated in the previous section of this recipe—we can clearly see which text in the file comes from which part of the code. These parts should be replaced with your own code to build custom electronic payment formats for Dynamics AX.

6
Integration with Microsoft Office

In this chapter, we will cover the following recipes:

- Creating an Excel file
- Reading an Excel file
- Creating a Word document from a template
- Creating a Word document with repeating elements
- Creating a Microsoft Project file
- Sending an e-mail using Outlook

Introduction

In most of the companies where Dynamics AX is implemented, people use Microsoft Office too. Dynamics AX maintains a very close relationship with Microsoft Office as it has a similar navigation, look and feel, out-of-the-box integration, and so on.

In this chapter, we will pay special attention to Microsoft Office applications, such as Excel, Word, Project, and Outlook. You will learn how to create and read various Office documents that can be used to export/import business data for further distribution or analysis. We will also see how personalized documents can be created within Dynamics AX from predefined templates.

Integration with Microsoft Office

Creating an Excel file

The Microsoft Office Excel format is one of the formats that has been supported by Dynamics AX right from its early versions. Since Dynamics AX 2009, almost every form has the Export to Excel function, which quickly allows you to load data on the screen into Excel for further analysis with powerful Excel tools. In Dynamics AX 2012, new Microsoft Office add-ins were introduced. They allow you to export data, edit it, and publish it back to Dynamics AX in a user-friendly manner.

If the add-ins have not been installed, you can still create an Excel document from the code. Dynamics AX holds a set of standard application classes prefixed with `SysExcel`. Basically, these classes are COM wrappers for Excel, and they contain additional helper methods to make the developer's tasks easier. The classes can be only used on the client tier and on those machines where Microsoft Excel is present.

In this recipe, we will demonstrate the use of the `SysExcel` classes. We will create a new Excel file from the code and will fill it with a customer list from the system.

How to do it...

Carry out the following steps in order to complete this recipe:

1. In the AOT, create a new job named `CreateExcelFile` with the following code snippet:

```
static void CreateExcelFile(Args _args)
{
    CustTable           custTable;
    SysExcelApplication excel;
    SysExcelWorkbooks   workbooks;
    SysExcelWorkbook    workbook;
    SysExcelWorksheets  worksheets;
    SysExcelWorksheet   worksheet;
    SysExcelCells       cells;
    SysExcelCell        cell;
    int                 row;

    try
    {
        excel = SysExcelApplication::construct();
```

```
            workbooks   = excel.workbooks();
            workbook    = workbooks.add();
            worksheets  = workbook.worksheets();
            worksheet   = worksheets.itemFromNum(1);
            cells       = worksheet.cells();
            cells.range('A:A').numberFormat('@');

            while select custTable
            {
                row++;
                cell = cells.item(row, 1);
                cell.value(custTable.AccountNum);
                cell = cells.item(row, 2);
                cell.value(custTable.name());
            }

            excel.visible(true);
    }
    catch
    {
        if (workbook)
        {
            workbook.close();
        }
        if (excel)
        {
            excel.quit();
        }
    }
}
```

Integration with Microsoft Office

2. Run the job and check the list of customers on the screen, as shown in the following screenshot:

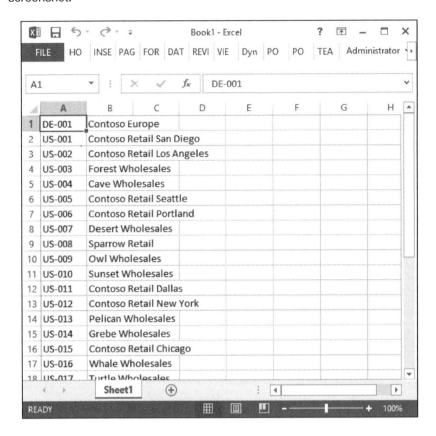

3. Save the list as a file for further use in the next recipe, say, `C:\temp\customers.xlsx`.

4. Close the Excel file once you're done.

How it works...

We start the code by creating the `SysExcelApplication` object, which represents an instance of Excel. Next, we get a collection of Excel documents that are stored in the `SysExcelWorkbooks` class. Initially, the collection is empty, so we have to create a new document by calling the `add()` method of the `SysExcelWorkbooks` class.

Once the document is ready, we get a reference to a collection of sheets within the document, and then we get a reference to the first sheet in the collection. This is where we start adding the data.

Next, we get a reference to a collection of cells within the sheet. We use the `SysExcelCells` class for this. The first column in the sheet will contain a customer's account number, so we have to make sure that it is formatted as text. To do this, we address the first column by using the A:A range and setting its format to @. This will prevent automatic Excel formatting. Sometimes, customer accounts can be expressed as numbers such as 1000 and 1001, and although they are stored in the system as text, Excel will automatically display them as numbers.

To display all the customers, we start looping through the `CustTable` table and fill the customer account number into the first column and the customer name into the second one, for each row. In this way, we populate as many rows as we have customers in the system.

Finally, we set the Excel instance to show up on the screen by calling its `visible()` method. We do this after all the data has been populated, to ensure that the user cannot interfere with the process.

All the code is placed in the `try/catch` block to ensure that in the case of any errors, the created Excel instance and the created document are closed and do not stay in memory.

Reading an Excel file

In Dynamics AX, data can be retrieved from Excel files with the help of the same `SysExcel` classes that we used to create Excel files. These classes provide a simple interface for developers to access and read data in Excel files.

In this recipe, we will demonstrate how to read Excel files using the `SysExcel` classes. We will read the file created in the previous recipe and display its contents in the **Infolog** window.

How to do it...

Carry out the following steps in order to complete this recipe:

1. In the AOT, create a new job named `ReadExcelFile` with the following code snippet (replace the filename with your own):

    ```
    static void ReadExcelFile(Args _args)
    {
        SysExcelApplication  excel;
        SysExcelWorkbooks    workbooks;
        SysExcelWorkbook     workbook;
        SysExcelWorksheets   worksheets;
    ```

Integration with Microsoft Office

```
        SysExcelWorksheet       worksheet;
        SysExcelCells           cells;
        COMVariantType          type;
        int                     row;
        CustAccount             account;
        CustName                name;
        #define.filename(@'C:\temp\customers.xlsx')

        try
        {
            excel = SysExcelApplication::construct();

            workbooks = excel.workbooks();
            workbooks.open(#filename);
            workbook   = workbooks.item(1);
            worksheets = workbook.worksheets();
            worksheet  = worksheets.itemFromNum(1);
            cells      = worksheet.cells();
            type = cells.item(row+1, 1).value().variantType();

            while (type != COMVariantType::VT_EMPTY)
            {
                row++;
                account = cells.item(row, 1).value().bStr();
                name    = cells.item(row, 2).value().bStr();
                info(strFmt('%1 - %2', account, name));
                type = cells.item(row+1, 1).value().variantType();
            }

            excel.quit();

        }
        catch
        {
            if (workbook)
            {
                workbook.close();
            }
            if (excel)
            {
                excel.quit();
            }
        }
    }
```

2. Run the job to display the contents of the file in the **Infolog** window, as shown in the following screenshot:

How it works...

We start the code by creating the `SysExcelApplication` object, which represents an instance of Excel. Next, we get a collection of Excel documents that are stored in the `SysExcelWorkbooks` class. Initially, the collection is empty and we open the previously created file, as the first document in the collection, by calling the `open()` method of the `SysExcelWorkbooks` class. Then, we get a reference to the opened document, which is expressed as the `SysExcelWorkbook` class.

Once the document is ready, we get a reference to a collection of sheets within the document and then we get a reference to the first sheet in the collection. This is where our data is located.

Next, we get a reference to a collection of cells within the sheet. We use the `SysExcelCells` class for this. We also use a `do while` statement to go through all the rows until the first cell of the next row is empty. Inside the statement, we read the customer account number from the first cell and the customer name from the second cell in each row, and output them to the **Infolog** window. The `value()` method of the `SysExcelCells` class returns an object of the `COMVariant` type, and we call its `bStr()` method to retrieve the textual data.

The `COMVariant` class is used to store various types of data when dealing with external objects. The objects could be of any type, such as string, integer, or decimal. In the cases where it is not known what type of data to expect in a cell, we can call the `variantType()` method to check what kind of data is stored in the cell, and depending on the result, we can use `bStr()`, `int()`, `float()`, or other relevant methods of the `COMVariant` class.

Finally, we close the instance of Excel by calling its `quit()` method.

Integration with Microsoft Office

All the code is placed in the `try/catch` block to ensure that in the case of any errors, the created Excel instance and the created document are closed and do not stay in memory.

Creating a Word document from a template

Microsoft Office Word allows presenting Dynamics AX data in a variety of formats. Using Word templates makes things even more easier. The newly introduced Microsoft Office add-ins also provide a user friendly way to do this.

If add-ins have not been installed, Dynamics AX still allows you to create Word documents from the code. Although there are no Dynamics AX application classes for Word as we have for Excel, Word documents can still be created using a very similar approach by calling the `COM` components directly. The only inconvenience is that IntelliSense in the code editor will not provide method suggestions. However, the methods and their parameters can be easily looked up in the online MSDN library.

In this recipe, we will create a simple Word document from a template. We will use the `COM` component model to read a Word template and fill it in with data from the system.

Getting ready

Before we start with the code, we have to create a new Word template. Open Microsoft Word, create a new blank document, and then create the following lines in the document (to create bookmarks, use the **Bookmark** button located in the toolbar under **Insert | Links**):

- Insert the bold text **To:** and then add a bookmark named **Customer**
- Insert the text **Thank you for contacting us.**
- Insert a blank line
- Insert the bold text **Kind Regards,**
- Insert a bookmark named **User**
- Insert a bookmark named **Company**
- Insert the bold text **Company address:**
- Insert a bookmark named **Address**

Save the file as `letter.dotx`.

The document should look identical to what is shown in the following screenshot:

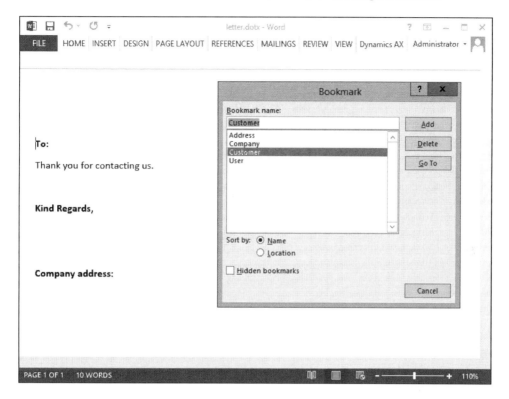

How to do it...

Carry out the following steps in order to complete this recipe:

1. In the AOT, create a new job named CreateWordDocument with the following code snippet (replace US-027 with your own customer account and make sure that the location of the letter.dotx template is correct):

    ```
    static void CreateWordDocument(Args _args)
    {
        Filename    template;
        CustTable   custTable;
        COM         word;
        COM         documents;
        COM         document;
        COM         bookmarks;
        COM         bookmark;
        COM         range;
    ```

```
void processBookmark(str _name, str _value)
{
    if (!bookmarks.Exists(_name))
    {
        return;
    }
    bookmark = bookmarks.Item(_name);
    range    = bookmark.Range();
    range.InsertAfter(_value);
}

#define.Word('Word.Application')
#define.template(@'C:\temp\letter.dotx');

custTable = CustTable::find('US-027');

try
{
    word = new COM(#Word);
}
catch (Exception::Internal)
{
    if (word == null)
    {
        throw error("Microsoft Word is not installed");
    }
}

try
{
    documents = word.Documents();
    document  = documents.Add(#template);
    bookmarks = document.Bookmarks();

    processBookmark('Customer', custTable.name());
    processBookmark('User', HcmWorker::find(
        DirPersonUser::current().worker()).name());
    processBookmark('Company', CompanyInfo::find().Name);
    processBookmark('Address',
        CompanyInfo::find().postalAddress().Address);

    word.Visible(true);
}
catch
```

```
        {
            if (document)
            {
                document.Close(false);
            }
            if (word)
            {
                word.Quit();
            }
        }
    }
```

2. Run the job to see the results. Note the data inserted in the template from the system near each bookmark, as shown in the following screenshot:

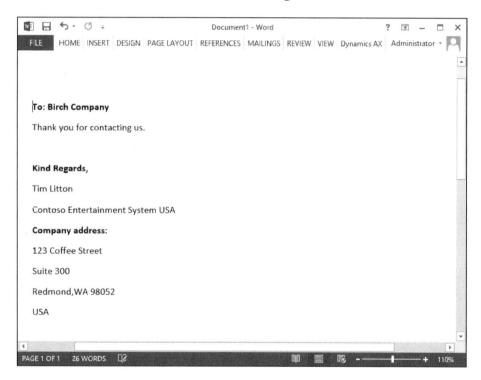

How it works...

In this recipe, in the declaration section we declare a number of COM objects for the Word application itself and its other elements. We also declare a local function to insert a value into the document near a predefined bookmark.

Integration with Microsoft Office

Next, we create a new instance of Word, get a reference to the document collection, and create a new document from the template. Then, we get a reference to the bookmark collection and start inserting the values into the document with the help of the previously defined function.

Finally, once the document is ready, we display it on the screen. Alternatively, we can call the `SaveAs()` method on the `document` object in order to save the document as a file without even showing it on the screen.

All the code is placed in the `try/catch` block to ensure that in the case of any errors, the created Word instance and the created document are closed and do not stay in memory.

Creating a Word document with repeating elements

Microsoft Office Word documents created from the Dynamics AX code, besides simple data output, can have more complex structures, such as a dynamic number of repeating elements. For example, a collection letter document can have a variable list of overdue invoices for different customers.

In this recipe, we will create a Word document with repeating elements. For this demonstration, we will display a list of customers in a dynamically-generated Word table.

Getting ready

For this example, we need to prepare a new Word template and save it as a file named `table.dotx`. The template will contain one bookmark named `Title` at the top and one table beneath, with a single row and two columns, shown as follows:

Chapter 6

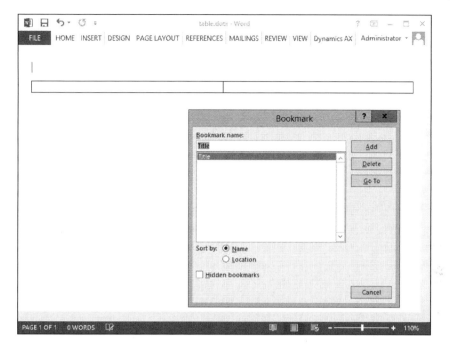

How to do it...

Carry out the following steps in order to complete this recipe:

1. In the AOT, create a new job named `CreateWordTable` with the following code snippet (make sure the location of the template is correct):

```
static void CreateWordTable(Args _args)
{
    CustTable       custTable;
    COM             word;
    COM             documents;
    COM             document;
    COM             bookmarks;
    COM             bookmark;
    COM             tables;
    COM             table;
    COM             rows;
    COM             row;
    COM             cells;
    COM             cell;
    COM             range;
    int             i;
```

```
void processBookmark(str _name, str _value)
{
    if (!bookmarks.exists(_name))
    {
        return;
    }
    bookmark = bookmarks.Item(_name);
    range    = bookmark.Range();
    range.InsertAfter(_value);
}

#define.Word('Word.Application')
#define.template(@'C:\temp\table.dotx');

try
{
    word = new COM(#Word);
}
catch (Exception::Internal)
{
    if (word == null)
    {
        throw error("Microsoft Word is not installed");
    }
}

try
{
    documents = word.Documents();
    document  = documents.Add(#template);
    bookmarks = document.Bookmarks();
    processBookmark('Title', 'Customers');

    tables = document.Tables();
    table  = tables.Item(1);
    rows   = table.Rows();

    while select custTable
    {
        i++;
        row   = rows.Item(i);
        cells = row.Cells();
        cell  = cells.Item(1);
        range = cell.Range();
```

```
                range.InsertAfter(custTable.AccountNum);
                cell   = cells.Item(2);
                range  = cell.Range();
                range.insertAfter(custTable.name());
                row = rows.Add();
            }

            row.Delete();
            word.Visible(true);
        }
        catch
        {
            if (document)
            {
                document.Close(false);
            }
            if (word)
            {
                word.Quit();
            }
        }
    }
```

2. Run the job to generate the document containing a list of customers, as shown here:

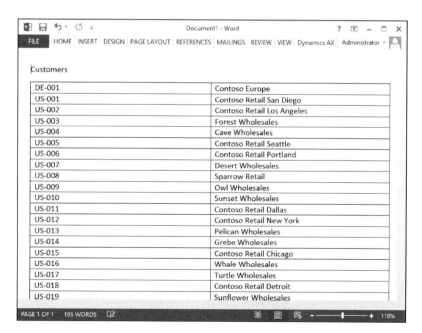

How it works...

In this recipe, we declare a number of COM objects that represent various elements, such as the Word application itself, a document collection, and bookmarks. We also declare the objects and their collections for handling the table, its rows, and cells. We also define a local helper function to insert a value into a document near a predefined bookmark.

After the declaration section, we create a new instance of Word, get a reference to the document collection, and create a new document from the template. Then, we get a reference to the bookmark collection and insert the document title with the help of the previously defined function.

Next, we get a reference to a table collection and then a reference to the first (and only) table in the collection. This is the table that we inserted into the template previously.

Finally, we select all the customers and insert their account numbers and names one by one into the document table.

All the code is placed in the `try/catch` block to ensure that in the case of any errors, the created Word instance and the created document are closed and do not stay in memory.

Creating a Microsoft Project file

Microsoft Project files are one of the many files that can be created in Dynamics AX by using the COM component model. Microsoft Project files can be very useful when it comes to presenting some kind of scheduling information, such as a project plan or production schedule.

In this recipe, we will create a new Microsoft Project file from the code. We will output a project's forecast data as a project plan in Microsoft Project.

Getting ready

For this recipe, we need to set up some data. Navigate to **Project management and accounting | Common | Projects | All projects**, select any of the open projects, click on **Hour forecasts** by going to **Plan | Forecast** in the action pane, in order to open the **Hours forecasts** form, and create several forecast lines similar to the ones shown in the following screenshot:

Chapter 6

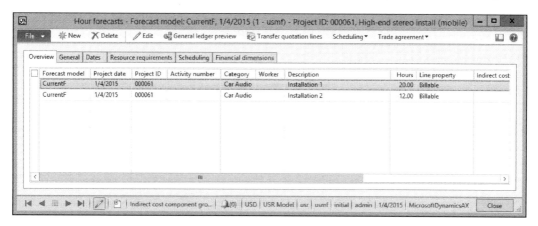

Note the project number and the forecast model, which will be required later in the code.

To update scheduling, navigate to **Scheduling | Resource scheduling** in the action pane of the **Hours forecasts** form and then click on the **OK** button to accept the default parameters and run the scheduling, as shown here:

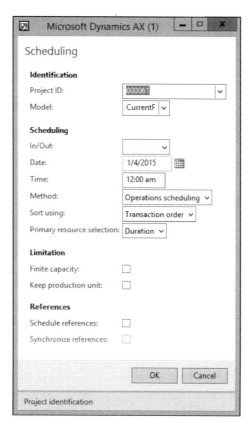

Integration with Microsoft Office

Now, the information in the **Scheduling** tab page of the **Hours forecast** form should look identical to what is shown in to the following screenshot:

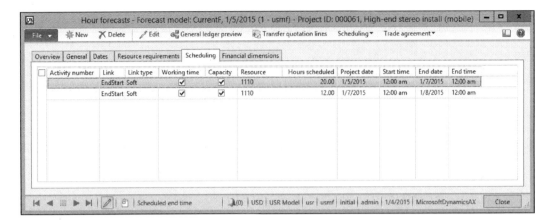

How to do it...

Carry out the following steps in order to complete this recipe:

1. In the AOT, create a new job named `CreateProjectFile` with the following code snippet (replace the project number and the forecast model with your own values):

```
static void CreateProjectFile(Args _args)
{
    ProjId                  projId = '000061';
    ProjForecastModelId     modelId = 'CurrentF';
    ProjTable               projTable;
    ProjForecastEmpl        forecastEmpl;
    COM                     msproject;
    COM                     projects;
    COM                     project;
    COM                     tasks;
    COM                     task;
    int                     n;
    #define.MSProject('MSProject.Application')

    projTable = ProjTable::find(projId);
    try
    {
        msproject = new COM(#MSProject);
    }
    catch (Exception::Internal)
```

```
        {
            if (msproject == null)
            {
                throw error("Microsoft Project is not installed");
            }
        }

        try
        {
            projects = msproject.Projects();
            project = projects.Add();
            tasks = project.Tasks();
            task = tasks.Add();
            task.Name(ProjTable.Name);
            task.OutlineLevel(1);

            while select forecastEmpl
                where forecastEmpl.ProjId == projTable.ProjId
                    && forecastEmpl.ModelId == modelId
            {
                task = tasks.Add();
                task.OutlineLevel(2);
                task.Name(forecastEmpl.Txt);
                task.Start(forecastEmpl.SchedFromDate);
                task.Duration(forecastEmpl.SchedTimeHours*60);
                if (n)
                {
                    task.LinkPredecessors(tasks.UniqueID(n));
                }
                n = task.UniqueID();
            }

            msproject.visible(true);
        }
        catch
        {
            if (msproject)
            {
                msproject.Quit(0);
            }
        }
    }
```

Integration with Microsoft Office

2. To test the code, run the job. Note the forecasted project hours displayed as a Microsoft Project plan, as shown in the following screenshot:

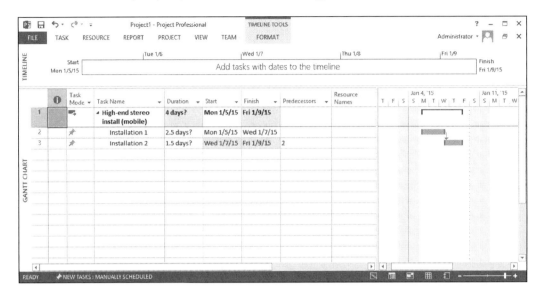

How it works...

In this recipe, we first declare a number of COM objects for handling various Microsoft Project elements. Then, we create a new instance of the Microsoft Project application, get a reference to the collection of projects, which is initially empty, and create a new project.

Once the project is ready, we get a reference to the collection of tasks and start adding individual tasks. The first task is a parent task and we set its name to the name of the selected project.

Next, we go through all the project hour forecast records and start adding each line as a new task in the document. Here, we set various task properties, such as name, start date, and duration. We also define every task to be dependent on the previous task by calling the `LinkPredecessors()` method with the number of the previous task, as an argument. Finally, once the document is ready, we display it on the screen.

All the code is placed in the `try/catch` block to ensure that in the case of any errors, the created Project instance and the created document are closed and do not stay in memory.

Chapter 6

Sending an e-mail using Outlook

In Dynamics AX, e-mails can be sent in several ways. One of them is to use Microsoft Office Outlook. The benefit of using Outlook is that the user can review e-mails and modify them, if required, before they are actually sent. Also, all the sent e-mails can be stored in the user's Outlook folders.

In this recipe, we will send an e-mail using Outlook. We will incorporate customer data from the system into a template in order to create the e-mail's text.

Getting ready

Before we start with the code, we need to create a new e-mail template. Navigate to **Organization administration | Setup**, open the **E-mail templates** form and create the following record:

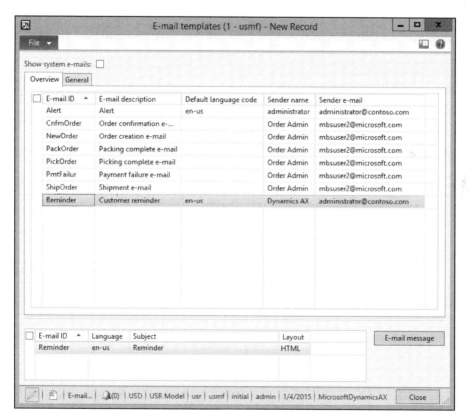

Integration with Microsoft Office

Next, click on the **E-mail message** button and enter the e-mail body, as shown in the following screenshot:

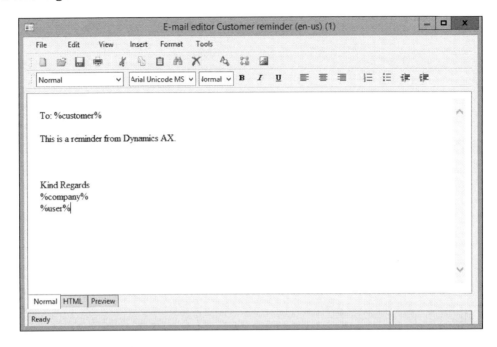

How to do it...

Carry out the following steps in order to complete this recipe:

1. In the AOT, create a new job named `SendCustReminderEmail` with the following code snippet (replace the customer account number with your own):

    ```
    static void SendCustReminderEmail(Args _args)
    {
        CustTable custTable;
        Map       mappings;

        custTable = custTable::find('US-027');

        mappings = new Map(Types::String, Types::String);

        mappings.insert('customer', custTable.name());
        mappings.insert('company', CompanyInfo::find().Name);
        mappings.insert('user', HcmWorker::find(
            DirPersonUser::current().worker()).name());
    ```

```
SysINetMail::sendEMail(
    'Reminder',
    custTable.languageId(),
    custTable.email(),
    mappings);
}
```

2. Run the job and a message similar to what is shown in the following screenshot will appear on the screen:

How it works...

In this recipe, we prepare a number of key-value mappings that will be inserted into the e-mail template. Then, we use the `sendEMail()` method of the `SysINetMail` class to send an e-mail using Outlook. This method accepts the following arguments:

- The name of the template
- The customer's language code
- The customer's e-mail address
- The prepared mapping

Note that depending on the version of Outlook, the **To...** field may not be populated automatically with the customer's e-mail address. This is due to a MAPI compatibility issue.

7
Using Services

In this chapter, we will cover the following recipes:

- Consuming the system query service
- Consuming the system metadata service
- Consuming an existing document service
- Creating a document service
- Consuming a document service
- Using an enhanced document service
- Creating a custom service
- Consuming a custom service
- Consuming an external service

Introduction

Dynamics AX provides many out-of-the-box services—programmable objects that can be used to communicate with application components or third-party applications. In order to meet complex business requirements, existing services can be customized or new services can be created from scratch.

The services are divided into three categories: non-customizable built-in system services, document services—which provide a standard approach for communicating between systems, and custom services—which allow you to expose any X++ logic as a service.

In this chapter, the various scenarios of creating and consuming all three types of services will be presented. The recipes in this chapter will demonstrate how services can be exposed and consumed using different techniques. All the examples, one way or another, will use the system currency information.

Consuming the system query service

The query service is one of the built-in system services in Dynamics AX. This service provides a set of operations that allow you to execute any AOT or dynamic query. The results are returned as an ADO.NET DataSet object. The query service cannot be customized and is hosted on the **Application Object Server** (**AOS**) at a fixed address.

In this recipe, we will create a .NET console application that will connect to the query service. The application will retrieve a list of currencies in the system, with the help of a dynamically created query.

Getting ready

Just before we start, we have to figure out the server name and the port that should be used while working with the services.

The server name can normally be found in the Windows OS settings. Navigate to **Control Panel** | **System and Security** | **System** and then look for **Computer name**, as shown in the following screenshot:

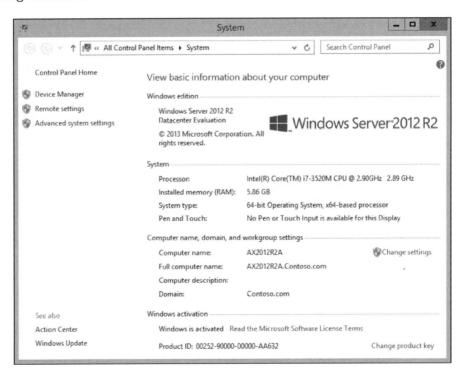

Chapter 7

In these demonstrations, as long as the AOS and the client code is on the same machine, it is also possible to use `localhost` as a server name regardless of the real server name. This effectively means the name of the current machine.

The port number can be found in **Microsoft Dynamics AX Server Configuration Utility**, which can be found by navigating to **Control Panel | Administrative Tools**. The port number is the one in the **Services WSDL port** field, as shown here:

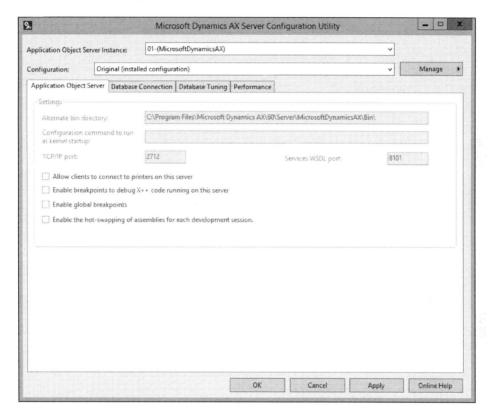

How to do it...

Carry out the following steps in order to complete this recipe:

1. In Visual Studio, create a new Visual C# Console Application project named `ConsumeSystemQueryService`.

Using Services

2. Add a new service reference named `QueryService` to the project as per what is shown in the following screenshot (replace `localhost:8101` with your machine name and port as described in the previous section):

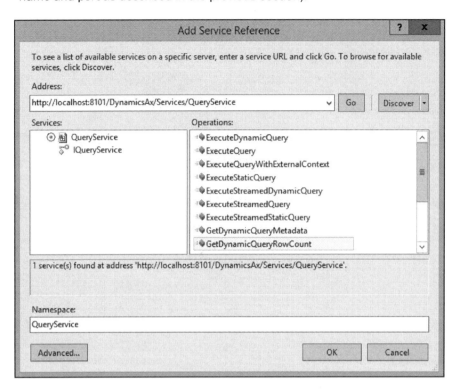

3. Add the following lines of code in the top section of the `Program.cs` file:

   ```
   using ConsumeSystemQueryService.QueryService;
   using System.Data;
   ```

4. Add the following code snippet to the `Main()` method:

   ```
   QueryServiceClient serviceClient;
   QueryMetadata query;
   QueryDataSourceMetadata currencyDataSource;
   QueryDataFieldMetadata field1, field2;
   Paging paging = null;
   DataSet result;

   query = new QueryMetadata();
   query.QueryType = QueryService.QueryType.Join;
   query.AllowCrossCompany = true;
   query.DataSources = new QueryDataSourceMetadata[1];
   ```

```csharp
currencyDataSource = new QueryDataSourceMetadata();
currencyDataSource.Name = "Currency";
currencyDataSource.Enabled = true;
currencyDataSource.FetchMode = FetchMode.OneToOne;
currencyDataSource.Table = "Currency";
currencyDataSource.DynamicFieldList = false;
currencyDataSource.Fields = new QueryFieldMetadata[2];
query.DataSources[0] = currencyDataSource;

field1 = new QueryDataFieldMetadata();
field1.FieldName = "CurrencyCode";
field1.SelectionField = SelectionField.Database;
currencyDataSource.Fields[0] = field1;

field2 = new QueryDataFieldMetadata();
field2.FieldName = "Txt";
field2.SelectionField = SelectionField.Database;
currencyDataSource.Fields[1] = field2;

serviceClient = new QueryServiceClient();

result = serviceClient.ExecuteQuery(query, ref paging);

serviceClient.Close();

foreach (DataRow row in result.Tables[0].Rows)
{
    Console.WriteLine(
        String.Format("{0} - {1}", row[0], row[1]));
}

Console.ReadKey();
```

Using Services

5. Run the program by clicking on *F5*. The results will be similar to what is shown in the following screenshot:

```
TWD - New Taiwan Dollar
TZS - Tanzanian Shilling
UAH - Hryvnia
UGX - Uganda Shilling
USD - US Dollar
UYI - Uruguay Peso en Unidades Indexadas
UYU - Peso Uruguayo
UZS - Uzbekistan Sum
VEF - Bolivar Fuerte
VND - Dong
VUV - Vatu
WST - Tala
XAF - CFA Franc BEAC
XAG - Silver
XAU - Gold
XCD - East Caribbean Dollar
XDR - SDR
XOF - CFA Franc BCEAO
XPD - Palladium
XPF - CFP Franc
XPT - Platinum
YER - Yemeni Rial
ZAR - Rand
ZWD - Zimbabwe Dollar
```

How it works...

We start the recipe by creating a new Visual C# Console Application project and adding a new service reference. We specify the **Web Services Description Language** (**WSDL**) address of the Dynamics AX query service in the **Address** field of the service reference. This address is not a service itself; it only holds all the required information about the service. The query service's WSDL address cannot be changed, and it is formatted as http://<servername>:<port>/DynamicsAx/Services/QueryService. Here, <servername> and <port> will be replaced with the AOS machine name and WSDL port number.

In this recipe, we replace <servername> with our machine name, which is localhost, and <port> with our service's WSDL port number, which is 8101, (defined in the Microsoft Dynamics AX Server Configuration Utility). The result is http://localhost:8101/DynamicsAx/Services/QueryService.

Just for information purposes, if you open the preceding address in a browser, say Internet Explorer, you will find that the definition of the actual query service address is net.tcp://localhost:8201/DynamicsAx/Services/QueryService.

Next, we continue with the code. All the logic goes into the Main() method of the application. In the code, we create a new query with the help of the QueryMetadata class, add a new data source based on the QueryDataSourceMetadata class, and define two fields in the data source that will be retrieved from the database. The query, data source and field classes, and their properties are very similar to the Query, QueryBuildDataSource, and QueryBuildFieldList classes in Dynamics AX.

Chapter 7

Finally, we call the query service with the created query as an argument. The service returns a `DataSet` object, and we go through each row in the first table and display its fields on the screen.

Consuming the system metadata service

The metadata service is another system service that allows clients to get the object's metadata information from the AOT, for example, table or field properties. Metadata services are not customizable and are hosted on the AOS at a fixed address.

In this recipe, we will create a .NET console application that will connect to the metadata service. The application will retrieve a few properties of the `Currency` and `ExchangeRate` tables.

How to do it...

Carry out the following steps in order to complete this recipe:

1. In Visual Studio, create a new Visual C# Console Application project named `ConsumeSystemMetadataService`.

2. Add a new service reference, named `MetadataService`, to the project (replace `localhost:8101` with your own address and port):

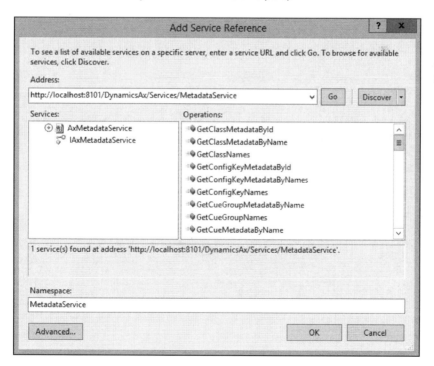

Using Services

3. Add the following line of code in the top section of the `Program.cs` file:

    ```
    using ConsumeSystemMetadataService.MetadataService;
    ```

4. Add the following code snippet to the `Main()` method:

    ```
    AxMetadataServiceClient serviceClient;
    TableMetadata[] tables;

    serviceClient = new AxMetadataServiceClient();
    serviceClient.Open();

    tables = serviceClient.GetTableMetadataByName(
        new string[] { "Currency", "ExchangeRate" });

    serviceClient.Close();

    foreach (TableMetadata table in tables)
    {
        Console.WriteLine(String.Format("{0}: {1}, {2}",
            table.Name,
            table.TitleField1.Name,
            table.TitleField2.Name));
    }

    Console.ReadKey();
    ```

5. Run the program by clicking on *F5*. The results will be similar to what is shown in the following screenshot:

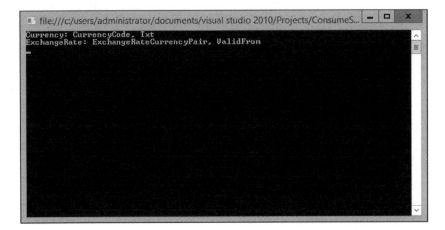

How it works...

In this recipe, we first create a new Visual C# Console Application project and then add a new service reference. We specify the WSDL address of the Dynamics AX metadata service in the `Address` field of the service reference. The metadata service's WSDL address cannot be changed, and it is formatted as `http://<servername>:<port>/DynamicsAx/Services/MetadataService`. Here, `<servername>` and `<port>` will be replaced with the AOS machine name and the WSDL port number.

In this recipe, we replace `<servername>` with our machine name, which is `localhost`, and `<port>` with our service's WSDL port number, which is `8101` (defined in the **Microsoft Dynamics AX Server Configuration Utility**). The result is `http://localhost:8101/DynamicsAx/Services/MetadataService`.

All the code resides in the `Main()` method of the application. Here, we create and open a connection to the service. Then, we call `GetTableMetadataByName()`—one of the many available operations. This method accepts a list of table names and returns information about them in a form of the `TableMetadata` class.

Finally, we close the connection to the service and then display we display the `TitleField1` and `TitleField2` properties of each object in the returned result on the screen.

Consuming an existing document service

In Dynamics AX, document services allow you to exchange data with external systems by sending and receiving XML documents, such as customers, sales orders, vendors, purchase orders, products, and so on.

In this recipe, we will explore how data can be retrieved from the system using one of the existing services. We will create a .NET console application that will get a currency description from the system using the read operation.

How to do it...

Carry out the following steps in order to complete this recipe:

1. In the AOT, locate the `CurrencyServices` service group.
2. Select the **Deploy Service Group** option from the right-click context menu. A number of messages will be displayed in the **Infolog** window, about the successful deployment.

Using Services

3. Navigate to **System administration | Setup | Services and Application Integration Framework | Inbound ports** in order to check the newly deployed service (note the value in the **WSDL URI** field), as shown in the following screenshot:

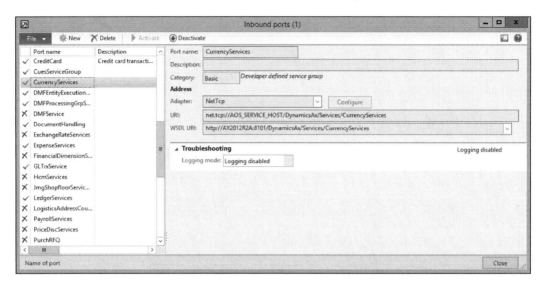

4. In Visual Studio, create a new Visual C# Console Application project named `ConsumeExistingDocumentService`.
5. Add a new service reference named `CurrencyServices` to the project.
6. Copy the address from the **WSDL URI** field into the **Address** field:

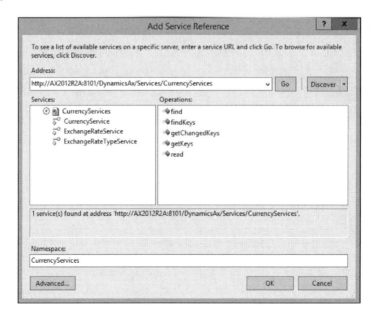

7. Add the following line of code in the top section of the `Program.cs` file:

   `using ConsumeExistingDocumentService.CurrencyServices;`

8. Add the following code snippet to the `Main()` method:

   ```
   CurrencyServiceClient serviceClient;
   AxdLedgerCurrency currency;

   KeyField keyField = new KeyField();
   keyField.Field = "CurrencyCode";
   keyField.Value = "LTL";

   EntityKey keys = new EntityKey();
   keys.KeyData = new KeyField[1] { keyField };

   serviceClient = new CurrencyServiceClient();

   currency = serviceClient.read(
       null, new EntityKey[1] { keys });

   serviceClient.Close();

   Console.WriteLine(String.Format("{0} - {1}",
       currency.Currency[0].CurrencyCode,
       currency.Currency[0].Txt));

   Console.ReadKey();
   ```

9. Run the program by clicking on *F5*. The results should be similar to what is shown in the following screenshot:

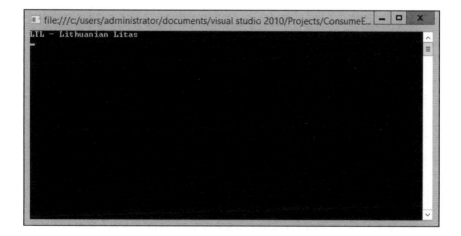

Using Services

How it works...

We start this recipe by deploying the `CurrencyServices` service group. This action reads the group's configuration, creates a new basic port in the **Inbound ports** form, and then activates the port. The existing port, if it exists, will be overridden.

The newly created port has two addresses. One of them is **WSDL URI**—the address that holds all the information about the service, and the other one is **URI**—the address of the actual service.

Next, we create a new Visual C# Console Application project and a new service reference. We provide the **WSDL URI** value from the **Inbound port** form as its address.

The `Main()` method starts by defining and creating a new `KeyField` instance. Here, we set the information that will be used to search—the field name and its value. Then, the key field is added to the table key list, which normally holds the number of elements that match the number of fields in the table's primary key.

Next, we create the service's client object and call its read operation with the table key list as an argument. The result is an `AxdLedgerCurrency` object, which represents the `Currency` table.

Lastly, we close the connection to the service and then display the currency code and its description on the screen.

There's more...

The previous example returns only one value matching the key provided. It can be slightly modified to return multiple results. Let's replace the code in the `Main()` method with the following code snippet:

```
CurrencyServiceClient serviceClient;

CriteriaElement criteriaElement = new CriteriaElement();
criteriaElement.DataSourceName = "Currency";
criteriaElement.FieldName = "CurrencyCode";
criteriaElement.Value1 = "A??";
criteriaElement.Operator = Operator.Equal;

QueryCriteria query = new QueryCriteria();
query.CriteriaElement =
    new CriteriaElement[1] { criteriaElement };

serviceClient = new CurrencyServiceClient();

AxdLedgerCurrency currency = serviceClient.find(null, query);
```

```
serviceClient.Close();

if (currency.Currency != null)
{
    foreach (AxdEntity_Currency c in currency.Currency)
    {
        Console.WriteLine(String.Format(
            "{0} - {1}",
            c.CurrencyCode,
            c.Txt));
    }
}

Console.ReadKey();
```

The difference is that now we use the `find` operation, which executes the provided query and returns the results. In the code, we define a query with a single data source and a filter on the `CurrencyCode` field, to find all the currencies that start with the letter A. The program's results will now be similar to what is shown in the following screenshot:

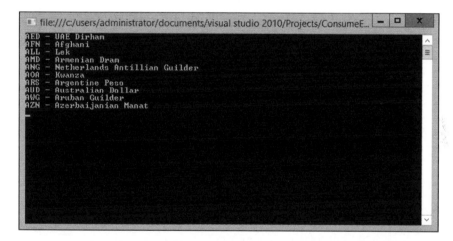

Creating a document service

In Dynamics AX, new document services can be created using the **AIF Document Service Wizard**. The developer has to provide a table and a query representing the document service, and the wizard generates all the objects required to run the service. Document services created by the wizard can be further customized to meet more complex requirements.

In this recipe, we will use the **AIF Document Service Wizard** to create a new document service for exposing currency information. Currency information is used for demonstration purposes only; Dynamics AX already contains an out-of-the-box currency document service.

Using Services

How to do it...

Carry out the following steps in order to complete this recipe:

1. In the AOT, create a new query named `CurrencyQuery`.
2. Add a new data source to the newly created query with the following properties:

Property	Value
Table	Currency
Name	Currency
Update	Yes

3. In the data source, change the property of the `Fields` node, as follows:

Property	Value
Dynamic	Yes

4. Open the **AIF Document Service Wizard** form, which can be found by navigating to **Tools | Wizards**. Click on the **Next** button on the first page, then enter the query name, and finally click on the **Next** button again, as shown here:

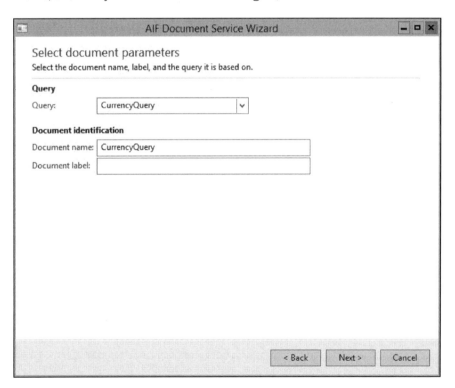

5. On the next page, leave the default names as is, mark the options as shown in the following screenshot, and click on the **Next** button:

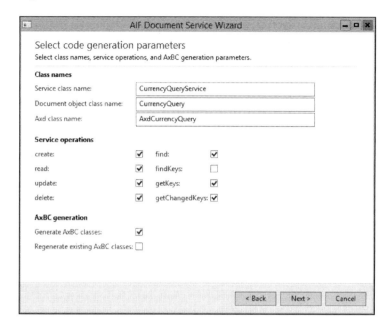

6. On the next page, review what will be generated by the system and click on the **Generate** button:

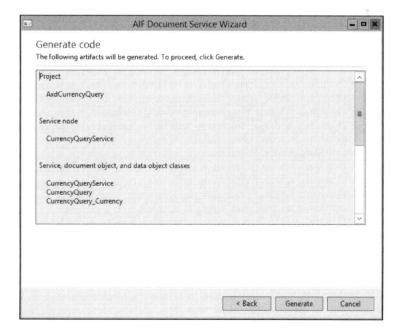

Using Services

7. On the last page, click on the **Finish** button to complete the wizard:

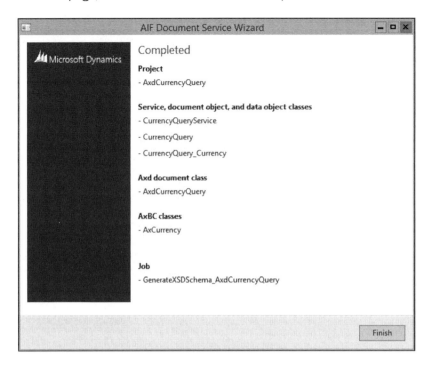

8. To review the newly created objects, locate and open the **AxdCurrencyQuery** private development project, which has been created by the wizard:

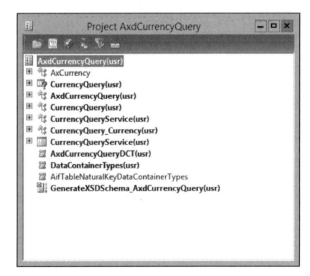

9. Compile the project to ensure that there are no errors.
10. In the AOT, create a new service group named `BasicCurrencyServices`.
11. In the service group, create a new service node with the following properties:

Property	Value
Name	CurrencyQueryService
Service	CurrencyQueryService

12. Deploy the service group by selecting the **Deploy Service Group** option from the service group's right-click context menu. The **Infolog** window will display a number of messages about the successful deployment.

13. Navigate to **System administration | Setup | Services and Application Integration Framework | Inbound ports** in order to view the newly deployed service, as shown in the following screenshot:

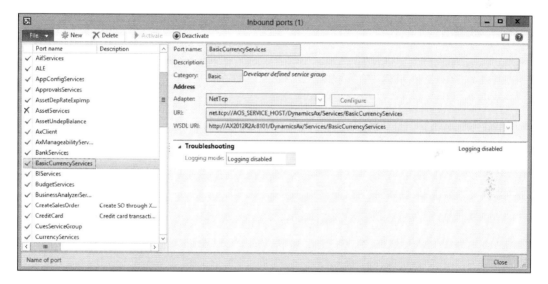

How it works...

We start the recipe by creating a new query. This query will be used by the service to return the data. The query contains only one data source linked to the `Currency` table. Although, in this recipe, we will only retrieve the data, setting the `Update` property of the data source to `Yes` will allow you to modify the data too. We also set the `Fields` node to be dynamic, to make sure that any field added to the table later will automatically appear in the query.

Using Services

Once the query is ready, we start the wizard. On the second page, we specify the query name and document name. On the third page, we select the operations to be implemented. And on the final two pages, we review which objects will be created and complete the wizard. The wizard creates a new private development project, with all the generated objects in it. At this point, everything is ready and we only need to create a new service group, add our service, and publish the group.

If everything is successful, we should see a new entry in the **Inbound ports** form. It is activated automatically, and we can use the address specified in the **WSDL URI** field to access the service.

Consuming a document service

In Dynamics AX, document services normally provide a number of predefined operations, such as `create`, `delete`, `read`, `find`, and `findKeys`. Each operation is responsible for some particular action; for example, `create` allows you to create a new document, `delete` allows you to delete a document, and so on. The `read` operation was demonstrated in the *Consuming an existing document service* recipe.

In this recipe, we will create a .NET console application to demonstrate how the `find` operation can be used. We will consume the service created in the *Creating a document service* recipe to list all the currencies in the system.

How to do it...

Carry out the following steps in order to complete this recipe:

1. In Visual Studio, create a new Visual C# Console Application project named `ConsumeBasicDocumentService`.
2. Add a new service reference named `BasicCurrencyServices` to the project.
3. Copy the address from the **WSDL URI** field, from the *Creating a document service* recipe, into the **Address** field, as shown here:

Chapter 7

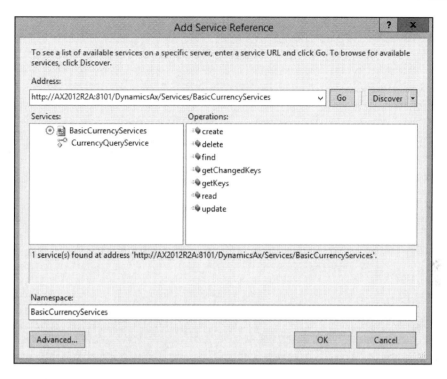

4. Add the following line of code in the top section of the `Program.cs` file:

   using ConsumeBasicDocumentService.BasicCurrencyServices;

5. Add the following code snippet to the `Main()` method:

   ```
   CurrencyQueryServiceClient serviceClient;

   CriteriaElement criteriaElement = new CriteriaElement();
   criteriaElement.DataSourceName = "Currency";
   criteriaElement.FieldName = "CurrencyCode";
   criteriaElement.Value1 = "";
   criteriaElement.Operator = Operator.NotEqual;

   QueryCriteria query = new QueryCriteria();
   query.CriteriaElement =
       new CriteriaElement[1] { criteriaElement };

   serviceClient = new CurrencyQueryServiceClient();

   AxdCurrencyQuery currency = serviceClient.find(null, query);
   ```

Using Services

```
        serviceClient.Close();

    if (currency.Currency != null)
    {
        foreach (AxdEntity_Currency c in currency.Currency)
        {
            Console.WriteLine(String.Format(
                "{0} - {1}",
                c.CurrencyCode,
                c.Txt));
        }
    }

    Console.ReadKey();
```

6. Run the program by clicking on *F5*. The results will be similar to what is shown in the following screenshot:

How it works...

In this recipe, we first create a new Visual C# Console Application project and then add a new service reference pointing to the address from the previous recipe.

The code in the `Main()` method creates a new query based on the `Currency` table and a filter on the `CurrencyCode` field. Here, we set the filter to not empty, that is, return all the records from the table.

To get the results, we call the `find` operation, which accepts the query as an argument and returns the `AxdCurrencyQuery` document. The last thing to do is to close the connection to the service and then display all the returned records on the screen.

Chapter 7

See also

- The *Creating a document service* recipe

Using an enhanced document service

In Dynamics AX, services can be exposed using basic or enhanced integration ports. Normally, simple services are exposed using basic ports. Conversely, enhanced ports are used in more complex scenarios. Enhanced ports offer additional capabilities compared to the basic integration ports. Enhanced ports can restrict data, execute complex preprocessing and post-processing rules, and be hosted on the Internet Information Services, and so on.

In this recipe, we will demonstrate how to create and consume a document service created in the *Creating a document service recipe*, using an enhanced integration port. We will use the document filtering feature of the enhanced port to restrict the range of data being exposed.

How to do it...

Carry out the following steps in order to complete this recipe:

1. Navigate to **System administration | Setup | Services and Application Integration Framework | Inbound ports** and create a new record, as follows:

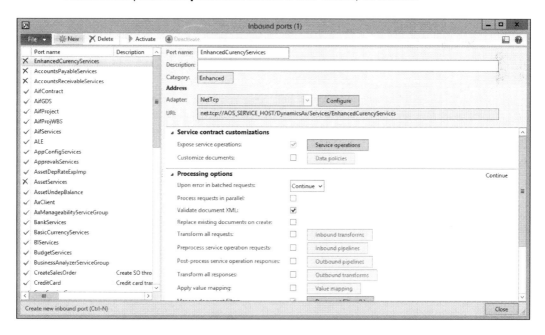

2. Click on the **Service operations** button to open the **Select service operations** form.

305

Using Services

3. Select all the `CurrencyQueryService` service operations that were previously created in the *Creating a document service* recipe:

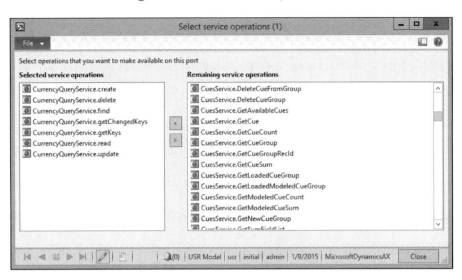

4. Close the **Select service operations** form.
5. In the **Inbound ports** form, expand the **Processing Options** tab page and open the **Document filters** form by clicking on the **Document filters** button.
6. In the opened form, click on the **Add** button, type `Currencies starting with B` into the **Description** field, and save the record. This is how the form will look:

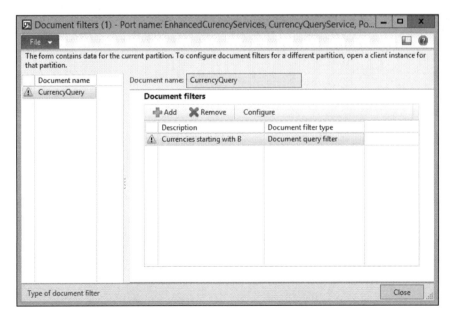

7. Click on the **Configure** button, while the newly created record is selected, and specify `B??` in the **Criteria** field, as follows:

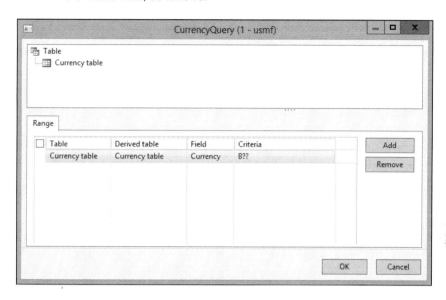

8. Close the **Query configuration** form and then close the **Document filters** form.
9. In the **Inbound ports** form, make sure that the **EnhancedCurrencyServices** record is selected and then click on the **Activate** button. The status should change as follows (note the value in the **WSDL URI** field):

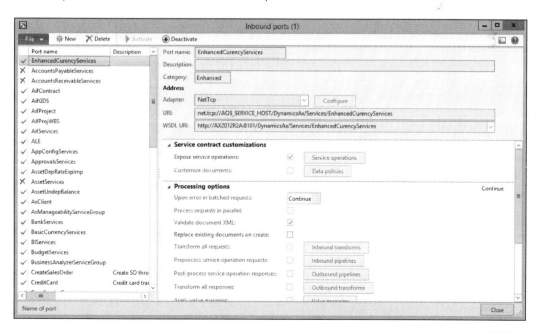

Using Services

10. In Visual Studio, create a new Visual C# Console Application project named `ConsumeEnhancedDocumentService`.
11. Add a new service reference named `EnhancedCurrencyServices` to the project.
12. Copy the address from the **WSDL URI** field into the **Address** field:

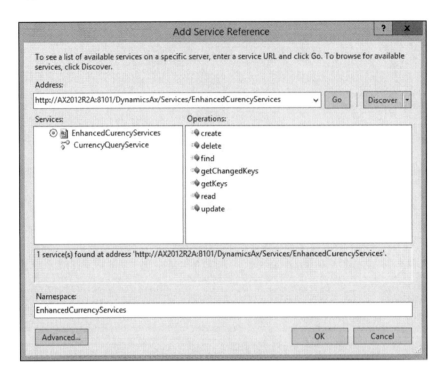

13. Add the following line of code in the top section of the `Program.cs` file:

    `using ConsumeEnhancedDocumentService.EnhancedCurrencyServices;`

14. Add the following code snippet to the `Main()` method:

```
CurrencyQueryServiceClient serviceClient;

serviceClient = new CurrencyQueryServiceClient();

EntityKeyPage keyPage = serviceClient.getKeys(null, null);

serviceClient.Close();

foreach (EntityKey key in keyPage.EntityKeyList)
{
    Console.WriteLine(key.KeyData[0].Value);
```

Chapter 7

```
    }

    Console.ReadKey();
```

15. Run the program by clicking on *F5*. The results will be similar to what is shown in the following screenshot:

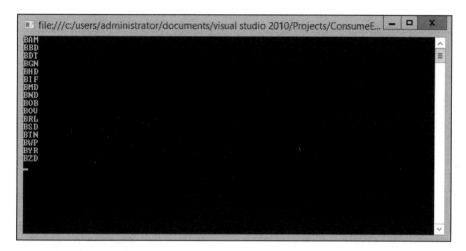

How it works...

In this recipe, no X++ code is required. In the **Inbound ports** form, we create a new entry and select the operations created in one of the previous recipes. Note that the **Category** field for manually created ports is set to **Enhanced** automatically, which means that the additional features will be available for this port. One of these is document filtering. To demonstrate its use, we create a new filter in order to limit the returned results to only the currencies that start with B. Once everything is ready, we activate the port.

At this stage, the service is ready. Next, we create a new Visual C# Console Application project and add a new service reference pointing to the address of the newly created port.

In the `Main()` method, we create a new service client object and call its `getKeys` operation. Document filters applied on enhanced ports are used only in the `getChangedKeys` and `getKeys` operations, so our operation returns only the entity keys that match the applied filters.

The last thing to do is to close the connection to the service and then go through the results and display them on the screen.

See also

- The *Creating a document service* recipe

Using Services

Creating a custom service

Custom services in Dynamics AX allows you to expose any X++ logic as a service. In order to expose X++ code as a service, we only need to add a special attribute to it. This allows us easily reuse the exiting code without any additional changes.

In this recipe, we will create a new custom service with a single, simple operation. The operation will accept currency code and return currency description.

How to do it...

Carry out the following steps in order to complete this recipe:

1. In the AOT, create a new class named `CustomCurrencyService` with the following code snippet:

   ```
   class CustomCurrencyService
   {
   }

   [SysEntryPointAttribute]
   public CurrencyName getCurrencyName(CurrencyCode _currencyCode)
   {
       return Currency::find(_currencyCode).Txt;
   }
   ```

2. Set the class' properties as follows:

Property	Value
RunOn	Server

3. In the AOT, create a new service with the following properties:

Property	Value
Name	CustomCurrencyService
Class	CustomCurrencyService

4. Expand the newly created service and select the **Add Operation** option from the **Operations** node's right-click context menu.

5. In the **Add service operations** form, select the **getCurrencyName** line by marking the **Add** checkbox and clicking on **OK**:

6. The service in the AOT will look similar to what is shown in the following screenshot:

7. In the AOT, create a new service group named `CustomCurrencyService`.
8. In the service group, create a new service node reference with the following properties:

Property	Value
Name	CustomCurrencyService
Service	CustomCurrencyService

9. Deploy the service group by selecting the **Deploy Service Group** option from its right-click context menu. The **Infolog** window will display a number of messages about the successful deployment.

Using Services

10. Navigate to **System administration | Setup | Services and Application Integration Framework | Inbound ports** in order to check the newly deployed service:

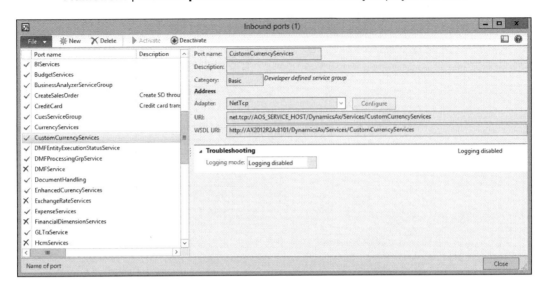

11. To verify the service, open the address specified in the **WSDL URI** field in a browser say Internet Explorer. The screen should look similar to this:

```
<?xml version="1.0" encoding="utf-8" ?>
- <wsdl:definitions name="CustomCurrencyServices" targetNamespace="http://tempuri.org/"
    xmlns:wsdl="http://schemas.xmlsoap.org/wsdl/" xmlns:wsx="http://schemas.xmlsoap.org/ws/2004/09/mex"
    xmlns:i0="http://tempuri.org/" xmlns:wsu="http://docs.oasis-open.org/wss/2004/01/oasis-200401-wss-wssecurity-utility-
    1.0.xsd" xmlns:wsa10="http://www.w3.org/2005/08/addressing" xmlns:wsp="http://schemas.xmlsoap.org/ws/2004/09/policy"
    xmlns:wsap="http://schemas.xmlsoap.org/ws/2004/08/addressing/policy"
    xmlns:msc="http://schemas.microsoft.com/ws/2005/12/wsdl/contract"
    xmlns:soap12="http://schemas.xmlsoap.org/wsdl/soap12/" xmlns:wsa="http://schemas.xmlsoap.org/ws/2004/08/addressing"
    xmlns:wsam="http://www.w3.org/2007/05/addressing/metadata" xmlns:xsd="http://www.w3.org/2001/XMLSchema"
    xmlns:tns="http://tempuri.org/" xmlns:soap="http://schemas.xmlsoap.org/wsdl/soap/"
    xmlns:wsaw="http://www.w3.org/2006/05/addressing/wsdl" xmlns:soapenc="http://schemas.xmlsoap.org/soap/encoding/">
  + <wsp:Policy wsu:Id="NetTcpBinding_CustomCurrencyService_policy">
    <wsdl:import namespace="http://tempuri.org"
      location="http://ax2012r2a:8101/DynamicsAx/Services/CustomCurrencyServices?wsdl=wsdl0" />
    <wsdl:types />
  + <wsdl:binding name="NetTcpBinding_CustomCurrencyService" type="i0:CustomCurrencyService">
  - <wsdl:service name="CustomCurrencyServices">
    - <wsdl:port name="NetTcpBinding_CustomCurrencyService" binding="tns:NetTcpBinding_CustomCurrencyService">
        <soap12:address location="net.tcp://ax2012r2a:8201/DynamicsAx/Services/CustomCurrencyServices" />
      - <wsa10:EndpointReference>
          <wsa10:Address>net.tcp://ax2012r2a:8201/DynamicsAx/Services/CustomCurrencyServices</wsa10:Address>
        - <Identity xmlns="http://schemas.xmlsoap.org/ws/2006/02/addressingidentity">
            <Upn>admin@Contoso.com</Upn>
          </Identity>
        </wsa10:EndpointReference>
      </wsdl:port>
    </wsdl:service>
  </wsdl:definitions>
```

How it works...

In Dynamics AX, any class can be exposed as a custom service. Here, we create a new one with a single method that accepts currency code and returns currency name. To enable the method as a service operation, we specify the `SysEntryPointAttribute` attribute at the top of the method, which will ensure that the method is available in the service operation list when creating service nodes. We also set the class to run on the server tier.

Next, we create a new service node and add the newly created operation to it. In order to deploy it, we also have to create a new service group that includes the created service. Once deployed, a new record is created in the **Inbound ports** form.

If everything is successful, the service is ready to be consumed. This will be explained in the next recipe.

See also

- The *Consuming a custom service* recipe

Consuming a custom service

Custom services are consumed in a way similar to any other Dynamics AX service. The difference is that each custom service can have a totally different set of operations, where system or document services always expose the same operations.

In this recipe, we will create a new .NET console application to demonstrate how to consume a custom service. We will use the service created in the *Creating a custom service* recipe, which returns a description of the provided currency.

How to do it...

Carry out the following steps in order to complete this recipe:

1. In Visual Studio, create a new Visual C# Console Application project named `ConsumeBasicCustomService`.
2. Add a new service reference named `CustomCurrencyServices` to the project.

Using Services

3. Copy the address from the **WSDL URI** field, from the *Creating a custom service* recipe, into the **Address** field:

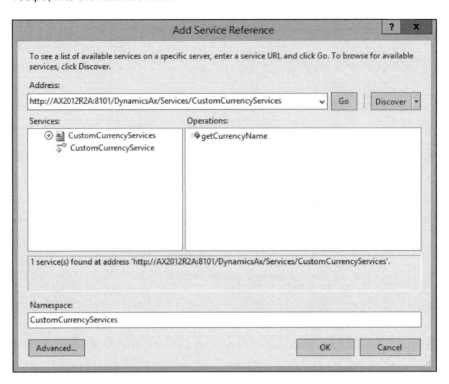

4. Add the following line of code in the top section of the `Program.cs` file:

    ```
    using ConsumeBasicCustomService.CustomCurrencyServices;
    ```

5. Add the following code snippet to the `Main()` method:

    ```
    CustomCurrencyServiceClient serviceClient;

    serviceClient = new CustomCurrencyServiceClient();

    string currencyName =
        serviceClient.getCurrencyName(null, "EUR");

    serviceClient.Close();

    Console.WriteLine(currencyName);

    Console.ReadKey();
    ```

6. Run the program by clicking on *F5*. The results will be similar to what is shown in the following screenshot:

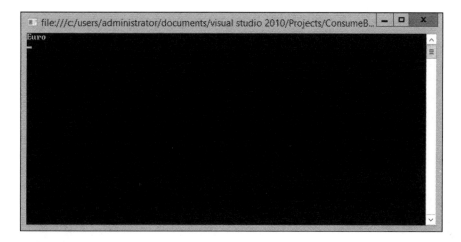

How it works...

We start this recipe by creating a new Visual C# Console Application project and adding a new service reference pointing to the address from one of the previous recipes.

The code in the Main() method is similar to code in the other recipes. Here, we create a new connection to the service and call its getCurrencyName operation to get the currency name.

See also

- The *Creating a custom service* recipe

Consuming an external service

In Dynamics AX, external services can be used in a variety of scenarios to retrieve information from external providers. This can be currency exchange rates, address information, logistics data, and many others. Such external services can be consumed directly from the X++ code, with the help of Visual Studio.

In this recipe, we will demonstrate how external services can be consumed from the X++ code. For demonstration purposes, we will use the service created in the *Creating a custom service* recipe, and we will assume that this service is an external service.

Using Services

How to do it...

Carry out the following steps in order to complete this recipe:

1. In Visual Studio, create a new Visual C# Class Library project named `ExtSrv`.
2. Delete `Class1.cs` from the project.
3. Add a new service reference named `CurServices` to the project.
4. Copy the address from the **WSDL URI** field, from the *Creating a custom service* recipe, into the **Address** field:

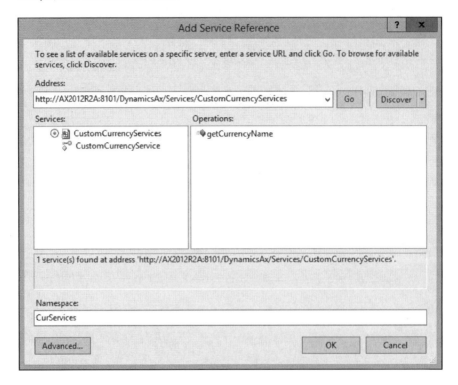

5. In Visual Studio, add the project to the AOT by selecting the **Add ExtSrv to AOT** option from the **File** menu.
6. Open the **Properties Window** from the **View** menu, change the following properties of the project, and save the project:

Property	Value
Deploy to Client	Yes
Deploy to Server	Yes

7. In Visual Studio, this is how the project will look:

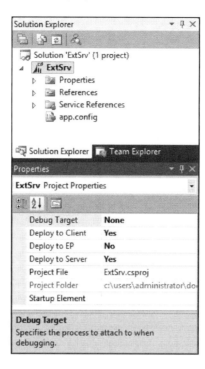

8. Restart the Dynamics AX client and verify that the **ExtSrv** project exists in the AOT by navigating to **Visual Studio Projects | C Sharp Projects**:

Using Services

9. Create a new job named `ConsumeExternalService` with the following code snippet:

```
static void ConsumeExternalService(Args _args)
{
    ClrObject serviceClientType;
    ExtSrv.CurServices.CustomCurrencyServiceClient serviceClient;
    System.Exception ex;

    try
    {
        serviceClientType = CLRInterop::getType(
            "ExtSrv.CurServices.CustomCurrencyServiceClient");
        serviceClient = AifUtil::CreateServiceClient(
            serviceClientType);
        info(serviceClient.getCurrencyName(null, "USD"));
    }
    catch (Exception::CLRError)
    {
        ex = CLRInterop::getLastException();
        info(ex.ToString());
    }
}
```

10. Run the job. The **Infolog** window will display the results, as shown here:

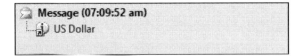

How it works...

In this recipe, we create a new Visual C# Class Library project and add a new service reference pointing to the address from the previous recipe.

Next, we add the project to the AOT and then change the deployment properties to make sure that the service is available for the X++ code running on both the server and client tiers.

To demonstrate how to consume the service, we create a new job. We start the job by defining the service reference created in Visual Studio. Then, we create the service client object and call its `getCurrencyOperation` operation, as if it was a regular X++ method.

See also

- The *Creating a custom service* recipe

8
Improving Development Efficiency

In this chapter, we will cover the following recipes:

- Creating a code editor template
- Modifying the Tools menu
- Modifying the right-click context menu
- Searching for an object in a development project
- Modifying the Personalization form
- Modifying the About Microsoft Dynamics AX dialog

Introduction

Microsoft Dynamics AX has its own integrated development environment called **MorphX**, which contains various tools for designing, modifying, compiling, and debugging code. Besides this, the system allows you to modify existing tools and create new tools in order to improve development experience and efficiency.

This chapter contains several recipes for this purpose. It explains how code editor templates can be created, how the **Tools** and right-click context menus can be modified, and how to search for objects within development projects. The chapter also discusses how we can modify the **Personalization** form and modify the **About Microsoft Dynamics AX** dialog.

Creating a code editor template

Code editor templates allow developers to reuse commonly used blocks of code. Dynamics AX already provides a number of out-of-the-box code templates for creating the `construct()`, `main()`, and `parm()` methods, various statements (such as `if`, `else`, and `switch`), code comments, and so on. The templates can be invoked by right-clicking anywhere in the code editor and navigating to **Scripts | template** from the context menu. It is also possible to activate the templates by simply typing the name of the template and pressing the *Tab* key. The existing templates can be modified and new templates can be created.

In this recipe, we will create a new code template for the `find()` method, which is normally created in most of the tables. The template will only be available in the table's methods, and it will automatically detect the current table name and use its primary key to determine the method's arguments.

How to do it...

Carry out the following steps in order to complete this recipe:

1. In the AOT, locate the `xppSource` class and create a new method with the following code snippet:

```
Source findMethod(TableName _tableName)
{
    str                 method;
    DictTable           dictTable;
    DictIndex           dictIndex;
    DictField           dictField;
    FieldName           fieldName;
    DictType            dictType;
    DictEnum            dictEnum;
    int                 fieldCount;
    int                 i;
    container           fields1;
    container           fields2;
    container           fields3;
    IdentifierName      varName;
    IdentifierName      varType;

    method =
        'static %1 find' +
            '(%2, boolean _forUpdate = false)%5' +
        '{%5' +
        '    %1 table;%5' +
```

```
            '%5' +
        '   if (%3)%5' +
        '   {%5' +
        '       if (_forUpdate)%5' +
        '           table.selectForUpdate(_forUpdate);%5' +
            '%5' +
        '       select firstOnly table%5' +
        '           where %4;%5' +
        '   }%5' +
        '   return table;%5' +
        '}';

    dictTable = new DictTable(tableName2id(_tableName));

    dictIndex = dictTable.indexObject(
        dictTable.replacementKey() ?
            dictTable.replacementKey() :
            dictTable.primaryIndex());

    if (dictIndex)
    {
        fieldCount = dictIndex.numberOfFields();

        for (i = 1; i <= fieldCount; i++)
        {
            dictField = new dictField(
                dictTable.id(),
                dictIndex.field(i));
            fieldName = dictField.name();
            varName = '_' + strLwr(subStr(fieldName,1,1)) +
                subStr(fieldName,2,strLen(fieldName)-1);

            if (dictField.typeId())
            {
                dictType = new DictType(dictField.typeId());
                varType  = dictType.name();
            }
            else if (dictField.enumId())
            {
                dictEnum = new DictEnum(dictField.enumId());
                varType  = dictEnum.name();
            }
            else
            {
```

```
                throw error(
                    strfmt(
                        "Field '%1' type is not defined",
                        fieldName));
            }

            fields1 += strFmt('%1 %2',
                varType,
                varName);
            fields2 += varName;
            fields3 += strFmt(
                'table.%1 == %2',
                fieldName,
                varName);
        }
    }

    source = strFmt(
        method,
        _tableName,
        con2Str(fields1,', '),
        con2Str(fields2, ' && '),
        con2Str(fields3, #newLine + strRep(' ', 14) + '&& '),
        #newLine);

    return source;
}
```

2. In the AOT, locate another class, `EditorScripts`, and create a new method with the following code snippet:

```
void template_method_find(Editor _editor)
{
    TreeNode   objNode;
    xppSource  xpp;
    Source     template;

    objNode = EditorScripts::getApplObjectNode(_editor);

    if (!objNode)
    {
        return;
    }

    _editor.gotoLine(1);
```

```
        _editor.firstLine();
        while (_editor.moreLines())
        {
            _editor.deleteLines(1);
            _editor.nextLine();
        }

        xpp      = new xppSource();
        template = xpp.findMethod(objNode.AOTname());
        _editor.insertLines(template);
    }
```

3. In the same class, find the `isApplicableMethod()` method and add the following lines of code at the bottom of the `switch` statement:

   ```
   case methodStr(EditorScripts, template_method_find):
       return (_aotNode &&
           _aotNode.treeNodeType().id() == #NT_DBTABLE);
   ```

4. To test the template in the AOT, create a new table or locate any table that does not have the `find()` method, for example, `CustCollectionsPool`.

5. Create a new method, then right-click anywhere in the editor, and navigate to **Scripts | template | method | find** in the context menu (alternatively, type `find` anywhere in the editor and click on the *Tab* key):

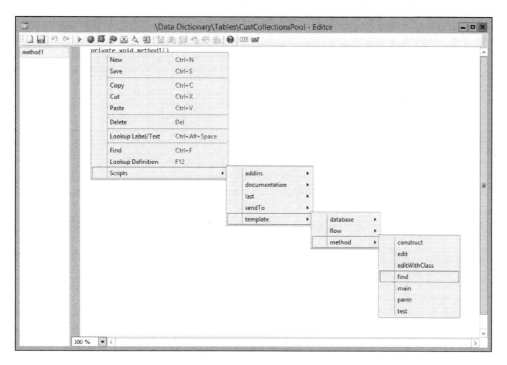

6. The code snippet shown in the following screenshot will be generated:

How it works...

Code templates are located in the xppSource class of a standard application. We start the recipe by creating a new method called findMethod() in that class. This new method holds all the code required to generate the find() method for a given table. The method accepts the table name as an argument, and this is the only thing we need.

Right after the variable declaration section, we initialize the method variable that contains the static code for creating the find() methods. The placeholders, %1, %2, and others, will be dynamically replaced with the following information:

- %1: The table name.
- %2: The list of arguments that depend on the number of fields in the table's primary key. The list contains a number of type/name pairs used as parameters for the method.
- %3: The list of fields in the if statement. The list consists of the method's parameters separated by &&. The statement is used to improve the method's performance so that no database query is executed if any of the primary fields are empty.
- %4: The list of fields in the where clause. The list consists of table fields from the primary key and the corresponding method parameters.
- %5: A new line symbol.

The method returns a dynamically generated code for the find() method for a given table.

In this recipe, to simplify the demonstration, the `findMethod()` method is created using a simple string formatting function, `strFmt()`. Alternatively, the template code can be formatted using various helper methods of the `xppSource` class, such as `beginBlock()`, `endBlock()`, `indent()`, and others. For more information, explore the other methods in the same class.

The next step is to create a link in the right-click context menu for the newly created template. This can be done simply by creating a new method in the `EditorScripts` application class. The method name should follow a special format, where each submenu is separated by underscores. In our example, we want our template to show up as **find** in **template | method**, so we name the method as `template_method_find()`.

The code in `template_method_find()` will be executed once the user activates the **find** template. In this method, we first call the code, which removes all the existing code from the user's editor window, and then we call the previously created `findMethod()` method to insert the generated code into the empty editor window.

Lastly, we modify the `isApplicableMethod()` method in the same class in order to ensure that the **find** option is only available in table methods. The method contains a big `switch` statement, where each case corresponds to one of the template methods. The method is called automatically for every template whenever the right-click context menu is opened. The conditions inside this method, depending on the current context, evaluate to either `true` or `false`, which subsequently determines the visibility of each template in the menu.

Modifying the Tools menu

In the AOT, Dynamics AX contains the **Menus** node, which holds all the user menus. Although most of them correspond to a specific module, there are several special system menus. For example, the **MainMenu** menu is a top-level menu that holds references to all the module menus and allows you to navigate throughout the system. The **GlobalToolsMenu** menu represents the **Tools** folder, which is under the **File** menu, in the user workspace and contains shortcuts to commonly used user functions. The **DevelopmentTools** menu represents the **Tools** menu in the Development Workspace and contains tools for developers.

In this recipe, we will demonstrate how the system menus can be modified. We will add a link to the **Online users** form in the **DevelopmentTools** menu.

How to do it...

Carry out the following steps in order to complete this recipe:

1. In the AOT, locate the **DevelopmentTools** menu.
2. Add a new separator at the top of the menu.

Improving Development Efficiency

3. Add a new menu item at the top of the same menu with the following properties:

Property	Value
MenuItemType	Display
MenuItemName	SysUsersOnline

4. The following screenshot shows how the **DevelopmentTools** menu will look:

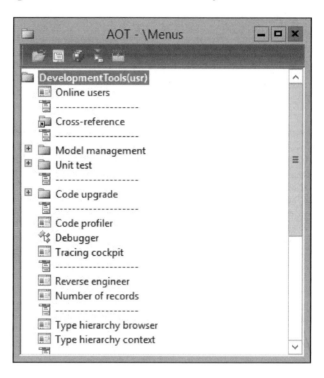

5. To test the menu, open the **Tools** menu in the Development Workspace window and note the newly added **Online users** option:

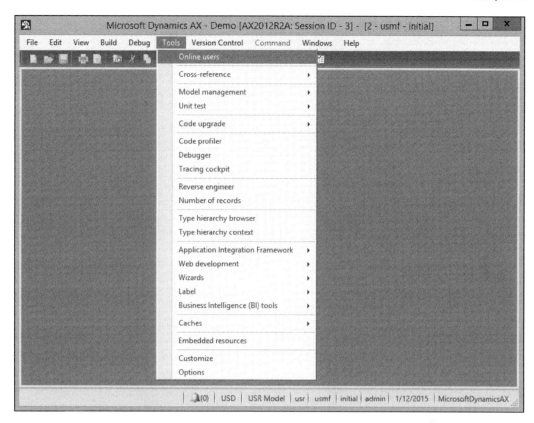

How it works...

In this recipe, we only need to add the desired menu item to the **DevelopmentTools** menu. For users, the menu item will be available under the **Tools** menu in the Development Workspace.

Modifying the right-click context menu

In the Development Workspace, many developer tools can be accessed from the right-click context menu in the AOT. Some of the tools, such as **Export**, **Delete**, and **Restore**, are common for all AOT objects. Some of the options are only available for specific objects; for example, the **Compile** function is only available for classes, tables, and other objects that contain code.

In this recipe, we will demonstrate how to modify the right-click context menu. We will add two new options to the right-click context menu for development projects nodes, which allows you to set the selected project as a startup project and clear it from the startup project.

Improving Development Efficiency

How to do it...

Carry out the following steps in order to complete this recipe:

1. In the AOT, create a new action menu item with the following properties:

Property	Value
Name	DevProjectStartupUpdateSet
Label	Set as the startup project

2. Create one more action menu item with the following properties:

Property	Value
Name	DevProjectStartupUpdateClear
Label	Clear startup project

3. In the AOT, create a new class with the following code snippet:

   ```
   DevProjectStartupUpdate
   {
   }

   static void main(Args _args)
   {
       UserInfo         userInfo;
       SysContextMenu   contextMenu;
       IdentifierName   projectName;

       if (!_args.menuItemName() ||
           !SysContextMenu::startedFrom(_args))
       {
           return;
       }

       contextMenu = _args.parmObject();

       switch (_args.menuItemName())
       {
           case menuitemActionStr(DevProjectStartupUpdateSet):
               projectName =
                   contextMenu.getFirstNode().treeNodeName();
               break;
   ```

```
            case menuitemActionStr(DevProjectStartupUpdateClear):
                projectName = '';
                break;
            default:
                return;
        }

        ttsBegin;

        select firstOnly forUpdate userInfo
            where userInfo.id == curUserId();

        userInfo.startupProject = projectName;

        if (!userInfo.validateWrite())
        {
            throw Exception::Error;
        }

        userInfo.update();

        ttsCommit;
    }

    static boolean isStartupProject(
        IdentifierName _projectName,
        UserId _userId = curUserId())
    {
        return (select firstOnly UserInfo
            where UserInfo.id == _userId
                && UserInfo.startupProject == _projectName).RecId ?
            true :
            false;
    }
```

4. For both menu items, set the following properties:

Property	Value
ObjectType	Class
Object	DevProjectStartupUpdate

Improving Development Efficiency

5. Add the newly created menu items to the `SysContextMenu` menu, as shown in the following screenshot:

6. In the AOT, find the `SysContextMenu` class, open its `verifyItem()` method, and locate the last `case` statement at the bottom. Add two new `case` statements just below the last `case` statement:

```
case menuitemActionStr(DevProjectStartupUpdateSet):
    if (firstNode.handle() != classNum(ProjectNode) ||
        !match(#pathProjects, firstNode.treeNodePath()))
    {
        return 0;
    }
    return !DevProjectStartupUpdate::isStartupProject(
        firstNode.treeNodeName());
case menuitemActionStr(DevProjectStartupUpdateClear):
    if (firstNode.handle() != classNum(ProjectNode) ||
        !match(#pathProjects, firstNode.treeNodePath()))
    {
        return 0;
    }
    return DevProjectStartupUpdate::isStartupProject(
        firstNode.treeNodeName());
```

7. To test the results, open the **Projects** window by clicking on **Project** in the toolbar of the Development Workspace, select any project, and select the newly created **Set as startup project** option, which is under **Add-Ins**, from the right-click context menu:

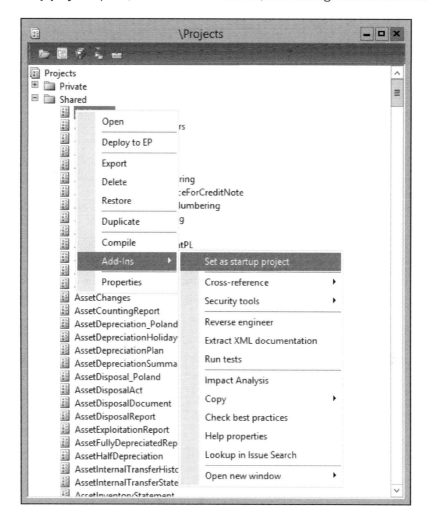

8. Restart the Development Workspace; you will notice that the previously set project opens automatically.

Improving Development Efficiency

9. To clear the startup project from the project window, select the same project again and choose the **Clear startup project** option, which is under **Add-Ins**, from the right-click context menu:

How it works...

We start this recipe by creating two new menu items. One of them is used to set the currently selected project as the startup project, and the other one is used to clear the current project from the startup project, if it was set before. Each of the menu items point to the class that, depending on the caller menu item, will update the `UserInfo` table with the startup project or clear it. The same class also contains the `isStartupProject()` helper method, which is used later to determine whether the given project is already defined as a startup project.

Next, we add the newly created menu items to the `SysContextMenu` menu, which is actually the right-click context menu for the AOT. In order to ensure that the menu items are displayed only for the project nodes, we modify the `verifyItem()` method of the standard `SysContextMenu` class. At the top level, this method has a `switch` statement with three cases (one for each type of menu item): display, action, and output. Inside each `case`, there is another `switch` statement with cases for the individual menu items located in the `SysContextMenu` menu—an item is displayed in the menu if a case returns `1`, and it is not visible if `0` is returned.

We add two additional cases for our menu items under the action case. Both the menu items will be visible only for project nodes. The menu item that is used to set the project as a startup project will be shown if the current project is not already defined as a startup project, and the menu item that is used to clear the startup project is only shown if the current project is defined as a startup project.

Searching for an object in a development project

In Dynamics AX, any development changes to the application normally have to be organized in development projects. The same object could belong to one or more projects, but Dynamics AX does not provide an easy way to determine which development projects a specific object belongs to.

In this recipe, we will create a class to search for an object in the development projects. The class is only for demonstration purposes, but it can be easily converted to a standalone tool and integrated into the right-click menu.

How to do it...

Carry out the following steps in order to complete this recipe:

1. In the AOT, create a new class with the following code snippet:

   ```
   class DevProjectSearch
   {
   }
   private boolean findChildren(
       TreeNode        _parent,
       UtilElementType _type,
       IdentifierName  _name)
   {
       TreeNode         child;
       TreeNodeIterator iterator;
       #TreeNodeSysNodeType

       iterator = _parent.AOTiterator();
   ```

```
            child = iterator.next();

            while (child)
            {
                if (child.treeNodeType().id() == #NT_PROJECT_GROUP)
                {
                    return this.findChildren(child, _type, _name);
                }
                else if (child.AOTname() == _name &&
                         child.treeNodePath() &&
                         child.utilElement().recordType == _type)
                {
                    return true;
                }
                child.treeNodeRelease();
                child = iterator.next();
            }
            return false;
        }

        void find(UtilElementType _type, IdentifierName _name)
        {
            TreeNode    projects;
            ProjectNode project;

            projects = SysTreeNode::getSharedProject();

            if (!projects)
            {
                return;
            }

            project = projects.AOTfirstChild();

            while (project)
            {
                if (this.findChildren(
                        project.loadForInspection(),
                        _type,
                        _name))
                {
                    info(project.AOTname());
                }
                project = project.AOTnextSibling();
            }
        }
```

2. To test the class, create a new job with the following code snippet:

   ```
   static void TestDevProjectSearch(Args _args)
   {
       DevProjectSearch search;
       search = new DevProjectSearch();
       search.find(UtilElementType::Table, tableStr(CustTable));
   }
   ```

3. Run the job to display the results in the **Infolog** window, as follows:

How it works...

In this recipe, we create a new class with several methods. The first method is `findChildren()` and is used for a recursive search operation within the AOT node. It accepts three parameters: a `TreeNode` object, an element type, and an element name. In this method, we go through all the children of the `TreeNode` object and check whether any of them match the provided element type and name. If any of the child nodes contain more nodes within, we use the same `findChildren()` method to determine whether any of its children match the element type and name.

The second method is named `find()` and is used for the actual search, for the given element type and name. The method goes through all of the shared development projects and calls the `findChildren()` method to determine whether the given element is in one of its nodes.

The class can be called from anywhere in the system, but in this recipe, to demonstrate how it works, we create a new job, define and instantiate the class, and use the `find()` method to search for the `CustTable` table in all the shared projects.

See also

▶ The *Modifying the right-click context menu* recipe

Modifying the Personalization form

The **Personalization** form allows users to customize their most often-used forms to fit their needs. Users can hide or move form controls, change labels, and so on. The setup is available for any Dynamics AX form and can be opened from the right-click context menu, by selecting the **Personalize** option.

For developers, this form can be very useful too. For example, it contains the handy **System name** field, which displays the name of the currently selected table field or method so that you don't need to search for it in the AOT. The **Information** tab provides details about the form itself, the caller object, and the menu item used, and it allows you to open those objects instantly in the AOT view. The last tab, **Query**, shows the tables used in the form's query; this is also very useful in facilitating a quick understanding of the underlying data structure.

In this recipe, we will demonstrate how to enhance the **Personalization** form. We will add a new button to the last tab page, which will open the selected table in the AOT.

How to do it...

Carry out the following steps in order to complete this recipe:

1. Open the `SysSetupForm` form in the AOT and find the following code in its `fillQueryTreeQueryDatasource()` method:

   ```
   formTreeItem = new FormTreeItem(
       nodeText, imagelist.image(#ImageDataSource), -1, null);
   ```

2. Replace it with the following code:

   ```
   formTreeItem = new FormTreeItem(
       nodeText,
       imagelist.image(#ImageDataSource),
       -1,
       queryBuildDataSource.table());
   ```

3. Add a new `ButtonGroup` control to the `QueryPage` tab, with the following property:

Property	Value
Name	ButtonGroup1

4. Add a new `Button` control to the created button group and set its properties, as follows:

Property	Value
Name	EditTable
AutoDeclaration	Yes

Property	Value
Text	Edit

5. Override the `clicked()` event method of the button with the following code snippet:

```
void clicked()
{
    FormTreeItem    formTreeItem;
    TableId         tableId;
    TreeNode        treeNode;
    #AOT

    formTreeItem = QueryTree.getItem(
        QueryTree.getSelection());

    tableId = formTreeItem.data();

    if (!tableId || !tableId2name(tableId))
    {
        return;
    }

    treeNode = infolog.findNode(
        #TablesPath +
        #AOTDelimiter +
        tableid2name(tableId));

    if (!treeNode)
    {
        return;
    }

    treeNode.AOTnewWindow();
}
```

6. In the `QueryTree` control, override the `selectionChanged()` event method with the following code snippet:

```
void selectionChanged(
    FormTreeItem _oldItem,
    FormTreeItem _newItem,
    FormTreeSelect _how)
{
    super(_oldItem, _newItem, _how);

    EditTable.enabled(
        tableid2name(_newItem.data()) ? true : false);
}
```

Improving Development Efficiency

7. To test the changes, open any form (for example, **Main accounts** located in **General ledger**), and then open the **Personalization** form by right-clicking anywhere on the form and selecting the **Personalize** option:

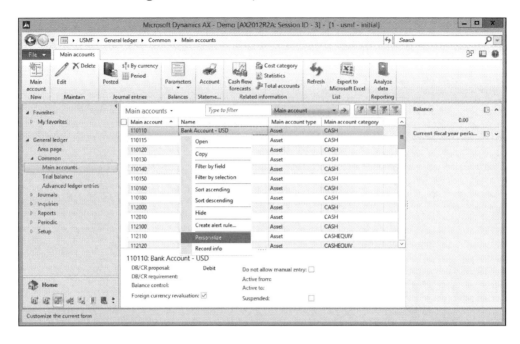

8. Go to the **Query** tab page and select one of the tables in the displayed query, as shown here:

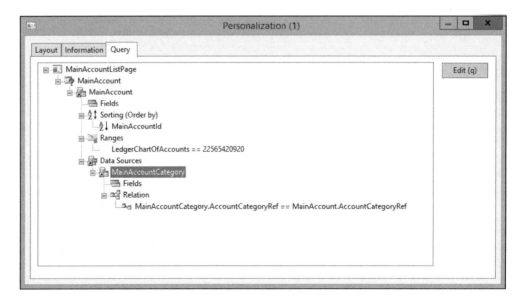

9. Click on the newly created **Edit** button to open the selected table in the AOT, as shown in the following screenshot:

How it works...

First, we modify the initialization of the `QueryTree` control. Normally, each tree node can hold some data. The query tree in the `SysSetupForm` form does not have any data associated with its nodes, so we have to modify the code and store the table number in each node that represents a table.

Next, we add a new button and override its `clicked()` method. In this method, we get the table number stored in the currently selected node—this is what we stored earlier—and search for that table in the AOT. We display it in a new AOT window, if found.

Finally, we override `selectionChanged()` on the `QueryTree` control to make sure that the button's status is updated upon node selection. In other words, the **Edit** button is enabled if the current tree node contains some data; otherwise, it is disabled.

In this way, we have modified the **Personalization** form to provide the developer with quick access to the underlying tables, directly in the AOT.

Improving Development Efficiency

Modifying the About Microsoft Dynamics AX dialog

The **About Microsoft Dynamics AX** dialog in Dynamics AX contains various information about the system. It shows kernel and application version numbers, localization information, links to other information, and so on. The dialog is available under the **Help** menu.

This dialog is also a good place to add any additional third-party information. In this recipe, you will learn how to modify the system in order to add a simple custom version number to the **About Microsoft Dynamics AX** dialog.

How to do it...

Carry out the following steps in order to complete this recipe:

1. In the AOT, find the `ApplicationVersion` class and create a new method with the following code snippet:

    ```
    static str usrAppl()
    {
        return '1.0.0';
    }
    ```

2. In the AOT, locate the `SysAbout` form and add a new `StaticText` control, with the following properties, at the bottom of **VersionInfoGroup**, which is located in **DetailGrp | MainGrp | RightGroup**:

Property	Value
Name	CustomVersion
AutoDeclaration	Yes
Width	Column width
Text	

3. The following screenshot shows how the form in the AOT will look:

4. Add the following line of code to the variable declaration section of the form's `run()` method:

   ```
   str usrVersionNumber = ApplicationVersion::usrAppl();
   ```

5. Add the following code snippet to the same method, right before `element.unLock(true)`:

   ```
   if (usrVersionNumber)
   {
       CustomVersion.text('Custom version: ' + usrVersionNumber);
   }
   ```

6. Navigate to **Help** | **About Microsoft Dynamics AX** and note the newly created **Custom version** control, as shown here:

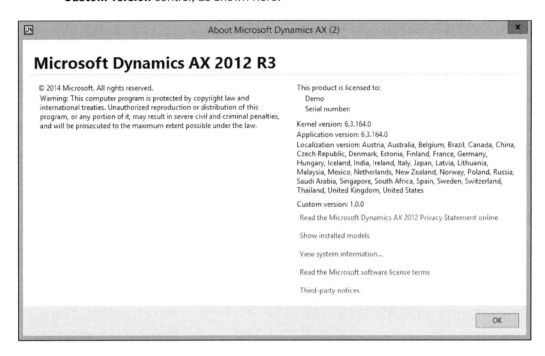

How it works...

The `ApplicationVersion` class is the place where the application version numbers are stored. For example, `applBuildNo()` returns the current application version. By modifying this class, Dynamics AX developers can modify original or custom version numbers. This class is called from the `SysAbout` form, which is actually the **About Microsoft Dynamics AX** dialog box.

In this recipe, we first create a new method in the `ApplicationVersion` class, which returns our version number. Normally, the number is updated with every new release.

Next, we modify the `SysAbout` form by adding a new control. Then, we modify the form's `run()` method to ensure that the number in the previously created method is displayed on the form.

Now, the **About Microsoft Dynamics AX** dialog box contains a new line that shows our custom version number.

9
Improving Dynamics AX Performance

In this chapter, we will cover the following recipes:

- Calculating code execution time
- Writing efficient SQL statements
- Caching a display method
- Using Dynamics AX Trace Parser
- Using SQL Server Database Engine Tuning Advisor

Introduction

It is quite common for many large Microsoft Dynamics AX installations to suffer from performance issues. These issues can be caused by insufficient hardware, incorrect configuration, ineffective code, and many other reasons.

There are lots of ways to troubleshoot and fix performance issues. This chapter discusses a few simple must-know techniques to write code properly and to deal with basic performance issues. This is in no way a complete guide to solving performance issues in Dynamics AX.

Calculating code execution time

When working on improving an existing code, there is always the question of how to measure the results. There are numerous ways to do this, for example, visually assessing the improvements, getting feedback from users, using the code profiler and/or trace parser, and various other methods.

Improving Dynamics AX Performance

In this recipe, we will discuss how to measure the code execution time using a very simple method, just by temporarily adding a few lines of code. In this way, the execution time of the old code can be compared with that of the new one in order to show whether any improvements were made.

How to do it...

Carry out the following steps in order to complete this recipe:

1. In the AOT, create a new job with the following code snippet:

    ```
    static void GetExecutionTime(Args _args)
    {
        int start;
        int end;

        start = WinAPI::getTickCount();
        sleep(1000); // pause for 1000 milliseconds
        end = WinAPI::getTickCount();

        info(strFmt("%1", end - start));
    }
    ```

2. Run the job to see how many milliseconds it takes to execute the code, as shown in the following screenshot:

How it works...

In this recipe, the `sleep()` command simulates the business logic which execution time is being measured.

The main element in the created job is the `getTickCount()` method of the standard `WinAPI` class. The method returns the `TickCount` property of the .NET environment, which is a 32-bit integer containing the amount of time, in milliseconds, that has passed since the last time the computer was started.

We place the first call to the `getTickCount()` method before the code we want to measure, and we place the second call right after the code. In this way, we know when the code was started and when it was completed. The difference between the times is the code execution time, in milliseconds.

Normally, using such a technique to calculate the code execution time does not provide useful information, as we cannot exactly tell whether the amount of time taken is right or wrong. It is much more beneficial to measure the execution time before and after we optimize the code. In this way, we can clearly see whether any improvements were made.

There's more...

The approach described in the previous section can be successfully used to measure a long-running code, such as numerous calculations or complex database queries. However, it may not be possible to assess the code that takes only a few milliseconds to execute.

The improvement in the code may not be noticeable, as it can be greatly affected by the variances caused by the current system conditions. In such cases, the code in question can be executed a number of times so that the execution times can be properly compared.

To demonstrate this, we can modify the previously created job as follows:

```
static void GetExecutionTimeLoop(Args _args)
{
    int start;
    int end;
    int i;

    start = WinAPI::getTickCount();
    for (i = i; i <= 100; i++)
    {
        sleep(1000); // pause for 1000 milliseconds
    }
    end = WinAPI::getTickCount();

    info(strFmt("%1", end - start));
}
```

Now, the execution time will be much longer and, therefore, easier to assess.

Writing efficient SQL statements

In Dynamics AX, SQL statements can often become performance bottlenecks. Therefore, it is very important to understand how Dynamics AX handles database queries and to follow all the best practice recommendations in order to keep your system healthy.

In this recipe, we will discuss some of the best practices to be used when writing database queries. For demonstration purposes, we will create a sample method with several scenarios and discuss each of them. The method will locate the CustGroup table record of a given customer account.

How to do it...

Carry out the following steps in order to complete this recipe:

1. In the AOT, locate the CustGroup table and create the following method:

```
static CustGroup findByCustAccount(
    CustAccount _custAccount,
    boolean _forupdate = false)
{
    CustTable custTable;
    CustGroup custGroup;

    if (_custAccount)
    {
        select firstOnly CustGroup from custTable
            where custTable.AccountNum == _custAccount;
    }
    if (custTable.CustGroup)
    {
        if (_forupdate)
        {
            custGroup.selectForUpdate(_forupdate);
        }

        select firstOnly custGroup where
            custGroup.CustGroup == custTable.CustGroup;
    }
    return custGroup;
}
```

2. In the same table, create another method with the following code snippet:

```
static CustGroup findByCustAccount2(
    CustAccount _custAccount,
    boolean     _forupdate = false)
{
    CustTable custTable;
    CustGroup custGroup;

    if (_custAccount)
    {
        if (_forupdate)
        {
            custGroup.selectForUpdate(_forupdate);
        }
        select firstOnly custGroup exists
            join custTable
                where custGroup.CustGroup == custTable.CustGroup
                    && custTable.AccountNum == _custAccount;
    }
    return custGroup;
}
```

How it works...

In this recipe, we have two different versions of the same method. Both methods are technically correct, but the second one is more efficient. Let's analyze each of them.

In the first method, we should pay attention to the following points:

- Verify that the _custAccount argument is not empty; this will avoid the running of an unnecessary database query.

- Use the firstOnly keyword in the first SQL statement to disable the effect of the read-ahead caching. If the firstOnly keyword is not present, the statement will retrieve a block of records, return the first one, and ignore the others. In this case, even though the customer account is a primary key and there is only one match, it is always recommended that you use the firstOnly keyword in the find() methods.

- In the same statement, specify the field list—we want to retrieve, instructing the system not to fetch any other fields that we are not planning to use. In general, this can also be done on the AOT query objects, by setting the `Dynamic` property of the `Fields` node to `No` in the query data sources and adding only the required fields manually. This can also be done in forms, by setting the `OnlyFetchActive` property to `Yes` on the form's data sources.
- Execute the `selectForUpdate()` method only if the `_forupdate` argument is set. Using the `if` statement is more efficient than calling the `selectForUpdate()` method with `false`.

The second method already uses all the discussed principles, plus an additional one, as follows:

- Both the SQL statements are combined into one using an `exists` join. One of the benefits is that only a single trip is made to the database. Another benefit is that no fields are retrieved from the customer table because of the `exists` join. This makes the statement even more efficient.

Caching a display method

In Dynamics AX, display methods are widely used to show additional information on forms or reports that come from different data sources, including special calculations, formatting, and more. Although they are shown as physical fields, their values are the result of various calculations.

The display methods are executed each time the form is redrawn. This means that the more complex the method is, the longer it will take to display the results on the screen. Normally, it is recommended that you keep the code in the display methods to a minimum.

The performance of the display methods can be improved by caching them. This is when the display method's return value is retrieved from a database or calculated only once and subsequent calls to retrieve the same value are made to the cache.

In this recipe, we will create a new cached display method. We will also discuss a few scenarios in order to learn how to properly use caching.

How to do it...

Carry out the following steps in order to complete this recipe:

1. In the AOT, locate the `CustGroup` table and create a new display method with the following code snippet:

    ```
    display Description displayPaymTermDescription()
    {
        return (select firstOnly Description from PaymTerm
            where PaymTerm.PaymTermId == this.PaymTermId).Description;
    }
    ```

2. Add the newly created method to the table's `Overview` group, right beneath the `PaymTermId` field, as shown in the following screenshot:

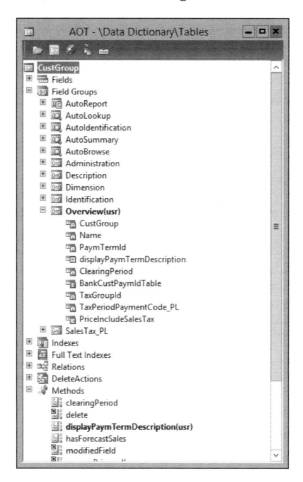

3. In the AOT, find the `CustGroup` form and override the `init()` method of its `CustGroup` data source with the following code snippet:

```
void init()
{
    super();
    this.cacheAddMethod(
        tableMethodStr(CustGroup,displayPaymTermDescription));
}
```

4. To test the display method, open the **Customer groups** form located in **Accounts receivable | Setup | Customers** and notice the newly create **Description** column, as shown here:

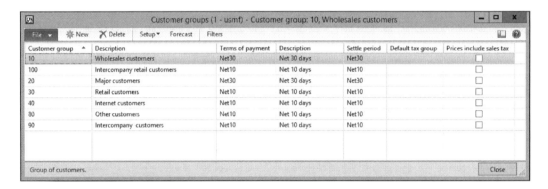

How it works...

In this recipe, we create a new display method on the `CustGroup` table to show the description of the group's payment terms. In the method, we use a query to retrieve only the `Description` field from the `PaymTerm` table. Here, we can use the `find()` method of the `PaymTerm` table, but that would decrease the display method's performance, as it returns the whole `PaymTerm` record while we only need a single field. In a scenario such as this, when there are only a few records in the table, it is not so important; however, in the case of millions of records, the difference in the performance will be noticeable.

We also add the method that we created to the **Overview** group in the table in order to ensure that it automatically appears on the overview screen of the **Customer group** form.

In order to cache the display method, we override the `init()` method of the `CustGroup` data source and call its `cacheAddMethod()` method to ensure that the method's return values are stored in the cache.

The `cacheAddMethod()` method instructs the system's caching mechanism to load the method's values into the cache for the records visible on the screen, plus some subsequent records. It is important that only the display methods that are visible in the overview screen are cached. The display methods located in different tab pages show a value from a single record at a time, and therefore it is not efficient to cache such methods.

Speaking about the display method caching, there are other ways to do this. One of the ways is to place the `SysClientCacheDataMethodAttribute` attribute at the top of the display method, as shown in the following code snippet:

```
[SysClientCacheDataMethodAttribute]
display Description displayPaymTermDescription()
{
    return (select firstOnly Description from PaymTerm
        where PaymTerm.PaymTermId == this.PaymTermId).Description;
}
```

In this case, the method will automatically be cached on any form where it is used without any additional code.

Another way is to change the `CacheDataMethod` property of the form's control to `Yes`. This will have the same effect as using the `cacheAddMethod()` method or the `SysClientCacheDataMethodAttribute` attribute.

Using Dynamics AX Trace Parser

Microsoft Dynamics AX has a feature that allows you to generate trace files of the client and server activity. It collects lots of useful information, such as user sessions, call trees, SQL statements, and execution durations. Such trace files can be analyzed with a tool called **Dynamics AX Trace Parser**, which displays all the trace information within the informative graphical user interface and allows developers to see what is happening behind the scenes and make appropriate decisions.

In this recipe, we will demonstrate how to use Dynamics AX Trace Parser. We will create and run a simple class that contains a simple SQL statement while running AX tracing. Then, we will analyze the generated trace using Trace Parser.

How to do it...

Carry out the following steps in order to complete this recipe:

1. In the AOT, create a new class with the following code snippet:

    ```
    class CustTransTracing
    {
    }
    static void main(Args _args)
    {
        CustTrans custTrans;

        select count(RecId) from custTrans
            where custTrans.Approved;

        info("Finished");
    }
    ```

2. Change the following property of the class:

Property	Value
RunOn	Server

3. Navigate to **Tools | Tracing cockpit**. Mark the **Bind parameters** checkbox and accept the default values for the rest of the parameters, as shown here:

Chapter 9

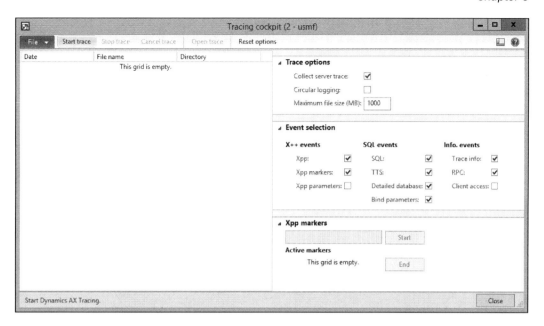

4. Click on **Start trace** and then save the trace file to, say, `C:\temp\trace.etl`.
5. Go back to the created class and run it.
6. Now, in the **Tracing cockpit** form, click on **Stop trace**:

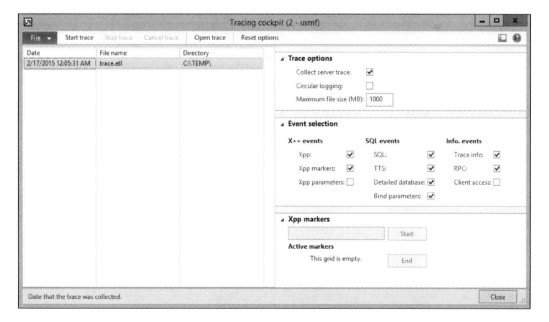

Improving Dynamics AX Performance

7. Open **Microsoft Dynamics AX 2012 Trace Parser** by clicking on **Open trace** (if required, select an existing database or register a new tracing database) and select your server session (**Ax32Serv.exe**) in the **Session** field at the top of the screen, as shown here:

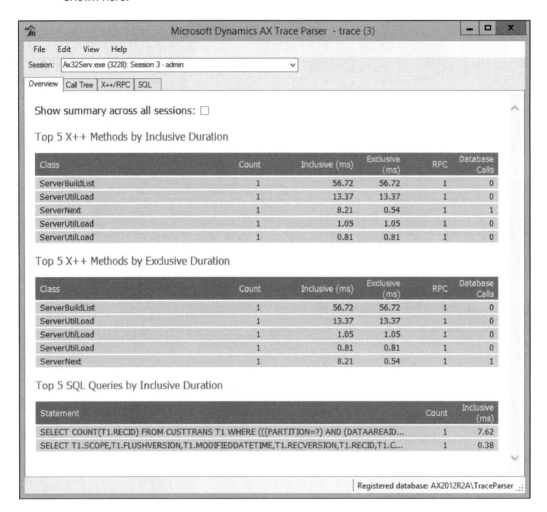

Chapter 9

8. Open the **SQL** tab page. The query will be displayed here. If there are too many records, apply the filter by typing `CustTrans` into the **Name Filter** field and marking the **Show Tables** checkbox to find your query, as shown in the following screenshot:

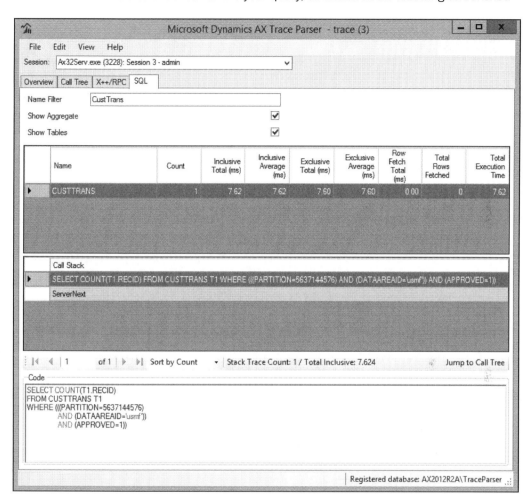

Improving Dynamics AX Performance

9. Click on **Jump to Call Tree** in order to display the query in the call stack, as shown in the following screenshot:

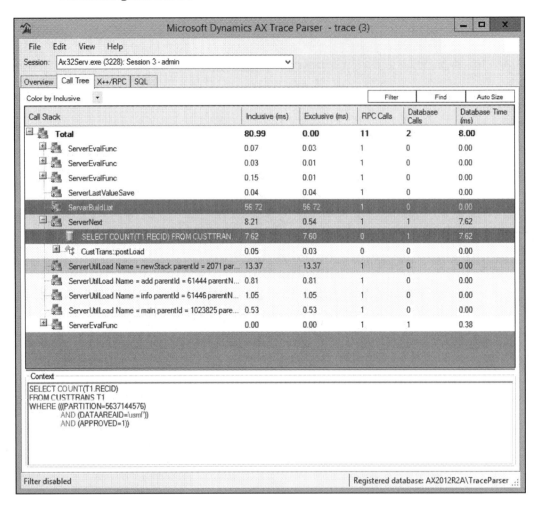

How it works...

The goal of this recipe is to demonstrate how we can trace X++ code and X++ SQL statements converted to actual database queries.

For this purpose, we create a simple class with the `main()` method containing a single SQL statement.

Then, we start the tracing, run the class, and stop the tracing, which generates the trace file with all the information we need. Note that tracing can also be started and stopped from the code by calling the `start()` and `stop()` methods of the `xClassTrace` class.

The next step is to open the file using Trace Parser. This tool provides a lot of information, but for the purpose of this recipe, we only search for our SQL statement in the **SQL** tab page. In this tab page, we can see the details of our query, along with its tracked execution times. We can see the class and method name that this SQL statement was called from. We can also see how the actual SQL statement, which has been executed in the database, looks. Such information is very useful to understand how Dynamics AX converts X++ code into SQL queries.

Additionally, it is possible to locate the SQL statement in the call stack by clicking on the **Jump to Call Tree** button. This view shows the code in question, in the context of other processes.

Note that the statement we used contains a non-indexed field in its `where` clause, which makes it inefficient. In the next recipe, we will demonstrate how to improve it.

See also

- The *Using SQL Server Database Engine Tuning Advisor* recipe

Using SQL Server Database Engine Tuning Advisor

SQL Server Database Engine Tuning Advisor allows developers to analyze and improve database queries. The tunning advisor examines query usage and recommends how it can be improved. Though most of the time the results of this tool are accurate, before making any database changes, it is recommended that you you double check them by using some other technique.

In this recipe, we will use Database Engine Tuning Advisor to analyze the query captured by Trace Parser from the previous recipe.

Improving Dynamics AX Performance

How to do it...

Carry out the following steps in order to complete this recipe:

1. Open **SQL Server Management Studio** and connect to the server where your Dynamics AX database resides.

2. Select the Dynamics AX database, create a new query, and copy the SQL statement from the previous recipe. Execute the query to ensure that it is error-free, as shown here:

3. Right-click anywhere in the query window, and from the right-click context menu, select **Analyze Query in Database Engine Tuning Advisor** and then click on **Start Analysis** and wait for the results, as shown in the following screenshot:

Chapter 9

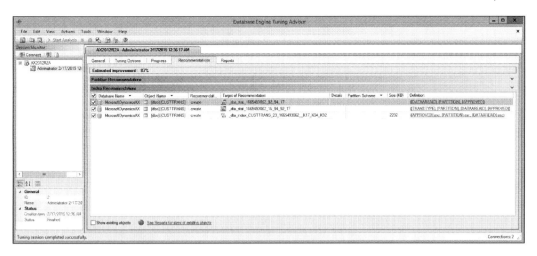

4. Observe the recommendations. Click on the last one, where the creation of a new index is recommended:

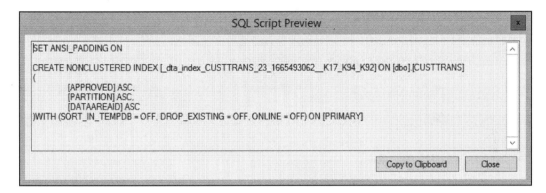

How it works...

The goal of this recipe is to demonstrate how we can use suggestions from Database Engine Tuning Advisor to improve the performance of SQL statements in Dynamics AX. As an example, we use the SQL statement from the previous recipe, which contains a non-indexed field in its `where` clause.

The Database Engine Tuning Advisor window can be opened from the **Tools** menu of **SQL Server Management Studio** or directly from the right-click context menu of the query window. In the latter case, it will automatically analyze a query specified in the query window.

Once the analysis is complete, the **Database Engine Tuning Advisor** window displays a list of recommendations, which can be reviewed by clicking on the value in the **Definition** column of the **Recommendations** tab page.

In this recipe, the tuning advisor suggests that you create database statistics and a new index. Here, the index is the most important element. In the **SQL Script Preview** window, we can see which fields are included in the index, which helps us to create the same index in Dynamics AX.

Normally, after creating indexes, we have to run Database Engine Tuning Advisor to check whether the estimated query's performance was improved.

See also

- The *Using Dynamics AX Trace Parser* recipe

Index

A

About Microsoft Dynamics AX dialog
 about 340
 modifying 340-342
Application Integration Framework (AIF) 40
Application Object Server (AOS) 286
Application Object Tree (AOT) 2
AssetConsistencyCheck class, methods
 description() 39
 executionOrder() 39
 helpText() 39
 run() 39
automatic lookup
 creating 164, 165
automatic transaction text
 modifying 233-235

B

browse
 building, for folder lookup 192, 193

C

checklist
 creating, for user friendly ledger budget setup 98-105
code editor template 320
code execution time
 calculating 343-345
color picker lookup
 creating 200-206
comma-separated value (CSV) files
 about 45
 creating 45-48
 reading 48-50

custom filter control
 creating 113-117
custom instant search filter
 creating 118-120
custom options
 displaying 181-184
custom service
 about 310
 consuming 313-315
 creating 310-313

D

data
 exporting, to XML file 40-43
 importing, from XML file 43, 44
data consistency
 checks, enhancing 36-39
date effectiveness feature
 using 52-56
development project
 object, searching in 333-335
Dialog class 58
dialog event
 handling 63-67
DialogField class 58
DialogGroup class 58
dialogs
 about 58
 creating, RunBase framework used 58-62
dialogSelectCtrl() method 67
DialogTabPage class 58
direct SQL statement
 executing 29-35
display method
 caching 348-351

document handling 14
document handling note
  adding 14-16
document service
  consuming 302-304
  creating 297-301
  enhanced document service, using 305-309
  existing document service, consuming 293-297
dynamic form
  building 68-73
Dynamics AX Trace Parser
  about 351
  using 351-357

E

editor template
  creating 320-325
efficient SQL statements
  writing 346-348
electronic payment format
  creating 252-260
e-mail
  sending, Outlook used 281-283
enhanced document service
  using 305-309
Excel file
  creating 262-265
  reading 265-268
existing document service
  consuming 293-297
external service
  consuming 315-318

F

file
  stored image, saving as 158-161
file selection
  lookup, building for 196-200
folder lookup
  browse, building for 192, 193
form
  about 57
  used, for building lookup 169-174

form, methods
  fileNameLookupFilename() 199
  fileNameLookupInitialPath() 199
  fileNameLookupTitle() 199
form splitter
  adding 73-78

G

general journal
  creating 214-218
  posting 222, 223
global lookup functions
  pickClass() 181
  pickDataArea() 180
  pickField() 181
  pickTable() 181
  pickUser() 181
  pickUserGroups() 181

I

image
  adding, to records 153-155
  displaying, as part of form 155-158
  preloading 130-134
  stored image, saving as file 158-161

J

journal 214
journal posting 222
journal processing
  examples 227, 228

L

last form values
  storing 82-85
ledger voucher
  creating 228-232
  posting 228-232
list, of custom options
  displaying 179, 180
lookup
  about 163
  building, based on record description 185-191

building, for file selection 196-200
building, form used 169-174
creating, dynamically 167-169
lookup columns 165, 166

M

macro
using, in SQL statement 27, 28
Make New Folder button
adding 195, 196
manual folder browsing lookup 194
methods, BudgetModelTree class
beginDrag() 96, 97
canMove() 97
dragOver() 96, 97
drop() 96, 97
stateDropHilite() 97
Microsoft Office Excel format 262
Microsoft Project file
about 276
creating 276-280
modal form
creating 78, 79
MorphX 319
multiple forms
modifying, dynamically 80-82
multiple records
processing 150, 151

N

normal table
using, as temporary table 19
number sequence
about 2
creating 2-7
number sequence handler
using 110-113

O

object
searching, in development project 333-335
OR operator
using 26
Outlook
used, for sending e-mail 281-283

P

Personalization form
about 336
modifying 336-339
primary key
renaming, Rename function used 8-11
project journal
processing 224-227
purchase order
about 236
creating 237, 238
posting 239-244

Q

query object
about 23
building 23-25

R

records
coloring 151-153
copying 19-22
image, adding to 153-155
merging 11-13
Rename function
used, for renaming primary key 8-11
repeating elements
Word document, creating with 272-276
right-click context menu
modifying 327-333
RunBase framework
used, for creating dialogs 58-62

S

sales order
creating 244-247
posting 247-252
segmented entry control
using 208-213
selected/available list
building 121-126
splitters 73
SQL Server Database Engine Tuning Advisor
about 357

using 358-360
SQL statement
macro, using in 27, 28
stored image
saving, as file 158-161
SysListPanelRelationTableCallback class
capabilities, demonstrating 126-129
SysListPanelRelationTable class
capabilities, demonstrating 126-129
SysQuery methods
value() 118
valueNot() 118
valueUnlimited() 118
system metadata service
consuming 291-293
system query service
consuming 286-291

T

template
Word document, creating from 269-271
temporary table
normal table, using as 19
Tools menu
modifying 325-327
Tree control
drag and drop functionality 92-96
performance 92
using 86-92
tree lookup
building 175-178

U

user friendly ledger budget setup
checklist, creating for 98-105

V

VendPaymJournalCreate job
creating 219-222
View details link
adding 106-108

W

Web Services Description Language (WSDL) 290
wizard
creating 137-149
wizard, AOT objects
MainAccountWizard class 148
MainAccountWizard display menu item 149
MainAccountWizard form 149
Word document
creating, from template 268-271
creating, with repeating elements 272-276

X

XML file
data, exporting to 40-43
data, importing from 43, 44

Thank you for buying
Microsoft Dynamics AX 2012 R3 Development Cookbook

About Packt Publishing

Packt, pronounced 'packed', published its first book, *Mastering phpMyAdmin for Effective MySQL Management*, in April 2004, and subsequently continued to specialize in publishing highly focused books on specific technologies and solutions.

Our books and publications share the experiences of your fellow IT professionals in adapting and customizing today's systems, applications, and frameworks. Our solution-based books give you the knowledge and power to customize the software and technologies you're using to get the job done. Packt books are more specific and less general than the IT books you have seen in the past. Our unique business model allows us to bring you more focused information, giving you more of what you need to know, and less of what you don't.

Packt is a modern yet unique publishing company that focuses on producing quality, cutting-edge books for communities of developers, administrators, and newbies alike. For more information, please visit our website at `www.PacktPub.com`.

About Packt Enterprise

In 2010, Packt launched two new brands, Packt Enterprise and Packt Open Source, in order to continue its focus on specialization. This book is part of the Packt Enterprise brand, home to books published on enterprise software – software created by major vendors, including (but not limited to) IBM, Microsoft, and Oracle, often for use in other corporations. Its titles will offer information relevant to a range of users of this software, including administrators, developers, architects, and end users.

Writing for Packt

We welcome all inquiries from people who are interested in authoring. Book proposals should be sent to `author@packtpub.com`. If your book idea is still at an early stage and you would like to discuss it first before writing a formal book proposal, then please contact us; one of our commissioning editors will get in touch with you.

We're not just looking for published authors; if you have strong technical skills but no writing experience, our experienced editors can help you develop a writing career, or simply get some additional reward for your expertise.

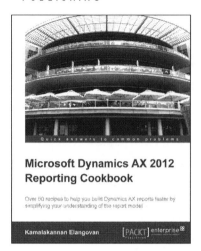

Microsoft Dynamics AX 2012 Reporting Cookbook

ISBN: 978-1-84968-772-0 Paperback: 314 pages

Over 50 recipes to help you build Dynamics AX reports faster by simplifying your understanding of the report model

1. Practical recipes for creating and managing reports.
2. Illustrated step-by-step examples that can be adopted in real time.
3. Complete explanations of the report model and program model for reports.

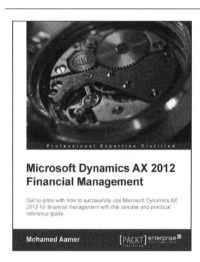

Microsoft Dynamics AX 2012 Financial Management

ISBN: 978-1-78217-720-3 Paperback: 168 pages

Get to grips with how to successfully use Microsoft Dynamics AX 2012 for the financial management with this concise and practical reference guide

1. Understand the financial management aspects in Microsoft Dynamics AX.
2. Successfully configure and set up your software.
3. Learn about real-life business requirements and their solutions.

Please check www.PacktPub.com for information on our titles

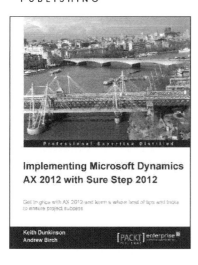

Implementing Microsoft Dynamics AX 2012 with Sure Step 2012

ISBN: 978-1-84968-704-1 Paperback: 234 pages

Get to grips with AX 2012 and learn a whole host of tips and tricks to ensure project success

1. Get the confidence to implement AX 2012 projects effectively using the Sure Step 2012 Methodology.
2. Packed with practical real-world examples as well as helpful diagrams and images that make learning easier for you.
3. Dive deep into AX 2012 to learn key technical concepts to implement and manage a project.

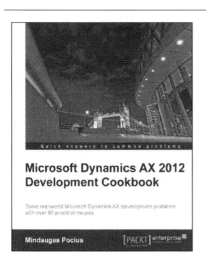

Microsoft Dynamics AX 2012 Development Cookbook

ISBN: 978-1-84968-464-4 Paperback: 372 pages

Solve real-world Microsoft Dynamics AX development problems with over 80 practical recipes

1. Develop powerful, successful Dynamics AX projects with efficient X++ code.
2. Proven recipes that can be reused in numerous successful Dynamics AX projects.
3. Covers general ledger, accounts payable, accounts receivable, project modules, and general functionality of Dynamics AX.

Please check www.PacktPub.com for information on our titles

Made in the USA
Columbia, SC
16 February 2018